INDIGENOUS DATA SOVEREIGNTY

TOWARD AN AGENDA

INDIGENOUS DATA SOVEREIGNTY

TOWARD AN AGENDA

Edited by
TAHU KUKUTAI AND JOHN TAYLOR

Australian
National
University

PRESS

Centre for Aboriginal Economic Policy Research
College of Arts and Social Sciences
The Australian National University, Canberra

RESEARCH MONOGRAPH NO. 38
2016

ANU PRESS

Published by ANU Press
The Australian National University
Acton ACT 2601, Australia
Email: anupress@anu.edu.au
This title is also available online at press.anu.edu.au

National Library of Australia Cataloguing-in-Publication entry

Title:	Indigenous data sovereignty : toward an agenda / editors: Tahu Kukutai, John Taylor.
ISBN:	9781760460303 (paperback) 9781760460310 (ebook)
Series:	Research monograph (Australian National University. Centre for Aboriginal Economic Policy Research) ; no. 38.
Subjects:	Indigenous peoples--Statistics.
	Aboriginal Australians--Legal status, laws, etc.
	Aboriginal Australians--Statistics.
	Records--Access control--Australia.
	Maori (New Zealand people)--Legal status, laws, etc.
	Maori (New Zealand people)--Statistics.
	Records--Access control--New Zealand.

Other Creators/Contributors:
                Kukutai, Tahu, editor.
                Taylor, John, 1953- editor.

Dewey Number: 305.89915

Cover design and layout by ANU Press.

Cover photograph: Preston Singletary and Lewis Tamihana Gardiner *Whale rider* 2007. Glass (blown and sand-carved), pounamu (New Zealand jade), pāua (New Zealand abalone), 20 x 24.5 x 6 inches (50.8 x 62.2 x 15.2 cm incl. base). Photo © Russell Johnson. This powerful collaborative work brings together the artistic traditions of Tlingit of the Northwest Coast of Canada and Māori of Aotearoa/New Zealand. It reflects the spirit of this book, showing another way in which indigenous peoples are collaborating across international borders to make themselves visible and heard.

Contents

List of figures

List of tables

Abbreviations

5D data	five 'Ds' of Indigenous Australian data
AATSIHS	Australian Aboriginal and Torres Strait Islander Health Survey
ABS	Australian Bureau of Statistics
AFN	Assembly of First Nations
AHMAC	Australian Health Ministers Advisory Group
AIAN	American Indian and Alaska Native
AIHW	Australian Institute of Health and Welfare
ANRC	Alaska Native Regional Corporation
ANU	The Australian National University
ANVSA	Alaska Native Village Statistical Area
APS	Australian Public Service
ARF	acute rheumatic fever
ASSA	Academy of the Social Sciences in Australia
AuSSA	Australian Survey of Social Attitudes
AWHI	Auckland Wide Healthy Homes Initiative
BIA	Bureau of Indian Affairs
CAEPR	Centre for Aboriginal Economic Policy Research
CANZUS	Canada, Australia, New Zealand and the United States
CCOH	Chiefs Committee on Health
COAG	Council of Australian Governments
CSIRO	Commonwealth Scientific and Industrial Research Organisation
CVD	cardiovascular disease
DD/PP	deficit data/problematic people

DHB	district health board
DSov	data sovereignty
DSuz	data suzerainty
ECOSOC	Economic and Social Council
FETP	Field Epidemiology Training Program
FNIGC	First Nations Information Governance Centre
GAS	Group A Streptococcal
GDP	gross domestic product
GIS	Geographical Information System
GP	general practitioner
HILDA	Household Income and Labour Dynamics in Australia
HUD	Department of Housing and Urban Development (US)
ICES	Indigenous Community Engagement Strategy
ICG	Indigenous community governance
ICT	information and communication technology
IDI	Integrated Data Infrastructure
IEAG	Independent Expert Advisory Group
IEM	Indigenous Engagement Manager
IGO	international governmental organisation
ILO	International Labour Organization
IMSB	Independent Māori Statutory Board
IP	intellectual property
IRB	institutional review board
IT	information technology
LSIC	Longitudinal Survey of Indigenous Children
MADSG	Metro Auckland Data Stewardship Group
MAE	Master of Applied Epidemiology
MAST	Maths as Story Telling
MCT	Minnesota Chippewa Tribe
MSB	Medical Services Branch
NAGATSIHID	National Advisory Group on Aboriginal and Torres Strait Islander Health Information and Data
NATSISS	National Aboriginal and Torres Strait Islander Social Survey

NCATSIS	National Centre for Aboriginal and Torres Strait Islander Statistics
NCEPH	National Centre of Epidemiology and Population Health
NGO	nongovernmental organisation
NHC	National Hauora Coalition
NHMRC	National Health and Medical Research Council
NHT	national health target
NIHB	Non-Insured Health Benefits
NSO	national statistics office
OCAP®	ownership, control, access and possession
OID	*Overcoming Indigenous disadvantage* report
OLS	ordinary least-squares
OTSA	Oklahoma Tribal Statistical Area
PHO	primary health care organisation
PISA	Programme for International Student Assessment
RHS	(First Nations and Inuit) Regional Health Survey
RNZCGP	Royal New Zealand College of General Practitioners
SAIR	State American Indian Reservation
SDG	Sustainable Development Goal
SDTSA	State Designated Tribal Statistical Area
TDSA	Tribal Designated Statistical Area
TMR	Te Mana Raraunga
TPP	Trans-Pacific Partnership
UBC	University of British Columbia
UN	United Nations
UNDRIP	United Nations Declaration on the Rights of Indigenous Peoples
UNPFII	United Nations Permanent Forum on Indigenous Issues
VET	vocational education and training
WIPO	World Intellectual Property Organization
YKC	Yawuru Knowing our Community survey

Contributors

Darin Bishop (Ngāruahine, Taranaki) is Team Leader of Organisational Knowledge at Te Puni Kōkiri, the Ministry of Māori Development. He has had a long involvement with the development of Māori statistics across the official statistics system and was formerly a researcher in the now disbanded Māori Statistics Unit at Statistics New Zealand. Along with former unit head Whetu Wereta, Darin played a critical role in the development of the Māori Statistics Framework.

Megan Davis is a Cobble Cobble Aboriginal woman from south-west Queensland. She is Professor of Law and Director of the Indigenous Law Centre at the University of New South Wales. She is also a Commissioner of the NSW Land and Environment Court and a Fellow of the Australian Academy of Law. Megan is the Chair and expert member of the United Nations Permanent Forum on Indigenous Issues and holds portfolios including Administration of Justice and Gender and Women. She is a former fellow of the United Nations High Commission for Human Rights and was one of the lawyers who drafted the United Nations Declaration on the Rights of Indigenous Peoples.

Dickie Farrar is the Chief Executive Officer of the Whakatōhea Māori Trust Board. She affiliates to Whakatōhea, Te Whānau ā Apanui, Te Aitanga ā Mahaki and Ngāti Porou. She has experience at a senior level in health, management and *iwi* development. She has held positions of general manager, CEO and directorships with a number of *iwi* organisations and Māori trusts.

James Hudson was raised in the Mataatua tribal region and is of the Ngāti Awa, Tuhoe, Ngāti Pukeko and Ngaitai tribes. In his early career, James practised environmental and commercial law, specialising in Māori land law and tribal corporate and governance structures and Treaty of Waitangi settlements. He then took up an academic research career specialising in Māori and indigenous governance, while completing his doctorate, and developed a Māori-specific indicators framework to measure tribal outcomes. James is currently the Principal Adviser (Evaluation) for the Independent Māori Statutory Board, Tāmaki Makaurau (Auckland), leading their monitoring and reporting of Māori outcomes.

Maui Hudson affiliates to Ngāruahine, Te Mahurehure and Whakatōhea and is currently a member of the Whakatōhea Māori Trust Board. Maui is Associate Professor in the Faculty of Māori and Indigenous Studies at the University of Waikato and has research interests in the areas of ethics, innovation, the interface between indigenous knowledge and science and indigenous data sovereignty.

Rawiri Jansen is of Ngāti Raukawa (Ngati Hinerangi) descent and was formerly a resource teacher of Māori language in the Hawkes Bay area before he completed his medical training in 2000. He has provided clinical teaching, Te Reo and Tikanga Māori programs for Māori health professionals throughout Aotearoa/New Zealand. He is past chairman of Te Ataarangi Trust (a national Māori language organisation) and is Chairperson of Te Ohu Rata o Aotearoa (Māori Medical Practitioners Association). Rawiri's main focus is on providing clinical leadership towards Māori health equity. He is currently a general practitioner in Auckland and Clinical Director for the National Hauora Coalition (a primary health care organisation).

Paul Jelfs is General Manager of the Population and Social Statistics Division of the Australian Bureau of Statistics (ABS) in Canberra. He has extensive experience in Commonwealth and state government agencies in both information management and service delivery. He has a background in public health and epidemiology and has driven large information initiatives such as the Australian Health Survey, national and state-based cancer information systems, national disability and mortality data collections and Aboriginal and Torres Strait Islander health and welfare information. Paul is the Senior Reconciliation Champion for the ABS.

Tahu Kukutai belongs to the Waikato, Ngāti Maniapoto and Te Aupouri tribes and is Associate Professor at the Institute of Demographic and Economic Analysis, University of Waikato. Tahu specialises in Māori and indigenous demographic research and has written extensively on issues of Māori and tribal population change, identity and inequality.

She also has an ongoing interest in how governments around the world count and classify populations by ethnic-racial and citizenship criteria. In a former life she was a journalist.

Raymond (Ray) Lovett is a National Health and Medical Research Council Early Career Fellow and Research Fellow with the Epidemiology for Policy and Practice group at the National Centre for Epidemiology and Population Health, The Australian National University. He also holds an adjunct Fellowship at the Australian Institute of Aboriginal and Torres Strait Islander Studies in the Indigenous Social and Cultural Wellbeing group. Ray is an Aboriginal (Wongaibon) epidemiologist with extensive experience in health services research and large-scale data analysis for public health policy development and evaluation.

Lesley McLean is coordinator of the tribal database for the Whakatōhea Māori Trust Board. She affiliates to Whakatōhea and Te Whānau ā Apanui. In her role, she is responsible for maintaining the data integrity of the tribal database, connecting *whānau* genealogies and linking them to local communities, as well as profiling Māori land within Whakatōhea's tribal region.

Frances Morphy is Honorary Associate Professor at the Centre for Aboriginal Economic Policy Research at The Australian National University and a 2015–16 Research Affiliate of the Center for Advanced Study in the Behavioral Sciences at Stanford University. An anthropologist and linguist by training, her current research concerns the intersection between anthropology and demography, with a focus on Aboriginal Australian populations.

Ian Pool is Emeritus Professor at Waikato University and Fellow of the Royal Society of New Zealand. He has analysed Māori populations since 1958, publishing numerous books and articles on Māori, most recently *Colonization and development, NZ 1769–1900: the seeds of Rangiatea* (2015, Springer). Other recent books include (co-authored) *The New Zealand family* (2007, AUP), (co-edited) *Riding the age waves* (2005, Springer) and *Age structural transitions: challenges for development* (2006, CICRED). He has also published widely on African demography, population change in Aotearoa/New Zealand and other issues. He has lived in eight countries and conducted missions for international agencies across francophone and anglophone Africa, Asia and the Pacific.

Desi Rodriguez-Lonebear is a citizen of the Northern Cheyenne Nation from Montana, USA. She is pursuing a dual PhD in demography at the University of Waikato and sociology at the University of Arizona. Her doctoral research focuses on the count and classification of American Indian tribal identity in US official statistics and tribal data systems. She is an appointed member of the US Census Bureau's National Advisory Committee and a Graduate Research Associate at the Native Nations Institute at the University of Arizona. She is a co-founder of the US Indigenous Data Sovereignty Network.

Diane E Smith is Senior Research Fellow and convenor of the Higher Degree by Research Program at The Australian National University's National Centre for Indigenous Studies. She has more than 40 years experience working with Indigenous Australian communities and organisations across Australia. She is a board member of the Australian Indigenous Governance Institute. Diane was a chief investigator for the Australian Indigenous Community Governance Research Project, the largest multidisciplinary comparative research investigation into Indigenous governance undertaken in Australia (anu.edu/caepr/ICGP) and author of the subsequent Indigenous Governance Toolkit (aigi.com.au). Her PhD (Anthropology, ANU) investigated Indigenous modes of networked governance and their intercultural articulation with the Australian state.

C Matthew Snipp is the Burnet C. and Mildred Finley Wohlford Professor of Humanities and Sciences in the Department of Sociology at Stanford University. He is also serving as the Chair of Native American Studies and is the current Director of the Center for Comparative Studies in Race and Ethnicity. His tribal affiliations are Oklahoma Cherokee and Choctaw.

John Taylor is Emeritus Professor at the Centre for Aboriginal Economic Policy Research at The Australian National University. He is a Fellow of the Academy of the Social Sciences in Australia and a Policy Associate of the Aboriginal Policy Research Consortium (International) based at the University of Western Ontario. He is a population geographer specialising in the demography of indigenous peoples.

Ceal Tournier is founding and current Chairperson of the First Nations Information Governance Centre (FNIGC) headquartered in Akwesasne, Ontario. She has been the FNIGC Saskatchewan representative since 1995 and Regional Representative Co-chair since 2002. Her background is in First Nations health and social services delivery. As General Manager of Health & Family Services Inc. for the Saskatoon Tribal Council, she is well acquainted with the needs of First Nations people, especially in regard to valid and quality data. She is a passionate advocate for the development of a framework that will see First Nations as controllers of their own destiny.

Maggie Walter is a member of the Palawa Briggs/Johnson Tasmanian Aboriginal family descended from the Pairrebenne people of Tebrakunna country, North Eastern Tasmania. She is Professor of Sociology and the Pro Vice-Chancellor of Aboriginal Research and Leadership at the University of Tasmania. She has published extensively in the field of race relations, inequality, and research methods and methodologies, and is passionate about Indigenous statistical engagement. Recent books include *Indigenous statistics: a quantitative methodology* (with C Andersen, Left Coast Press, 2013) *Inequality in Australia: discourses, realities and directions* (with D Habibis, 2nd edn, Oxford University Press, 2014). She is also the editor of *Social research methods* (3rd edn, Oxford University Press, 2013).

Mandy Yap is a Research Fellow at the Crawford School of Public Policy at The Australian National University. She was previously a Research Officer at CAEPR and a researcher at the National Centre for Social and Economic Modelling, working on social exclusion, ageing, diabetes modelling and women and fertility issues. Her current research interests include the role of gender equality in development and methodologies around constructing indicators of quality of life and wellbeing. Her doctoral research aims to develop culturally relevant and gender-sensitive indicators of wellbeing working with the Yawuru community in Western Australia.

Eunice Yu is a Yawuru woman from Broome, Western Australia. She has been employed at the Kimberley Institute since 2008, undertaking strategic research to inform innovative policy development. Prior to this, Eunice worked for the Australian Government in various administrative and managerial positions. She has extensive experience at the community level in the areas of culture, sports, education, child care and youth. She currently serves as a board member of the Kimberley Development Commission and sits on the Roundtable for Aboriginal and Torres Strait Islander Statistics with the Australian Bureau of Statistics.

Preface

The twin problems of lack of reliable data and information on indigenous peoples and the biopiracy and misuse of their traditional knowledge and cultural heritage are issues that have been grappled with in the process of drafting and negotiating the United Nations Declaration on the Rights of Indigenous Peoples (UNDRIP). It is ironic that even with the emergence of the global 'data revolution' these problems persist in many countries where indigenous peoples live.

The United Nations Permanent Forum on Indigenous Issues in its first and second sessions (2002, 2003) already recognised that a key challenge faced by national and international bodies is the lack of disaggregated data on indigenous peoples. The absence or lack of data that reflect where and how many indigenous peoples there are, and how they are faring in relation to the realisation of their individual and collective rights is directly related to the weakness of governments and intergovernmental bodies in formulating and implementing indigenous-sensitive decisions and programs.

Several expert meetings and forum sessions have come up with recommendations on how data collection and data disaggregation on indigenous peoples can be done and how and what indicators should be used to measure implementation of the Millennium Development Goals, and now the newly adopted Sustainable Development Goals, in relation to realising indigenous peoples' rights. Data should be generated to measure how the rights of indigenous peoples to access and ownership of lands, territories and resources are being met; how their participation in decision-making and control over their own development processes are progressing; what control over data and knowledge they are achieving; and what discrimination and exclusion they experience in regard to their social, economic and cultural rights.

In terms of approaches and methodologies, it was stressed in these UN forums that indigenous peoples should control these data and that their effective participation in data gathering and research should be ensured. Furthermore, resulting data should be available for use by them in policy articulation, in planning and in monitoring and evaluation efforts.

Unfortunately, there is still a long way to go before such data collection and disaggregation are done in most countries outside Canada, Australia, New Zealand, the United States and a few Latin American countries. A common problem raised by governments is the lack of financial and technical resources to carry this out. Another unfounded fear, which is repeatedly expressed by some governments, is that generating disaggregated data can exacerbate discrimination and data differentiation can lead to conflicts.

Such concerns and fears should not be used to deny indigenous peoples their right to self-determination (Article 3, UNDRIP), which is their right to determine their political status and to pursue freely their economic, social and cultural development. This right necessarily includes their right to have data and information collected, by them or jointly with them, that reflect their past and present realities and provide the basis for their pursuit of self-determined economic, social and cultural development.

The concept of data sovereignty, which is elaborated in this book, is linked with indigenous peoples' right to maintain, control, protect and develop their cultural heritage, traditional knowledge and traditional cultural expressions, as well as their right to maintain, control, protect and develop their intellectual property over these.

The emergence of the global data revolution and associated new technologies can be a double-edged sword for indigenous peoples. If indigenous peoples have control over what and how data and knowledge will be generated, analysed and documented, and over the dissemination and use of these, positive results can come about. The collection and disaggregation of data on indigenous peoples and the documentation and transmission of their knowledge to younger generations can be facilitated. They can be the primary beneficiaries of the use of data, their knowledge and their cultural heritage.

If, however, indigenous peoples lose control because there are no existing laws and policies that recognise their rights and regulate the behaviour of institutions and individuals involved in gathering and disseminating data and knowledge, marginalisation, inequality and discrimination will persist. The respect of their right to have their free, prior and informed consent obtained before data are gathered and disseminated is crucial to prevent this from happening.

The efforts of the various authors in this book to theorise about and conceptualise data sovereignty, and provide case study examples of its links to the realisation of the rights of indigenous peoples, are pioneering and laudable. I hope this book will initiate further debates about how the data revolution can be harnessed to facilitate the collection and disaggregation of data on indigenous peoples. I also hope that this book will inspire more indigenous peoples to assert and actualise their rights to control, own and further develop their knowledge and cultural heritage and to effectively transmit these to the younger generations.

Victoria Tauli-Corpuz
UN Special Rapporteur on the Rights of Indigenous Peoples
Baguio City
Philippines

1

Data sovereignty for indigenous peoples: current practice and future needs

Tahu Kukutai and John Taylor

Origins of a conversation

In July 2015, an international group of scholars, representatives of indigenous organisations and government personnel from the CANZUS group of Anglo-settler democracies—Canada, Australia, Aotearoa/New Zealand and the United States—gathered in Canberra to participate in a workshop, 'Data sovereignty for indigenous peoples: current practice and future needs'. The purpose of the workshop, sponsored by the Academy of the Social Sciences in Australia (ASSA) and the Centre for Aboriginal Economic Policy Research (CAEPR) at The Australian National University, was to identify and develop an indigenous data sovereignty agenda, leveraging international instruments such as the United Nations Declaration on the Rights of Indigenous Peoples (UNDRIP).[1] In an age when data permeate our lives daily, issues relating to data consent, use, ownership and storage have become increasingly complex. While indigenous peoples have long claimed sovereign status over their lands and territories, debates about 'data sovereignty' have been dominated by national

---

1   See: un.org/esa/socdev/unpfii/documents/DRIPS_en.pdf.

governments and multinational corporations focused on issues of legal jurisdiction. Missing from those conversations have been the inherent and inalienable rights and interests of indigenous peoples relating to the collection, ownership and application of data about their people, lifeways and territories. This book is the first to engage with the topic of data sovereignty from an indigenous standpoint, drawing on papers and discussions from the Canberra workshop. Although it is focused on the CANZUS states, the intended audience is global and varied. It includes indigenous communities grappling with issues of identity, representation, participation and development; governments, agencies and nongovernmental organisations (NGOs) seeking to formulate a response; and researchers trying to theorise and conceptualise a rapidly emerging field.

The multifaceted nature of indigenous data sovereignty gives rise to a wide-ranging set of issues, from legal and ethical dimensions around data storage, ownership, access and consent, to intellectual property rights and practical considerations about how data are used in the context of research, policy and practice. Similarly, the scope of the indigenous data ecosystem is vast and includes data generated or held by indigenous communities and organisations, governments, the public sector, international governmental organisations (IGOs), NGOs, research institutions and commercial entities. As the beginning point of a conversation on indigenous data sovereignty, this book does not try to comprehensively cover all facets. Rather, we have focused on the areas for which we have collective expertise—as data users in research, policy, planning and governance contexts—leaving aside legal, ethical, commercialisation and technological issues for future exploration.

The broad aim of this book is to stimulate new thinking and uncover emergent practice regarding the generation of demographic, wellbeing and community development information in ways that better respond to the self-determination aspirations of indigenous peoples. To do so it also considers the implications of UNDRIP for the collection, ownership and application of statistics pertaining to indigenous peoples and what these might mean for indigenous peoples' sovereignty over data about them, their territories and ways of life.

The importance of data for the advancement of indigenous self-determination and development has been emphasised by indigenous NGOs (Tebtebba Foundation 2008), communities and tribes. The UN Permanent Forum on Indigenous Issues (UNPFII) has held a number of gatherings to discuss data collection and disaggregation (UNPFII 2004), indicators of wellbeing (UNPFII 2006) and development that encompasses culture and identity (UNPFII 2010). At these events, indigenous representatives have raised concerns about the relevance of existing statistical frameworks for reflecting their world views and have highlighted their lack of participation in data collection processes and governance. As a result, the collection of data on indigenous peoples is viewed as primarily servicing government requirements rather than supporting indigenous peoples' development agendas. The content of this volume thus provides a timely supplement to a call from the UNPFII that states should follow through on their commitments, made at the UN's 2014 World Conference on Indigenous Peoples, to give practical effect to the free, prior and informed consent provisions of UNDRIP, to empower indigenous partnership and aspirations and to incorporate these into the post-2015 UN development agenda (Taylor & Kukutai 2015).

Aside from informing UN-level discussions, the moment is opportune to critique the demography–policy nexus in nation-state settings and to reflect on how the statistical portrayal of indigenous peoples might be transformed (Kukutai & Taylor 2012). In the CANZUS states, national statistics offices (NSOs) are actively engaged in a process of census modernisation and transformation. For many decades, the census has been the 'gold standard' for population estimates and projections, particularly for subpopulations and small geographic areas, both of which include indigenous peoples (Bell 2015; Kukutai et al. 2015). However, NSOs are increasingly looking for alternatives to the traditional 'footwork' census through the use of rolling surveys, population registers and administrative data, along with greater use of digital technologies. In Canada, the decision to replace the 2011 long-form census with the voluntary National Household Survey had a major and detrimental impact on the quality, coverage and disaggregation of indigenous data (Smylie & Firestone 2015). In 2015, the newly elected Canadian Government acted quickly to reintroduce the long-form census. In Aotearoa/New Zealand, Statistics New Zealand has developed the Integrated Data Infrastructure (IDI), which links individual-level census records with data across the government system in preparation for a shift to a fully administrative census. While the IDI data are anonymised, other data-linking initiatives occurring within and across government agencies in Aotearoa/New Zealand are not anonymised and are intended for use for operational purposes such as 'targeted' interventions. Shifts such as these have major implications for the control, quality and comprehensiveness of indigenous data and are likely to be a key area of focus in future discussions about indigenous data sovereignty.

The most recently published best estimate puts the total world population of indigenous peoples at 302 million (Hall & Patrinos 2012: 10–12), comprising thousands of distinct polities encapsulated by some 70 countries. In saying that, the definitional means for arriving at such composite figures are many and varied and a definitive global demography remains unknown and is probably unknowable. Whatever the case, UNDRIP has now established a new set of international standards for relations between indigenous peoples and whichever nation-states encapsulate them and Articles 3, 4, 5, 15(i), 18, 19, 20(i), 23, 31, 32, 33, 38 and 42 of UNDRIP all raise urgent questions about the manner in which these nations statistically represent their indigenous citizens.

Of the countries that encapsulate the thousands of indigenous groups around the world it is estimated that more than half (55 per cent) do not separately identify indigenous people in their national statistical collections (NIDEA 2015). In those that do (including the CANZUS states), the tendency has been to generate crude social binaries (indigenous/non-indigenous) as input to public policy. However, the legal and moral framework that allowed for such simplification of complex and varied forms of indigenous cultural and political organisation has shifted in recent times such that many indigenous polities are asserting their own statistical identity and ownership of information in ways that this volume explores. In particular, UNDRIP now emphasises the rights of indigenous peoples to maintain and strengthen their institutions, cultures and traditions and to pursue their wellbeing in keeping with their own needs and aspirations. It also promotes their full and effective participation in all matters that concern them. Given this acknowledgement of wide-ranging rights it is not surprising that indigenous peoples and signatory governments have started to contemplate what exactly endorsement of UNDRIP might mean for the usual practice of government business.

This questioning arises from Article 42 of the declaration, which calls on states to promote the full application of UNDRIP provisions and to follow-up on their effectiveness. Current discussion here is focused on an 'implementation gap', where even good intentions by nation-states in the form of legislative and administrative changes might fail to deliver the benefits that indigenous peoples seek (Malezer 2009). But what do we mean by enjoying the benefit of those rights, and what does this have to do with the work of statistical agencies and information in general? The particular rights in question that have direct implications for the collection of statistical information are contained in Articles 18, 19, 23 and 31 while the overall focus of UNDRIP on the rights of indigenous 'peoples' as opposed to state-identified indigenous 'populations' adds a further dimension—a demography of indigenous 'population' may be well suited to the provision of citizen rights but it does not provide for the expression of indigenous interests in inherent and proprietary rights as 'peoples'. Thus, while not denying some role for centralised data collection, what indigenous peoples are seeking is a right to identity and meaningful participation in decisions affecting the collection, dissemination and stewardship of all data that are collected about them. They also seek mechanisms for capacity building in their own compilation of data and use of information as a means of promoting their full and effective participation in self-governance and development planning.

Organisation of the book

The contributions to this volume range widely over the issues outlined above. Deliberately, most of the papers are from indigenous authors, not least because indigenous peoples themselves are the ones at the vanguard of conceptual development and emerging practice in this area. UNDRIP provides something of a unifying theme for the book—a sort of test of whether data that are collected on indigenous peoples and the processes involved are meeting the benchmarks laid out therein, although this test is more often implicit than explicit. Accordingly, the book is structured to move from global considerations around the meaning of data sovereignty, colonial impacts on indigenous data sovereignty and the setting of new international standards for achieving indigenous aspirations through to individual case studies of the ways in which indigenous groups are giving practical meaning to data sovereignty.

The book is organised into four parts. The first comprises three chapters that examine key concepts and historical underpinnings. In Chapter 2, Megan Davis provides a personal reflection on the role of data in progressing the aims of indigenous peoples from her unique position as Chair of the UNPFII. It is clear from deliberations at the UN that indigenous engagement in the setting of relevant indicators will be a key issue in the post-2015 UN development agenda built around the new Sustainable Development Goals (SDGs). There is the prospect of a separate Indigenous Sustainable Development Index to sit alongside the SDGs, in line with a growing demand for the UNPFII to increase its focus on indigenous peoples' development agendas. As Davis notes, this requires the production of more nuanced data and information than currently exist and greater input from indigenous peoples themselves. One development here has been the 'Indigenous Navigator' project (indigenousnavigator.org) involving the International Labour Organization (ILO); Tebtebba Foundation; the Asia Indigenous Peoples Pact; the Forest Peoples Programme; the International Work Group for Indigenous Affairs and the European Commission. The navigator project provides survey tools and resources with which to report indigenous community perspectives on the implementation of indigenous rights, including whether or not indigenous rights to development are being met.

In Chapter 3, Matthew Snipp provides a more conceptual inquiry into the origin and meaning of the term 'data sovereignty' and an argument for its particular application to indigenous peoples via rights to self-determination. He notes its emergence as a twenty-first-century idea prompted by the effect of internet technologies on weakening impediments to information exchange that were previously imposed by geographic boundaries. In this context, sovereignty reflects the desire and ability of nation-states to continue to manage information in ways that are consistent with their laws, practices and customs. Such ability has long been beyond the reach of indigenous nations, who are smaller, poorer and politically weaker than the settler states that typically surround them. As long as this remains the case, it makes little sense to talk about a fully postcolonial world. Nonetheless, thinking of postcolonialism as a continuum, instead of a simple binary, does make it possible to consider how indigenous peoples might claim greater control over data connected to them. Snipp advances three preconditions for data decolonisation: that indigenous peoples have power to determine who should be counted among them; that data must reflect the interests and priorities of indigenous peoples; and that tribal communities must not only dictate the content of data collected about them, but also have the power to determine who has access to these data. This requires the building of indigenous expertise in the production and management of data and the formation of governance arrangements that allow for institutional oversight of research and data collection in indigenous communities.

In providing historical context for the volume, Ian Pool (Chapter 4) introduces the idea of a data continuum on the understanding that precolonial data existed and continue to exist. He argues that achieving data sovereignty is more than just a technical problem as colonialism marginalised or even expunged extant indigenous epistemologies. Indigenous peoples thus saw their data sovereignty submit to data suzerainty under colonial and postcolonial regimes. Ironically, as they now attempt to reform the colonial order's knowledge systems using techniques of data collection and analysis more grounded in their own cultural heritage, indigenous peoples face the potential of neo-data suzerainty from the globalisation of information systems and 'big data'.

The second part of the book includes three chapters that critique ongoing postcolonial statistical systems. In Chapter 5, Maggie Walter argues that population statistics are imbued with meaning derived from the dominant social norms, values and racial hierarchies of colonising nation-states. Her Google search for 'indigenous statistics' reveals an overwhelming focus on what she terms the five 'Ds' of Indigenous Australian data (5D data): disparity, deprivation, disadvantage, dysfunction and difference. The dearth of data on indigenous peoples that present an alternative narrative to the 5Ds serves to cement a 'deficit data–problematic people' correlation. As a consequence, indigenous people are largely invisible except as statistically informed pejorative stereotypes. In effect, the politics of data are embedded in 'who' has the power to make determinations and who controls the narratives surrounding indigenous peoples' lives. Currently, it is not indigenous peoples themselves. In the context of government reporting, Walter argues for a greater focus on the creation of data in a 'recognition space' between indigenous concepts of identity and wellbeing, and more mainstream constructs. Importantly, several of the issues raised by Walter were also identified in recommendations of the Royal Commission into Aboriginal Deaths in Custody in Australia 25 years ago (RCIADIC 1991: recommendations 2.53 & 2.63).

Frances Morphy's Chapter 6 offers an insightful critique of the demographic categories used to define indigenous peoples, as well as suggestions for how these might better capture indigenous forms of sociality. In achieving data sovereignty over 'naming', indigenous peoples face two kinds of challenges. One is how to determine the nature of data to be collected, including how to 'name' the indicators that measure indigenous realities. The other, and perhaps bigger, challenge is the transformation of power relations required to give effect to indigenous world views. Morphy argues for the prioritisation of indicators that reflect indigenous peoples' own local understandings of their social world over indicators that have been constructed according to hegemonic Global North categories. In the demographic practices of the Global North, there is a characteristic statistical 'silence' concerning levels of indigenous sociality beyond the household (echoing a point made by Ian Pool regarding the absence of Māori *whanaungatanga*, or kinship ties, in national accounts). Likewise, there is an absence of indicators concerning the nature and extent of connection to place. For indigenous peoples, the intrinsic connection between collective identity and place is one factor that distinguishes them from settler societies and goes to the heart of a rights-oriented demography.

Elaborating further on forms of sociality, Diane Smith (Chapter 7) notes that land rights and native title regimes in Australia have created a plethora of self-governing arrangements, but there remains the unresolved question of how to leverage rights bestowed in this way to pursue self-defined agendas. While ownership of data is crucial, a fundamental issue is to first establish who is the 'self' in 'self-determine-nation'. There is growing demand from Indigenous Australian polities for local data to support local planning and, while much can be accessed from conventional sources, data are not captured in ways that provide for 'culture-smart information'. 'Culture-smart' data require internal mandates from groups that, in turn, enable internally informed decision-making as the essence of sovereignty.

The third section of the book brings together, for the first time, case studies from across the CANZUS states that showcase the varied ways in which indigenous communities and organisations are asserting their own form of sovereignty over data. In Chapter 8, Ceal Tournier, on behalf of the First Nations Information Governance Centre, recalls how First Nation principles of 'ownership, control, access and possession' of data in Canada became trademarked as OCAP® under the auspices of a regionally representative steering committee that became the First Nations Information Governance Centre (FNIGC). This initiative was a political response to colonialism and the role of knowledge production in reproducing colonial relations. Much of the impetus for OCAP® came from the sorry history of research and information gathering involving First Nations people. Since 2010 FNIGC has operated on behalf of First Nations to ensure that OCAP® is applied through a certification process for research projects, surveys and information management systems. The FNIGC story is a stunning illustration of how sovereignty can be realised in relation to data, information and knowledge as part of a broader goal of self-determination.

Turning to Aotearoa/New Zealand, Maui Hudson, Dickie Farrar and Lesley McLean elaborate on key aspects of data sovereignty from the perspective of Whakatōhea *iwi* (tribe) in the Bay of Plenty region (Chapter 9). They argue that the pressing need for Whakatōhea is for equality of access to existing data to evolve its role as a treaty partner within a rapidly shifting data landscape. As government agencies move away from data collection based on individual consent towards linked individual-level administrative data, questions arise around the collective rights of *iwi* to unit-record access. The appetite for access to unit-record data reflects a growing statistical skills base among Māori, along with a growing appreciation of the power of data to inform internal governance and planning and external advocacy. In this evolving datascape, only culturally sensitive data might be seen as sovereign for *iwi*; other types of data could have flexible ownership arrangements, and jurisdiction over data may be regarded as partially shared.

Working in a slightly different legislative and policy setting, James Hudson (Chapter 10) provides an 'insider's' view of why and how the Independent Māori Statutory Board (IMSB) developed the 'Māori Plan' for Tāmaki Makaurau/Auckland. Established in 2010, the IMSB has statutory responsibility to promote issues of social, economic, cultural and environmental significance for Māori in Auckland. As the country's economic powerhouse, Auckland encompasses one-third of the national population, one-quarter of all Māori and a substantial migrant population (40 per cent of the populace were born overseas). Many of the issues faced by Māori in Auckland are distinctive to the region. A central motivation for the Māori Plan was to embed Māori aspirations for wellbeing in the overall 'Auckland Plan', which is Auckland Council's long-term strategy to promote social, economic, environmental and cultural wellbeing for all. Hudson observes that for the Māori Plan to be seen as useful and relevant to Māori, it needed to be founded on Māori philosophies and principles and meet the needs of both *mana whenua* (customary tribes) and *mataawaka* (the wider Māori population) in Auckland. The exercise highlighted the considerable data gaps that exist for Māori at the regional level, especially in the areas of environment and culture. The Māori Plan underlines a tension that has long existed between the interests and statistical reporting requirements of government and indigenous perspectives about what constitute useful and meaningful data.

In Chapter 11, Rawiri Jansen provides an interesting example of how the rise of an indigenous professional class in Aotearoa/New Zealand is generating new opportunities for data-sharing and data access using the experience of an Auckland-based Māori primary health care organisation as a case study. It shows how data can be mobilised to inform action 'by Māori for Māori'. Aotearoa/New Zealand is likely the only jurisdiction in the world to have achieved a fully pro rata share of medical undergraduate entry for its indigenous population, and the momentum that lies behind such an achievement is reflected in the density of Māori medical practitioners. This is bringing Māori expertise and focus into health care delivery systems with data collection, analysis and reporting tools now operating to address excessively high rates of rheumatic fever among Māori school children; to monitor real-time functioning of Māori primary care networks; to develop data-sharing platforms with other services that impact on Māori health, such as housing; and to negotiate system-wide data-sharing protocols.

Ray Lovett (Chapter 12) examines similar issues in Australia but with more focus on the capacities of indigenous people to participate in data creation and manipulation. He argues that statistics developed from an indigenous 'frame of view' and with greater engagement by indigenous people in data conceptualisation, design, collection, analysis and reporting would enhance the utility of information for Indigenous Australian nations. However, to achieve this requires a quantum increase in professionally trained Indigenous statisticians in a professional field that has struggled with student enrolments generally in recent years. One solution is to make coursework in statistics more relevant to indigenous world views, and two examples in this area are provided from a field-based epidemiology program and a proposed national survey involving statistical training for participating Aboriginal medical services. Lovett also highlights a need for official statistical agencies to address non-indigenous barriers to indigenous participation in data initiatives by making more meaningful use of existing statistical skills among indigenous professionals.

In Chapter 13, Mandy Yap and Eunice Yu provide a concrete example of what indigenous data sovereignty can look like in practice at the local level. Following determination of their native title in 2006, and subsequent signing of agreements in 2010, the Yawuru native title holders of Broome in Western Australia recognised an immediate need for data about themselves to secure their social, economic, cultural and environmental attributes as key components of regional planning. Several initiatives were embarked on concurrently. First came a survey of all Indigenous people and dwellings in the town to create a unit-record baseline. The second project addressed the development of an instrument to measure local understandings of Yawuru wellbeing (*mabu liyan*). The third initiative involved the construction of a geographic information system to digitally map places of cultural, social and environmental significance to inform a cultural and environmental management plan. Finally, a documentation project has been undertaken to collate and store all relevant legal records, historical information, genealogies and cultural information. This includes a Yawuru language revitalisation program.

In the final case study, from the United States, Desi Rodriguez-Lonebear reports on early findings from a survey of American Indian tribal leaders who note that reliance on others for data undermines their tribal sovereignty (Chapter 14). However, contestation over identity and tribal membership remains a primary issue due to decades of federal Indian policy, including deliberate termination, forced removal, relocation, assimilation and the eugenic application of 'blood quantum'. The diverse contexts of American Indian lives now demand new means of negotiating tribal identity but, ironically, this must take place in the face of the absolute sovereignty of tribes to determine their membership. Rodriguez-Lonebear also reminds us that while data are often seen as products of a digital age, indigenous peoples have long and rich histories of data collection and preservation, and these histories provide a solid foundation for the pursuance of indigenous data sovereignty in contemporary settings.

The concluding part of the book presents the views and practices of NSOs in Australia and New Zealand in regard to the production and application of indigenous statistics. In Chapter 15, Paul Jelfs outlines the Aboriginal and Torres Strait Islander enumeration and engagement activities of the Australian Bureau of Statistics (ABS). The main vehicle for improving the quality and relevance of Australian Indigenous statistics is the Indigenous Community Engagement Strategy involving Indigenous Engagement Managers in each jurisdiction. The ABS has also instituted a twice-yearly round table on Indigenous statistics to gather grassroots feedback on their activities from selected Indigenous people. The Reconciliation Action Plan also promotes career pathways for Indigenous people within the organisation. As for the future, the focus is on how to better generate data that more closely reflect Indigenous world views while still meeting government objectives. The ABS is seeking advice from Statistics New Zealand on this issue. Also under development are plans to establish strength-based reporting of the Aboriginal and Torres Strait Islander population, moving away from simply measuring disadvantage and gaps with respect to the non-Indigenous population. A key question to arise here is how NSOs might adapt their practices to meet new multiple objectives. For just over a century, the ABS has provided data for federal and state and territory tiers of government. In recent decades, it has also provided for a third tier: local government. The question now arises as to what its responsibilities might be in meeting the needs of newly emerging forms of Indigenous governance. Various forms of Indigenous incorporation exist or are required under Australian law, but the populations and geographic areas that they represent are not accommodated by current statistical frameworks, to say nothing about general agency obligations to give effect to the provisions of UNDRIP under Article 42.

In the final chapter, Darin Bishop (Chapter 16) reflects on his involvement in Māori data initiatives within the public sector— notably with the Māori Statistics Framework. Internationally, the framework is often regarded as an exemplar for NSOs, but, as Bishop notes, its development was long and often fraught. Initial attempts were unsuccessful because of a failure to adequately conceptualise

Māori indicators. The lesson learnt was to think beyond Western models of wellbeing and the confines of existing data. The shift away from a 'closing the gaps' approach to Māori development towards one focused on Māori potential provided an opportunity to also reframe the conversations around Māori statistical needs. While official Māori statistics provide many of the data for measuring socioeconomic outcomes, significant data gaps continue to exist in relation to Māori *whānau* (families) and households, Māori living overseas, Māori business activities, cultural outcomes and small-area data. Echoing the sentiments of other contributors, Bishop points to the need for an independent Māori voice in the official statistics system and for more Māori to be involved in crucial decision-making stages of the statistical cycle. Bishop also raises the important issue of appropriate 'units of measurement'. As one reviewer for this volume pointed out, the insistence on using the individual as the primary— often only—statistical unit of measurement is one of the embedded practices that cripples the ability of the CANZUS states to effectively address indigenous issues. The tendency of NSOs to see individuals as the primary units of measurement and aggregate from that level (for example, to households) means that governments are severely limited in their capacities to develop policies that are genuinely responsive to the collective conceptions that inform indigenous aspirations and agendas.

Key findings

The proposition that UNDRIP has implications for indigenous data sovereignty is overwhelmingly affirmed by the chapters in this book. Given the lack of strategic academic attention previously afforded this issue, discussions are necessarily preliminary and exploratory. It is clear that further work is needed to refine definitions, concepts, theory and applications. There is further scope to articulate the distinction between sovereignty as it relates to digital spaces and the forms of data stored in those spaces. Nonetheless, it is clear that indigenous peoples are positioning themselves and organising to give practical expression to various forms of indigenous data sovereignty at all scales at which indigenous polities are formed: international, national, regional and local/tribal. Likewise, (some) NSOs are starting to consider how their practices in relation to the collection and management of data pertaining to indigenous peoples might need to change, although, as Chapters 15 and 16 show, state agencies remain constrained by their structural focus on 'populations', rather than 'peoples', and by their ultimate function to service the needs of national governments. While there is some nod to the involvement and needs of indigenous peoples in data gathering, there is a clear implementation gap with respect to key provisions of UNDRIP. For its part, the UN, through the UNPFII, has recognised the need for alternative metrics to the post-2015 SDGs with some form of indigenous development index. There is also recognition of the need for a much greater level of community involvement and partnership in the gathering of culturally relevant information.

There are consequences in all of this for the epistemology of social science and, indeed, for any research activity that involves the collection or use of data on indigenous peoples, their territories and ways of life. While many of these issues have already been explored from an indigenous standpoint, by Tuhiwai-Smith (1999) and more recently by Walter and Andersen (2013), the breakthrough here is to link these arguments back to UNDRIP, to which the CANZUS group of states are signatories. By assembling a volume that is dominated by leading CANZUS-based indigenous social scientists and end-user data practitioners, we provide a degree of authenticity and voice that is unusual, if not unprecedented, in considerations of indigenous statistics.

An overarching conclusion of the collected papers is to reaffirm the assertion of UNDRIP that indigenous peoples have a right to self-determination that emanates from their inalienable relationships to lands, waters and the natural world, and that to give practical effect to this right requires a relocation of authority over relevant information from nation-states back to indigenous peoples. While the Western idea of 'data sovereignty' can be seen as a product of the digital age and nation-state jurisdiction over such data (Snipp, this volume), indigenous nations are asserting their own claims to data sovereignty, which are rooted in their inherent rights to self-determination as sovereign entities predating European settlers. Indigenous data sovereignty thus refers to the proper locus of authority over the management of data about indigenous peoples, their territories and ways of life. Early expressions of indigenous data sovereignty can be seen in indigenous oral traditions, which included a complex set of rights and responsibilities concerning the use of community-held information.

The contemporary expression of indigenous data sovereignty is made most forcefully in the Canadian case study (FNIGC, this volume) through the application of First Nations' principles and practices of ownership, control, access and possession (OCAP®) in relation to data that are about First Nations peoples. However, it should be recognised that the manner of application of these principles and practices will necessarily vary between jurisdictions and between indigenous polities. In Canada, the United States and Aotearoa/New Zealand there are clearly identifiable indigenous polities (First Nations, tribes and *iwi*, respectively) whose rights, including sovereign rights, have been established through treaty processes. The political landscape of the Australian settler state, and of Indigenous polities within it, is vastly different, although the prospect of treaty settlements has long been canvassed. While the achievement of indigenous data sovereignty requires a decolonisation of existing nation-state statistical systems, more thought and political work need to go into identifying and validating appropriate loci of indigenous data sovereignty, especially (among the CANZUS states) in Australia. In Canada, as we have seen, this has been given clear expression through the work of FNIGC. In the United States, the newly formed US Indigenous Data Sovereignty Network is pursuing similar goals and has identified four focus areas: data for sovereignty, data collection and access, data storage and security and data as intellectual property (USIDSN 2016). In Aotearoa/ New Zealand, the Māori Data Sovereignty network, Te Mana Raraunga (TMR) has developed a charter that provides the most complete expression to date of the basis for indigenous data sovereignty (see Appendix 1.1). It recognises that data form a living *taonga* or treasure and identifies six key ways through which to advance Māori data sovereignty:

1. asserting Māori rights and interests in relation to data
2. ensuring data for and about Māori can be safeguarded and protected
3. requiring the quality and integrity of Māori data and their collection
4. advocating for Māori involvement in the governance of data repositories

5. supporting the development of Māori data infrastructure and security systems

6. supporting the development of sustainable Māori digital businesses and innovations.

In raising issues of indigenous data sovereignty, this volume invites further scrutiny and debate on what is emerging as a major knowledge gap in the social sciences. Closing this particular gap requires substantial change and innovation including: the devising of new methods for the international measurement of indigenous development and wellbeing; meeting the challenge of embracing indigenous epistemologies; the analysis of legal and practical limits to data sovereignty, including the impact of free-trade agreements such as the Trans-Pacific Partnership (TPP) Agreement; the construction of models for developing data governance and capacity; exploring the implications of individual versus collective rights for data linkage, sharing and use; and consideration of the threats and opportunities presented by census transformation programs and the advent of 'big data' and open data. This volume signals the beginning point in an ongoing conversation initiated by and for indigenous peoples. There is much work yet to be done.

References

Bell M (2015). W(h)ither the census? *Australian Geographer* 46(3):299–304.

Hall G & Patrinos H (2012). *Indigenous peoples, poverty, and development*, Cambridge University Press, New York.

Kukutai T & Taylor J (2012). Postcolonial profiling of indigenous peoples in Australia and Aoteoroa/New Zealand. *Espace Populations Sociétés* 2012-1:13–27.

Kukutai T, Thompson V & McMillan R (2015). Whither the census? Continuity and change in census methodologies worldwide, 1985–2014. *Journal of Population Research* 32(3):3–22.

Malezer L (2009). *Dialogue with states regarding respect for and application of the UN Declaration and follow up on its effectiveness*, paper presented at the International Expert Group Meeting on the Role of the United Nations Permanent Forum on Indigenous Issues in the Implementation of Article 42 of the United Nations Declaration on the Rights of Indigenous Peoples, United Nations Department of Economic and Social Affairs, New York, 14–16 January 2009.

National Institute of Demographic and Economic Analysis (NIDEA) (2015). Unpublished data from the Ethnicity Counts? Project, NIDEA, University of Waikato, Hamilton, waikato.ac.nz/nidea/research/ethnicitycounts.

Royal Commission into Aboriginal Deaths in Custody (RCIADIC) (1991). *Royal Commission into Aboriginal Deaths in Custody (RCIADIC) national report: overview and recommendations*, Commissioner E Johnson, Australian Government Publishing Service, Canberra.

Smylie J & Firestone M (2015). Back to basics: identifying and addressing underlying challenges in achieving high quality and relevant health statistics for indigenous populations in Canada, *Statistical Journal of the IAOS* 31(1):67–87.

Taylor J & Kukutai T (2015). *Indigenous data sovereignty and indicators: reflections from Australia and Aotearoa New Zealand*, paper presented at the UNPFII Expert Group Meeting on The Way Forward: Indigenous Peoples and Agenda 2030, United Nations Department of Economic and Social Affairs, New York, 22–23 October 2015.

Tebtebba Foundation (2008). *Indicators relevant for indigenous peoples: a resource book*, Tebtebba Foundation, Baguio City, Philippines.

Tuhiwai-Smith L (1999). *Decolonizing methodologies: research and indigenous peoples*, Zed Books, London and New York.

United Nations Permanent Forum on Indigenous Issues (UNPFII) (2004). *Report of the workshop on data collection and disaggregation for indigenous peoples*, E/c.19/2004/1, United Nations Permanent Forum on Indigenous Issues, New York, 1–21 May 2004.

United Nations Permanent Forum on Indigenous Issues (UNPFII) (2006). *Report of the meeting on indigenous peoples and indicators of wellbeing*, E/c.19/2006/CRP.3, United Nations Permanent Forum on Indigenous Issues, Ottawa, 22–23 March 2006.

United Nations Permanent Forum on Indigenous Issues (UNPFII) (2010). *Report of the meeting on indigenous peoples: development with culture and identity—Articles 3 and 32 of the United Nations Declaration on the Rights of Indigenous Peoples*, E/c.19/2010/14, United Nations Permanent Forum on Indigenous Issues, New York, 19–30 April 2010.

United States Indigenous Data Sovereignty Network (USIDSN) (2016). Website. Native Nations Institute, Tuscon, nni.arizona.edu/news/articles/us-indigenous-data-sovereignty-network.

Walter M & Andersen C (2013). *Indigenous statistics: a quantitative research methodology*, Left Coast Press, Walnut Creek, CA.

Appendix 1.1

Te Mana Raraunga — Māori Data Sovereignty Network Charter

He whenua hou, Te Ao Raraunga
Te Ao Raraunga, He whenua hou[2]

Preamble

With respect to the inherent rights that we as Māori have by virtue of our inalienable relationships with the land, water and the natural world, we assert that:

- Data is a living tāonga and is of strategic value to Māori.
- Māori data refers to data produced by Māori or that is about Māori and the environments we have relationships with. Māori Data includes but is not limited to:

---

2 'Data is a new world, a world of opportunity.'

- Data from organisations and businesses
- Data about Māori that is used to describe or compare Māori collectives
- Data about Te Ao Māori that emerges from research
- Māori data is subject to the rights articulated in the Treaty of Waitangi and the UN's Declaration on the Rights of Indigenous Peoples,[3] to which Aotearoa New Zealand is a signatory.
- Data Sovereignty typically refers to the understanding that data is subject to the laws of the nation within which it is stored.
- Indigenous Data Sovereignty perceives data as subject to the laws of the nation from which it is collected.
- Māori Data Sovereignty recognises that Māori data should be subject to Māori governance.
- Māori Data Sovereignty supports tribal sovereignty and the realisation of Māori and Iwi aspirations.

Purpose

The purpose of Te Mana Raraunga is to enable Māori Data Sovereignty and to advance Māori aspirations for collective and individual wellbeing by:

- asserting Māori rights and interests in relation to data,
- ensuring data for and about Māori can be safeguarded and protected,
- requiring the quality and integrity of Māori data and its collection,
- advocating for Māori involvement in the governance of data repositories,
- supporting the development of Māori data infrastructure and security systems,
- supporting the development of sustainable Māori digital businesses and innovations.

---

3   Consistent with the rights articulated in the Mataatua Declaration, WAI 262 (Nga Puhi doc.), and the Outcome Document of UNDRIP.

Where necessary, Te Mana Raraunga will utilise the expertise of its members to provide Māori data governance functions over relevant datasets **in the absence of** mandated Māori governance entities. Te Mana Raraunga will support the establishment of appropriate protocols for iwi authority over data.

Te Mana Raraunga will advocate for resourcing to support the development of capacity and capability across the Māori data ecosystem including:

1. **Data rights and interests.** Establishing the nature of Māori rights and interests to government collected administrative data, survey, census and research data derived from indigenous tāonga are central to realising aspirations in the Mataatua Declaration, the WAI262 claim, and the UNDRIP. Articulating these rights and interests in an intellectual property framework is necessary to realise commercialisation opportunities and benefit sharing agreements for hapū, iwi and/or Māori entities.[4]

2. **Data governance.** There is a wealth of data pertaining to Māori individuals, whānau, households, hapū, iwi, entities and te Taiao that is collected by the state as part of the Official Statistics System (OSS), crown agencies and government organisations, through commercial transactions, social media, telecommunications (including satellites) and other means. Only a small proportion of these data sources are currently accessible to Māori for our own purposes and benefit. Māori involvement in data governance and data management is essential to ensure data is used for projects that support beneficial outcomes for Māori.

3. **Data storage and security.** As more businesses and entities have moved to cloud-based models of data storage, this has raised concerns around the security and privacy of data that are stored offshore, and the legal and privacy frameworks that the data are subject to, including the issue of data sovereignty. TMR supports the development of Māori data infrastructure and security systems to support the realisation of Māori data sovereignty.

4. **Data Collection, Access and Control:** Māori should be involved in decisions about the collection of and access to Māori data, analysis and interpretation. Use of data for research should also be

---

4   As set out by the World Intellectual Property Organization (WIPO).

consistent with frameworks for Māori research ethics (i.e. Te Ara Tika). Using data requires that data is made available in a usable form and that we have the workforce who can be actively engaged in the design, collection, processing, analysis and dissemination of data to meet our own needs.

Guiding principles

Te Mana Raraunga recognises the need to advance discussions about Māori Data Sovereignty at both governance (mana) and operational levels (mahi). The work of Te Mana Raraunga will support the realisation of rangatiratanga, kotahitanga, manaakitanga and kaitiakitanga.

Mana-Mahi Framework

Whanaungatanga and Whakapapa: Whanaungatanga denotes the fact that in Māori thinking and philosophy relationships between man, Te Ao Turoa (the natural world) and spiritual powers inherent therein, and Taha Wairua (spirit) are everything. Whakapapa evidences those linkages and identifies the nature of the relationships.

Rangatiratanga: Rangatiratanga speaks to the hapū, iwi/Māori aspiration for self-determination, to be in control of our own affairs and to influence those taking place within our iwi boundaries. This is especially true for activities that have the potential to affect our people (ngā uri whakaheke) or our environment (whenua/moana). Rangatiratanga can be expressed through leadership and participation. Data supports the expression of Rangatiratanga and Rangatiratanga can be expressed through data in terms of the OCAP®[5] principles of ownership, access, control and possession.

Kotahitanga: Kotahitanga speaks to a collective vision and unity of purpose while recognising the mana of rangatira from individual hapū and iwi. The foundations of kotahitanga can be found in our whakapapa and reflected in our relationships with each other. It is

---

5   The OCAP principles are trademarked by the First Nations Information Governance Centre and mean that First Nations control data collection processes in their communities and how the data are used. See: fnigc.ca/ocap.html.

important that we make space to identify our collective aspirations for indigenous data sovereignty and advocate for activities that benefit all Māori.

Manaakitanga: Manaakitanga can be expressed through the responsibility to provide hospitality and protection to whānau, hapū, iwi, the community and the environment. The foundations of manaakitanga rely on the ability of Māori to live as Māori, to access quality education, to have good health, to have employment opportunities and to have liveable incomes. Ethical data-use has the potential to contribute greatly to Māori aspirations.

Kaitiakitanga: Kaitiakitanga speaks to the hapū, iwi responsibility to be an effective steward or guardian and relates to actions that ensure a sustainable future for all people. Underpinning our existence is the need to protect and enhance Māori knowledge and practices, to strengthen whānau, hapū and iwi and to create sustainable futures. Kaitiaki have a social contract and are responsible to the communities they serve. Identifying appropriate data guardians and the principles by which they will operate is a key consideration.

Membership and mandate

Te Mana Raraunga advocates for Māori Data Sovereignty at a national level. Te Mana Raraunga is open to participation from Māori and iwi data users, ICT [information and communication technology] providers, researchers, policymakers and planners, businesses, service providers and community advocates that share this charter.

A working group advances Te Mana Raraunga's work programme with support from a part-time administrator. The working group will meet with key Māori and iwi representatives and liaise with government agencies including the New Zealand Data Futures Forum to support the realisation of Māori Data Sovereignty.

An inaugural meeting on Māori Data Sovereignty was held at Hopuhopu on 19th October 2015 where the formation of Te Mana Raraunga as a Māori Data Sovereignty Network was accepted by the participants and the contents of the charter discussed.

The charter was approved in Te Rangimarie at Papakura Marae on 5 April 2016.

Part 1: Decolonising indigenous data

2

Data and the United Nations Declaration on the Rights of Indigenous Peoples

Megan Davis

Introduction

It is well understood that the existence of relevant information is a vital precondition for devising adequate policy responses to address inequalities and to monitor the effectiveness of measures to overcome discrimination, both within and between countries, as well as for identifying additional gender-based discrimination. Yet, on many occasions, the situation of indigenous peoples remains invisible within national statistics. This is especially true in many developing countries, which often have weak institutional capacities as well as limited financial resources to collect statistics and disaggregate among the various ethnic, linguistic, religious and other groups that may be present in the country. Another factor complicating data collection for indigenous peoples is that, in many countries, particularly in Africa and Asia, the formal identification and recognition of indigenous peoples is still pending, and disaggregation of data based on ethnicity may be considered, for various reasons, controversial. This chapter provides an overview of the issues pertaining to indigenous peoples and data from a United Nations (UN) perspective—in particular, drawing on the work of the UN Permanent Forum on Indigenous Issues (UNPFII) and the UN Declaration on the Rights of Indigenous Peoples (UNDRIP).

The problem of data and indigenous peoples and the United Nations

Data have emerged as a major concern of the UNPFII, which is a functional commission of the Economic and Social Council (ECOSOC), a body constituted by both indigenous experts and representatives of states.[1] The resolution establishing the UNPFII as an advisory body to ECOSOC empowered the forum with a broad-ranging mandate to discuss indigenous issues relating to economic and social development, culture, the environment, education, health and human rights. According to the mandate, the UNPFII is expected to: 1) provide advice and recommendations on indigenous issues to ECOSOC, as well as to programs, funds and agencies of the UN through ECOSOC; 2) raise awareness and promote the integration and coordination of activities relating to indigenous issues within the UN system; and 3) prepare and disseminate information on indigenous issues. Therefore, data from UN member states and UN programs, agencies and funds are critical to the effective functioning of the forum.

A corollary to this is the unique composition of the forum. It has 16 members who are independent experts and serve for a term of three years. Eight members are indigenous and eight are state members. The indigenous members are appointed by the president of ECOSOC and represent the seven indigenous regions of the world: Africa; Asia; Central and South America and the Caribbean; the Arctic; Central and Eastern Europe, the Russian Federation, Central Asia and Transcaucasia; North America; and the Pacific. The state members are elected by ECOSOC on the basis of the five UN regional groups: Africa, Asia, Eastern Europe, Latin America and the Caribbean, and Western Europe and other states. This is a novel approach to representation in the UN but it means that the UNPFII has access to more nuanced and layered information about the composition of indigenous populations

---

1   Establishment of a Permanent Forum on Indigenous Issues, Economic and Social Council Resolution 2000/22, UN Doc. E/RES/2000/22 (2000).

than it would have through UN member states, who utilise conventional ways of conveying information about indigenous peoples through official statistics that are not disaggregated.

There are two brief points to be made about the UNPFII. While the forum is seen as a major development in the international legal activism of indigenous peoples, it has also been met with some scepticism in indigenous circles. These critics argue that the UNPFII domesticates indigenous issues within Western political structures and rigid working procedures and agendas to control the dissemination of information about human rights violations against indigenous peoples and to avoid consideration of indigenous peoples' right to self-determination (see, e.g., Havemann 2001: 9; Stewart-Harawira 2005: 18). The second point relates to indigenous identity. Not all states acknowledge indigenous populations. During the early period of the UN's engagement with indigenous peoples, a working definition was developed in Jose Martinez Cobo's *Study on the problem of discrimination against indigenous populations* to traverse the politics of indigeneity:

> Indigenous communities, peoples and nations are those which, having a historical continuity with pre-invasion and pre-colonial societies that developed on their territories, consider themselves distinct from other sectors of the societies now prevailing on those territories, or parts of them. They form at present non-dominant sectors of society and are determined to preserve, develop and transmit to future generations their ancestral territories, and their ethnic identity, as the basis of their continued existence as peoples, in accordance with their own cultural patterns, social institutions and legal system.
>
> This historical continuity may consist of the continuation, for an extended period reaching into the present of one or more of the following factors:
>
> a. Occupation of ancestral lands, or at least of part of them;
> b. Common ancestry with the original occupants of these lands;
> c. Culture in general, or in specific manifestations (such as religion, living under a tribal system, membership of an indigenous community, dress, means of livelihood, lifestyle, etc.);
> d. Language (whether used as the only language, as mother-tongue, as the habitual means of communication at home or in the family, or as the main, preferred, habitual, general or normal language);

e. Residence on certain parts of the country, or in certain regions of the world;

f. Other relevant factors.

> On an individual basis, an indigenous person is one who belongs to these indigenous populations through self-identification as indigenous (group consciousness) and is recognized and accepted by these populations as one of its members (acceptance by the group) … This preserves for these communities the sovereign right and power to decide who belongs to them, without external interference. (Martinez Cobo 1986–87: 379–82)

The definition of 'indigenous peoples' not infrequently is an issue for some states at the UNPFII. UNDRIP did not adopt a definition of 'indigenous peoples'; self-identification is emphasised.

In the formative days of the UNFPII, it was immediately apparent that data were the significant barrier to the work of the forum and the UN in general. For this reason, a UN expert group meeting was organised to examine the issue further. According to the Officer-in-Charge of the UN Statistics Division, 'consideration of the issue of indigenous peoples and data collection was ground-breaking work'. In 2004, he identified indigenous peoples as an 'important emerging theme in social statistics'.[2] From the outset, indigenous participants identified culturally specific data and standardised data to ensure that indigenous peoples were provided with data that were useful for them. In addition, the workshop report noted that participants emphasised qualitative and quantitative data *combined* as necessary to conceptualise indigenous peoples' issues and the underlying causes. The workshop participants argued:

> Research should be carried out in partnership with indigenous peoples and the use of qualitative data in the form of case studies, reports of special rapporteurs, community testimonies, etc., would allow Governments, non-governmental organizations, indigenous organizations and the United Nations system to bring in their experience and expertise. Many experts agreed that case studies provided opportunities, which could often be extrapolated into broader lessons. Case studies allowed for the use of both qualitative and quantitative data, which provided a holistic view of the welfare of distinct peoples.[3]

---

2   Report of the Workshop on Data Collection and Disaggregation for Indigenous Peoples, United Nations Doc. E/C.19/2004/2 [11]: 10.

3   ibid. [13]: 4–5.

On the other hand, there was caution expressed that case studies could be problematic because of the paucity of standardised data to compare with the non-indigenous population. For this reason:

[A] wide range of sources and types of data were desirable in building a complete profile of a people and also noted was the desirability of having trained indigenous peoples engaged in the full range of work concerning data collection, such as planning, collecting, analysing and report writing.[4]

The outcomes of the expert group meeting included the following questions relevant to data sovereignty:

- For whom are we collecting data?
- How do we collect the data?
- What should be measured?
- Who should control information?
- What are the data for?
- Why do indigenous peoples in resource-rich areas experience poor social conditions and a lack of social services?
- To what degree is remoteness responsible?

In terms of the challenges moving forward, indigenous participants identified the following obstacles and barriers:

a. Data collection was as much a political as a logistical exercise.

b. Currently available data for the most part did not adequately explain social conditions; there are gaps to be addressed.

c. Currently available data did not adequately incorporate environmental concerns.

d. Varying definitions of 'indigenous' could pose a problem in collecting data.

e. Standard forms of questions used would not always accurately reflect the situation of indigenous peoples—for example, indigenous family and social patterns were sometimes very different from the profile of the rest of the population.

f. Drifting and mobility in ethnic identity provided inconsistencies when comparing the population longitudinally.

---

4   ibid.: 4–5.

g. Some statistical offices pointed out the inadequate or inaccurate reporting of indigenous identity, often as a result of misunderstanding of questions or limited opportunities to identify as belonging to more than one race or ethnicity.

h. Indigenous peoples who migrated to other countries (either voluntarily or as a result of expulsion or fleeing conflict) were often faced with the dilemma of no longer having the opportunity of identifying as indigenous in their new country. This issue was also one for the new host country and was increasingly complex because of the increasing amount of migration, both documented and undocumented.

i. The fact that indigenous peoples often resided in areas affected by war and conflicts posed an additional challenge in terms of data collection.

j. Collecting statistics on indigenous languages was useful but did not give a complete picture of the population, especially as languages were lost as a result of urbanisation, discrimination and other factors. Recording ethnic affiliation remains a problem for statisticians.

k. Lack of vital or service statistics disaggregated by ethnic group, gender and age group made it difficult to assess adequately the health situation, standard of living and coverage of health services for indigenous peoples, as well as to set priorities for action and the evaluation of impacts on these populations.

l. The challenge for public health was to translate social and cultural information into practical information to promote the welfare of indigenous communities and individuals.

m. The economic situation of indigenous peoples was very often underrepresented in official statistics, because they often belonged to informal economies, which were reported inadequately.

n. While some data collection work and dissemination had been done in the Americas and in the circumpolar regions, in particular, limited data had been made available for Asia, Africa, the Caribbean and parts of the Pacific.[5]

---

5   ibid.: 9.

It is important to stress that the expert group observed that during the meeting many of the discussions were 'intertwined' with the issue of racial discrimination. Indigenous participants were concerned that statistics, 'although seemingly neutral', could be applied for the benefit and the detriment of indigenous peoples.

The UNPFII continues to focus on the issue of data collection and has made various recommendations towards this end. In its most recent session in 2016, the forum recommended states actively engage with indigenous peoples, in both developed and developing countries, in the development of key indicators on indigenous peoples to be included in the overall indicators for the post-2015 development agenda. In addition, the UN system has made calls to states and others within the international system to collect statistics on the situation of indigenous peoples. Most recently, in the *Outcome document of the World Conference on Indigenous Peoples*, adopted by the UN General Assembly on 22 September 2014, member states were called on to:

> commit themselves to working with indigenous peoples to disaggregate data, as appropriate, or conduct surveys and to utilizing holistic indicators of indigenous peoples' well-being to address the situation and needs of indigenous peoples and individuals, in particular older persons, women, youth, children and persons with disabilities.[6]

Despite these calls, to date, there have been few examples of concerted efforts to collect such data on the situation of indigenous peoples, and far fewer global efforts to collect data in a way that can allow for comparisons to be made across regions and contexts.

It is, however, worth mentioning some examples. Several countries have made progress with regard to disaggregation of data in their population, including on indigenous peoples. For example, the Government of Canada gathers statistical data on First Nation, Inuit and Métis people as part of its official census in areas such as population, education, health, employment, income and housing. These data can be compared with the statistical data collected for non-indigenous populations in the country, and generally reveal disparities in terms of social and economic outcomes. Chapters by Jelfs (this volume) and Bishop (this volume) also outline in some detail the substantial

---

6   Outcome document of the high-level plenary meeting of the General Assembly known as the World Conference on Indigenous Peoples, UN Doc. A/Res/69/2: para. 10.

developments that have occurred in Australia and New Zealand. At a regional level, the Economic Commission on Latin America and the Caribbean has made efforts to 'democratise information'. With the support of a number of UN agencies, donor agencies and private funders, the commission has established a comprehensive database, which provides sociodemographic data on indigenous peoples in the region, including data disaggregated by sex and age, as well as data on internal migration, health, youth and the territorial distribution of inequalities (see ECLAC n.d.). The basis of much of this work is the inclusion by most countries in Latin America of an 'indigenous identifier' in their 2000 census round, thus building data through the self-identification of individuals as being a member of an indigenous community (Del Popolo, Oyarce amd Ribotta 2015). There is yet to be a genuine global effort to collect data on the situation of indigenous peoples.

UNDRIP and data collection

UNDRIP provides the common framework of the normative content of the rights of indigenous peoples and is therefore important to understanding the issues of indigenous data sovereignty. The declaration represents a global consensus regarding the rights of indigenous peoples and was adopted by the UN General Assembly, with affirmative votes by the overwhelming majority of member states, in September 2007. UNDRIP is a non-binding declaration of the General Assembly, or 'soft' international law. An aspirational document, UNDRIP provides a framework that states can adopt in their relationship with indigenous peoples and that may guide them in the development of domestic law and policy. The text creates no new rights in international law nor does it create any binding legal obligations in domestic legal systems. Many of the articles in UNDRIP are recognised in other international instruments and/or are affirmations of putative international norms as well as evolving human rights standards pertaining to indigenous peoples.[7] UNDRIP is also replete with rights that are not commonly accepted as binding legal standards.

---

7   See, generally, Anaya (2009: 61–3); Wiessner (1999).

UNDRIP is fundamentally a human rights instrument, and it is worth noting that there are certain difficulties in measuring human rights achievements in terms of quantitative data or statistics, given that assessing the enjoyment of human rights will always contain a strong qualitative element. Nonetheless, experiences in developing indicators to measure progress in implementing human rights in other contexts have shown that it is possible to gather statistically useful data for human rights compliance.

UNDRIP covers a range of rights, including civil and political rights, economic and social rights, and others, such as rights that are viewed as fundamental for indigenous peoples—that is, rights to lands, territories and natural resources and rights to self-determination, autonomy and participation. It can be viewed as a relatively 'complete' reflection of the substantive rights of indigenous peoples. The rights recognised in UNDRIP are deliberately grouped into several identifiable themes—the rights to: self-determination; life, integrity and security; cultural, religious, spiritual and linguistic identity; education and public information; participatory rights; lands and resources. It should be noted, however, that UNDRIP in its entirety can be read as an expression of what the right to self-determination means in practical terms for indigenous peoples.

The cluster of Articles 1–6 recognises general principles surrounding rights to nationality, self-determination, equality and freedom from adverse discrimination. This cluster includes Article 3, which affirms the indigenous right to self-determination, and Article 4, which extends this right to self-government and autonomy in relation to internal and local affairs. Articles 7–10 recognise rights to life, integrity and security. Articles 11–13 pertain to culture, spirituality and linguistic identity, including the right to practice and revitalise cultural traditions and customs as well as the right to maintain, protect and develop past, present and future manifestations of indigenous culture.

Articles 14–17 deal with indigenous rights to education, information and labour rights, including the right of all children to education by the state as well as the right to establish and control indigenous educational systems and institutions. Articles 18–23 are participatory rights that enable special measures for immediate, effective and continuing improvement of indigenous economic and social conditions in the areas of employment, vocational training and retraining, housing, sanitation, health and social security. This section also provides that states shall take measures to ensure that indigenous women and children enjoy the full protection and guarantees against all forms of violence and discrimination.

Articles 24–31 deal with lands, territories and resources. Indigenous peoples have the right to own, develop, control and use the lands and territories they have traditionally owned or otherwise occupied or used. This includes the right to the full recognition of their laws, traditions and customs, land-tenure systems and institutions for the development and management of resources, and the right to effective measures by states to prevent any interference with, alienation of or encroachment on these rights. Articles 32–36 explain how the right to self-determination can be implemented, including matters relating to internal local affairs such as culture, education, information, media, housing, employment, social welfare, economic activities, land and resources and the environment. This section empowers indigenous peoples with the right to determine citizenship in accordance with customs and tradition. Most notably, it empowers indigenous peoples to promote and maintain traditional judicial customs, procedures and practices.

UNDRIP also gives guidance to states on how these substantive rights can be implemented within domestic legal and political systems. Article 37 recognises the right of indigenous peoples to conclude treaties, agreements or other constructive arrangements with states. Article 38 provides that the state, in cooperation with indigenous peoples, shall take appropriate measures including legislative measures to achieve the ends of UNDRIP; and Article 39 states that indigenous peoples have the right of access to financial and technical assistance from states for the enjoyment of the rights recognised in UNDRIP. Articles 40–46 are implementation provisions expounding the role of the state and international organisations in recognising the rights provided in UNDRIP. Article 46 of the declaration renders all the articles subject to existing international and domestic law. This means that the rights are relative and must be balanced with the rights of others.

The most important rights underpinning the framework of UNDRIP are the two key provisions on the right to self-determination:

Article 3

Indigenous peoples have the right of self-determination. By virtue of that right they freely determine their political status and freely pursue their economic, social and cultural development.

Article 4

Indigenous peoples, in exercising their right to self-determination, have the right to autonomy or self-government in matters relating to their internal and local affairs, as well as ways and means for financing their autonomous functions.

UNDRIP was developed with the active participation of indigenous peoples themselves, and reflects indigenous peoples' own priorities, views and concepts of wellbeing and culturally appropriate development. In this context, UNDRIP's affirmation of universal human rights standards that apply to indigenous peoples across the world, and that have been supported by states and indigenous peoples across the world, addresses an important element of data collection: the existence of universally acceptable standards for measurement to allow for cross-country comparison.

Measuring implementation of the human rights standards affirmed in UNDRIP will require the collection of both objective and subjective data (also referred to as 'fact-based' and 'judgment-based' data). These elements are complementary and mutually reinforcing, and both present important opportunities for the collection of data spearheaded by indigenous peoples themselves.

With respect to objective data, relevant information will include the existence of laws, policies and programs, as well as concrete actions, in line with the provisions of UNDRIP—for example, the existence of constitutional recognition of indigenous peoples, the total of lands demarcated in favour of indigenous peoples, the number of indigenous students with access to bilingual education programs, and so on. Collecting such data can often be conducted through a 'desk review' or through a review of available administrative data collected by the state or other sources. However, collection of such data by indigenous peoples themselves will also be essential, especially in countries with limited technical and financial capacities, or political will, to gather such information, and overcoming this constraint remains one of the major challenges for the UNPFII and allied agencies.

For its part, subjective data will measure, generally through the use of a survey or questionnaire, to what extent indigenous peoples perceive that their rights are being implemented—for example, whether their views have been reflected in a development plan and the perceived security of tenure of the lands and resources under traditional ownership. Collecting subjective data presents additional challenges in terms of resources and maintaining consistent data collection, but it also presents important opportunities for indigenous-driven efforts and for ensuring that indigenous peoples' rights and priorities are reflected in the data collected.

A first step in collection of data on the situation of indigenous peoples will be the development of appropriate indicators and surveys based on UNDRIP that can be applied in local contexts around the world. A second step is to train indigenous peoples, but also states, non-governmental organisations (NGOs) and others, in the collection of such data and to provide them with the tools necessary to do so. Finally, it is necessary that some entity at the global or regional level—perhaps within the UN—compiles, analyses and publishes the data.

A very interesting emerging example is the 'Indigenous Navigator' project being developed by a collection of UN organisations and NGOs, including the International Work Group for Indigenous Affairs, the Asia Indigenous Peoples Pact, the Forest Peoples Programme, the International Labour Organization (ILO) and the Tebtebba Foundation. The project has developed a framework and set of tools and indicators for indigenous peoples themselves to systematically monitor the level of recognition and implementation of their rights. The project uses as a basis for measurement the rights affirmed in UNDRIP and has devised a set of indicators that relate to clusters of rights covered by UNDRIP, including lands and resources, languages, self-government, participation, consultation and consent and recognition of identity. The project is now in a pilot phase and no doubt the information that emerges from the data collection process will be highly useful in various other contexts.

Conclusion

As part of its future work, the UNPFII has discussed the formulation of an indigenous peoples' index, based on the human rights affirmed in UNDRIP. At its annual session in 2015, the UNPFII held a panel discussion on this issue. It concluded that in establishing indicators, the focus should be on the vision and world views of indigenous peoples, based on collective rights, such as those to identity, land, territories and resources, free, prior and informed consent and indigenous women's participation in local, national and international decision-making processes. The forum will continue this work, building on positive experiences that already exist around the world, and it hopes to draw on the support of UN agencies, national statistics offices, academics and others, including and especially indigenous peoples themselves, to collaborate in this effort.

References

Anaya SJ (2009). *International human rights and indigenous peoples*, Aspen Publishers, New York.

Del Popolo F, Oyarce AM and Ribotta B (2015). *Sistema de Indicadores Sociodemográfico de Poblaciones y Pueblos Indígena de América Latina—SISPPI. Guia para el usuario* [*System of sociodemographic and population indicators and indigenous peoples of Latin America— SISPPI. User guide*], Santiago: CELADE/CEPAL—Fondo Indígena, celade.cepal.org/redatam/PRYESP/SISPPI/SISPPI_notastecnicas.pdf.

Economic Commission for Latin America and the Caribbean (ECLAC) (n.d.). *Indigenous peoples and Afro-descendants in Latin America and the Caribbean data bank—PIAALC*, ECLAC, Port of Spain, www.cepal.org/en/indigenous-peoples-and-afro-descendants-latin-america-and-carribean-data-bank-piaalc.

Havemann PL (2001). The participation deficit: globalization, governance and indigenous peoples. *Balayi: Culture, Law and Colonialism - Indigenous Peoples in the International Sphere* 3:9–36.

Martinez Cobo J (1986–87). *Study of the problem of discrimination against indigenous populations*, UN Doc. E/CN.4/Sub.2/1986/7, United Nations, New York, www.un.org/development/desa/indigenouspeoples/publications/2014/09/martinez-cobo-study/#more-7242.

Stewart-Harawira M (2005). *The new imperial order: indigenous responses to globalization*, Zed Books, London.

Wiessner S (1999). Rights and status of indigenous peoples: a global comparative and international legal analysis. *Harvard Human Rights Journal* 12:57.

3

What does data sovereignty imply: what does it look like?

C Matthew Snipp

Indigenous people have long struggled to retain their rights as autonomous self-governing people. These struggles have sometimes involved litigation, sometimes political manoeuvring and, too often, violence and bloodshed. In the United States, for example, various groups of native people waged war against Europeans virtually from the early days of first contact in the sixteenth century until the last battle was fought with the US Army in 1890. In the twenty-first century, another form of aboriginal sovereignty is at stake: data sovereignty.

Defining data sovereignty

The term 'data sovereignty' is a uniquely twenty-first-century expression that arises directly from the explosive growth of information associated with the internet and the spread of mobile phone technology. Quite simply, data sovereignty means managing information in a way that is consistent with the laws, practices and customs of the nation-state in which it is located. Privacy laws, for example, vary from one country to another. In recognition of the variability, data sovereignty means that information that would be illegal to provide in one location might be perfectly legal to disclose in another nation. In 2010, the search engine Google became famously embroiled in a controversy with Chinese authorities over their censorship practices. Google executives were loath to allow the Chinese Government to censor search results and to access email accounts managed by the company. This led the company to move its offices to Hong Kong and caused them to cede the large and lucrative Chinese market to their competitor Baidu.com (Helft & Barboza 2010).

The Chinese example notwithstanding, vast amounts of data are now accessible from virtually any far-flung part of the world. Geographic boundaries that once impeded the flow of information from one location to another are largely irrelevant. In the twentieth century, shutting down radio and television broadcasts and disabling telephone services across physical landlines could easily limit access to information. By comparison, mobile phone technology, satellite phones and internet access make the control of information vastly more difficult for smaller nations with resources more limited than the Government of China and a handful of other large, powerful and wealthy nations such as the United States. These smaller and less wealthy nations of course include indigenous people. There are vast differences among these groups in their size, their wealth and especially their powers as sovereign entities. However, suffice to say, in all instances, they are smaller, poorer and weaker than the settler states that typically surround them.

That indigenous people are typically poorer than the surrounding settler state has important implications for data sovereignty. This is because collecting data that can be turned into information and later organised into meaningful knowledge is a costly process. Censuses and surveys are very costly to conduct and even unobtrusive video surveillance must be processed to condense it and make it intelligible. This, too, often means that indigenous communities must forgo having access to certain types of information about themselves or must rely on outsiders with the requisite resources to obtain this information. Of course, relying on outsiders typically involves significant compromises over the control of data and therefore data sovereignty. Thus, these compromises entail important questions about from whom data are collected, the content of these data, the purposes for which these data are to be used and who will ultimately control access to these data. These questions are critical for understanding the vestiges of colonial dependency of indigenous people on the settler state.

Data from whom?

Before the collection of data can begin, a fundamental question must be asked—and answered—and that is: from whom will information be obtained? This is not a trivial question because it defines the universe and sampling frame for surveys, the subjects eligible to participate in experiments and who will and will not be counted in a census, just to name a few examples. For the purpose of collecting data from indigenous people, this question invokes the deeply complex question of 'who is (and is not) indigenous?'

Defining indigeneity

The question of 'who is indigenous' is deeply complex because it involves issues that must be addressed simultaneously and independently. On one hand, indigeneity is a group characteristic that defines the qualities of a collectivity. On the other hand, it is also a personal characteristic that either binds together or sets apart individuals from the larger collective of people deemed to be 'indigenous'. The experience of American Indians in the United States provides a good example of this duality, and it is a simpler example than in other parts of the world. For instance, in the United States, indigeneity is defined by the presence of ancestors occupying this part of the Western Hemisphere prior to 1492. In contrast, indigeneity in other continents such as Asia or Africa might hearken back to the earliest presence of *Homo sapiens*, long before recorded knowledge. Needless to say, this makes indigeneity virtually impossible to establish. So, for the sake of convenience in these regions, indigeneity simply means a presence prior to the arrival of European colonists, thereby making colonial contact one of the hallmarks of indigeneity everywhere in the world. Smith (1999) describes this as research through 'imperial eyes'.

Although 1492 benchmarks indigeneity in the Western Hemisphere, the settler states that now occupy and control this region typically complicate indigeneity with their own views of who is and is not indigenous. In Mexico, for example, a person is not indigenous unless they are capable of speaking an indigenous language such as Zapotec. In the United States, the federal government and the Congress in particular have determined that an American Indian is any person who belongs to a federally recognised tribe. Returning to the aforementioned duality of indigeneity, this begs the questions of what constitutes a 'federally recognised tribe' and how does one 'belong' to such an entity? The latter question has a very direct bearing on data sovereignty because the US Supreme Court has ruled that a determination of who 'belongs' to a tribe is a fundamental right that inheres in the political sovereignty of the tribes themselves. That is, in the Supreme Court decision of *Santa Clara Pueblo v. Martinez* (436 US 49 [1978]), the justices reasoned that by their retained rights of self-government, the ability of the tribes to determine what conditions must be met to qualify for tribal membership was a fundamental part of their sovereign powers. Although the court ruled that tribes may determine the conditions of membership, and there is a plethora of different conditions for different tribes, the court has not ruled on what constitutes a federally recognised tribe (Lerma 2014).

Instead, the legislative and executive branches of the federal government have taken a more active role in this determination. A complete account of how tribes have gained federal recognition is beyond the scope of this essay. However, several details are worth noting in relation to data sovereignty and especially for the determination of indigeneity.

Most tribes have received federal recognition by dint of their resistance to the expansion of the United States in the eighteenth and nineteenth centuries. This resistance led to treaties and other agreements that bestowed federal recognition. However, there also were many tribes that were too small to resist or simply acquiesced to the presence of American settlers and their demands for land. The existence of such groups was belatedly acknowledged in 1978 when the Bureau of Indian Affairs set forth a process for heretofore 'unrecognised tribes' to gain federal recognition. At that time, 356 groups requested federal recognition (BIA 2013). However, as of late 2013, only 17 of these cases had been resolved and granted federal recognition. Another nine were granted recognition by acts of Congress. Thirty-four petitions were denied and the remainder are still pending in review.

There is a multiplicity of conditions that the tribes may impose for membership. Frequently, there is some sort of descent requirement that establishes a minimum amount of American Indian heritage as measured by 'blood quantum'. Full-blood quantum indicates a fully indigenous maternal and paternal heritage. One-quarter blood quantum is a common standard that was first established by the Bureau of Indian Affairs (BIA) in 1933 and has been widely adopted by tribal governments. One way of thinking about this requirement is that it involves being able to document having one full-blood grandparent if the remaining grandparents are not indigenous. Political theorist Will Kymlicka (1995: 23) argues that such rules are fundamentally racist and manifestly unjust. Still, these rules remain widely accepted by a large number of American Indian tribes.

Returning to the subject of data sovereignty, it should be clear that the matter of from whom data should be collected is bound up in legal principles and bureaucratic regulations connected with the sovereign political rights of indigenous people. One might imagine that having established these elaborate edifices, the US Government would be assiduously cognisant of them whenever data are to be solicited from American Indians. One would be very wrong to make this assumption.

The US Census Bureau is the single largest and most comprehensive source of information about American Indians and Alaska Natives, as well as Native Hawaiians.[1] This information is collected in conjunction with the decennial census and a very large survey known as the American Community Survey. The Census Bureau embeds categories of indigeneity within its question about racial heritage—the same question used to identify other racial groups in American society. It takes virtually no heed whatsoever of the sovereign political status of American Indians beyond an instruction to 'print principal or enrolled tribe' for persons who indicate they are American Indians. Persons who do not report a tribe are tabulated simply as 'Tribe not reported', and about 20 per cent of persons reporting to be an American Indian did not report a tribe in 2010 (Liebler & Zacher 2013).

The tribes would have it otherwise. The author of this essay spent over nine years on a committee established by the Census Bureau to offer advice on how the bureau collects and disseminates information about race and ethnicity. The American Indians on this committee repeatedly requested the Census Bureau pay greater heed to enrolment status than

---

1   The legal and political status of Alaska Natives is slightly different to that of American Indians. The legal and political status of Native Hawaiians is substantially different to that of the other two groups.

a vague instruction by adding a question about enrolment status or clarifying the meaning of 'enrolment'.[2] The Census Bureau steadfastly refused these requests, usually citing insufficient questionnaire space for an additional question or instructions. Verifying enrolment or conducting follow-up contacts with persons who did not report a tribe were dismissed out of hand as too costly.[3]

Data dissemination

The US Census Bureau does not entirely disregard the sovereign status of American Indian tribes but it is only an afterthought in the dissemination of data, not in its collection. That is, the Census Bureau does publish data for geographic areas specifically identified with American Indians—that is, reservations. It also works with tribal communities living in areas where there is some other geographic connection, such as Alaska Native villages or the former Indian Territory known today as the state of Oklahoma. In fact, there is a substantial list of geographic units recognised by the Census Bureau:

- Alaska Native Village Statistical Areas (ANVSAs)
- Alaska Native Regional Corporations (ANRCs)
- Oklahoma Tribal Statistical Areas (OTSAs)
- OTSA Tribal Subdivisions
- Tribal Designated Statistical Areas (TDSAs)
- Tribal Census Tracts and Tribal Block Groups (on federally recognised reservations only)
- State American Indian Reservations (SAIRs)
- State Designated Tribal Statistical Areas (SDTSAs).

Missing from this, however, are cities where the majority of American Indians now reside. One reason for this omission is that, in most cities, with the exception of Minneapolis, American Indians are not clustered in ethnic enclaves like other minorities. Nonetheless, the fact that the Census Bureau pays little heed to tribal enrolment, and only incidental

2   To date, the Census Bureau has never defined, much less clarified, the meaning of 'principal tribe'.

3   In 2017, the Census Bureau will field test a tribal enrolment question but this will be too late to be incorporated into the 2020 census. However, it may possibly inform thinking about questionnaire construction in the American Community Survey and the 2030 census.

attention to American Indians in urban areas, means that tribes do not have a precise accounting of their membership. This is also because many census-identified American Indians (especially in cities) do not claim tribal citizenship. As a result, there is a substantial mismatch between the numbers of American Indians counted in the census and the enrolment number reported by the tribes. For example, in 2001, the BIA reported there were 1,816,504 enrolled tribal members.[4] A year earlier, the Census Bureau enumerated 4.1 million persons who were identified as American Indians and/or Alaska Natives in the 2000 census.[5]

While it is true that tribes could initiate their own data collection efforts and determine for themselves from whom data were obtained, censuses and surveys are expensive and tribal communities typically lack the resources and expertise to mount such operations. Administrative data can sometimes be deployed for some purposes, but, again, this type of information can often be difficult to repurpose for other applications and may be incomplete and subject to clerical errors and related problems. And, again, it misses completely those persons residing away from tribal lands.

Although this discussion has focused almost exclusively on the American Indian experience in the United States, it should be remembered that similar accounting difficulties exist around the world wherever indigenous people are located. As Davis (this volume) reminds us, there is perhaps no better illustration of these difficulties than the challenge faced by Martinez Cobo as he struggled with a working definition of who might be covered by the United Nations Declaration on the Rights of Indigenous Peoples (UNDRIP). In spite of the apparent specificity of conditions laid, the prevailing view today is that no formal universal definition of the term is necessary and, for practical purposes, the understanding of the term commonly accepted is the one provided by Martinez Cobo (UN 2004: 4).

---

4   The BIA issues biennial reports. The preceding report was issued in 1999.
5   The discrepancy in these numbers and in earlier BIA reports led to a review of and long hiatus in the reports. The BIA stopped issuing these reports after 2005 and renewed their publication in 2013, using census data instead to produce their estimates.

Data about what and for what?

Data content

Assuming there is some agreement about from whom data are to be obtained, there is the next matter of the content domains connected with the data. These domains may vary a great deal depending on the uses for which the data are intended, while their purpose may also vary depending on whether the end-user is the indigenous community or the settler state. Again, the experiences of American Indians in the United States are instructive.

Whether indigenous communities or agencies of settler states collect data likely makes a vast difference to the content of that data. Needless to say, the motivations for data collection by settler states are often vastly different than those behind data collection by indigenous communities. Settler states may be motivated by the perceived need to monitor and exercise surveillance over indigenous communities. In some cases, this surveillance may be for law enforcement or military purposes. In other instances, this surveillance may be more benign and involve data collection for the provision of social services or other forms of community development.

On the other hand, indigenous communities may wish to take stock of their communities for purposes that are rather different to those of the settler state. Indeed, access to and control of data for indigenous communities are two means of exercising a measure of autonomy and independence from surrounding settler states. Indigenous communities may wish to assess the specific needs of their community, especially when outside authorities are willing to provide no more than nonspecific aggregate information. This kind of information can be invaluable for the purpose of planning community development projects and making the case for certain types of assistance from outside authorities and nongovernmental organisations (NGOs). Indigenous communities also might seek more intangible sorts of information such as community attitudes, which might concern the desirability of projects such as bridge construction or even more volatile matters such as political beliefs (Clifford 2013).

In the United States, American Indian tribes typically lack the resources to routinely collect data of any description, especially the sort that can be obtained from surveys or censuses. Many tribes do, however, collect information in the course of delivering services of one sort or another, such as housing assistance, job training or social services. However, this information typically pertains to only the most needy tribal members. In some instances, data obtained from the US Census Bureau provide baseline information about education, employment, income and similar characteristics for the geographic units described above. However, the Census Bureau routinely refuses to provide data for geographical areas smaller than the ones already listed.[6] Furthermore, the Census Bureau has steadfastly refused to collect information it regards as 'subjective' attitudinal data. Consequently, for tribes to obtain information about community attitudes, they must either obtain financial resources elsewhere or rely on the traditional sources of rumour and hearsay.

For other minorities—such as African Americans, Asians and Hispanics—there are national polls and surveys that produce a great deal of information about the attitudes, beliefs and even mental health of these groups. The National Survey of Black Americans, for example, included questions about their use of mental health services and their religious commitment. The Latino National Survey conducted in 2006 asked questions about ethnic identity and political ideology. A comparable survey of American Indians and Alaska Natives has never been conducted in the United States. While a national survey of American Indians would not yield tribe or community-specific information, such a survey might nonetheless be informative about a broad range of issues affecting American Indians, especially compared with other groups in American society.

One likely reason that a national survey of American Indians has not been undertaken is logistics. Outside tribal lands, locating and surveying American Indians are challenging using conventional survey methods. American Indians and Alaska Natives make up slightly less than 2 per cent of the total US population. In addition, outside tribal lands, they tend not to live in large residential clusters like African Americans and Hispanics. Unlike other minority groups, they are not

---

6   The Census Bureau refuses such requests citing the protection of data confidentiality as the reason. More will be said about this issue below.

residentially segregated, although they are spread throughout poor and working-class neighbourhoods. Using conventional sampling frames means that very large numbers of respondents must be contacted and screened to obtain a sample of sufficient size and power to yield informative results. Needless to say, this is prohibitively costly. Put another way, assuming a 50 per cent response rate, it would take about 100,000 calls to obtain a sample with 9,000 respondents.

Privacy and confidentiality

Fielding a national survey of indigenous people, such as the National Aboriginal and Torres Strait Islander Social Survey in Australia (see Jelfs, this volume), would be a very significant development for American Indians. However, the content of these sorts of surveys, along with the typically small size of most indigenous communities, raises other concerns—namely, those connected with the privacy and confidentiality of the data. Privacy and confidentiality are fundamental issues connected with data sovereignty because settler states and indigenous communities alike may have laws and regulations designed to manage the privacy and confidentiality of data, especially personally identifiable data. Furthermore, there may be public attitudes and expectations associated with data for indigenous people.

Concerns about 'privacy' speak to the data content that is collected from individuals. Information that is considered 'private' frequently includes financial and health information, but, in the case of indigenous communities, it may involve other sorts of activities such as participation in religious and other ceremonies, hunting and gathering practices or support for community development projects. While this information might be invaluable for tribal leaders, academics and others lacking a vested interest in these activities, collecting this information may be viewed as intrusive at a minimum or even threatening and potentially harmful. The leaders of indigenous communities are often mindful of privacy concerns and may be in a position to prevent intrusive data collection. Some American Indian communities have established institutional review boards (IRBs) that must approve a project before research can be carried out in their communities.

However, these boards are no guarantee that data, once collected, will not be shared with others for unauthorised purposes. In one notable instance, the Havasupai tribe in Arizona shared blood samples in

1990 with researchers from Arizona State University interested in using this material for diabetes research. However, the DNA extracted from this blood was widely shared with other researchers with little or no interest in diabetes. According to a story that appeared in *The New York Times*, 'their blood samples had been used to study many other things, including mental illness and theories of the tribe's geographical origins that contradict their traditional stories' (Harmon 2010). The tribe eventually won a lawsuit that ordered a return of the blood samples and halted further research with them, along with a punitive damages award of US$700,000 that was paid by the university. However, the scientist who originally obtained these samples insisted that she did nothing wrong by sharing them with colleagues and maintained this position even after the courts sided with the tribe.

While concerns about privacy relate to the collection of information, confidentiality relates to how data are managed after they are collected—especially when respondents are promised anonymity in exchange for their cooperation. In the United States, data collected by the federal government are typically regarded as confidential except in the instance where they are considered a matter of public record such as in government budgets. Title 13 of the US Code compels individuals to respond to the decennial census and the American Community Survey, but it also imposes strict penalties on Census Bureau employees who disclose personally identifiable information. Similarly, the *Confidential Information Protection and Statistical Efficiency Act*[7] enacted in 2002 provides broad protections of confidentiality across all federal statistics agencies.

While the US federal government vigilantly protects the confidentiality of respondents from whom it collects information, this vigilance does not always serve the purposes of tribal communities who wish to use these data. The litmus test used by federal agencies before publishing data is a determination about whether the data are personally identifiable through 'deductive disclosure'. Deductive disclosure means that personal characteristics can be combined in a way that associates them with specific individuals. For instance, there might be only one Native Hawaiian living in the town of Dubuque, Iowa

---

7   *Confidential Information Protection and Statistical Efficiency Act*, Public Law 107–347, 116 Stat. 2899, 44 USC § 101.

(a small town in the American Midwest). If the Census Bureau then reports that the median personal income of Native Hawaiians living in Dubuque is $20,000, anyone acquainted with this person who knows their ethnic identity also will know their personal income. Consequently, the Census Bureau and other federal statistics agencies routinely suppress information they deem deductively disclosable.

In most instances, this is a lawful and entirely reasonable practice. Nonetheless, it can be problematic for indigenous communities under the following circumstances. In small indigenous communities, tribal officials, for instance, may wish to demonstrate the prevalence of a particular problem—for example, that the income of every family in the community is below the official poverty threshold. However, it is frequently the case that income data for small communities are routinely suppressed due to concerns about deductive disclosure. While it is certainly desirable to show the extent of poverty in these places, it has to remain an article of faith because the data to empirically demonstrate this problem are routinely withheld by the Census Bureau. Small tribal communities may voluntarily offer their consent to have such information disclosed, but exceptions are not allowed under existing federal policies. Consequently, there is a great deal of data collected by the Census Bureau and other agencies, such as the Indian Health Service, that are not accessible to smaller tribal communities. Even large tribes may encounter this problem. The Navajo Nation, one of the largest tribes in the United States, is organised around units known as chapter houses. Data for chapter houses are virtually non-existent because they are too small to meet thresholds imposed by the Census Bureau to avoid deductive disclosure.

Technological solutions?

Indigenous control of data collection and dissemination is the obvious solution to the problems enumerated above—that is, the essential problems associated with exercising data sovereignty entail indigenous people being in control of data content. This involves being able to dictate what information is collected under what circumstances and then being able to determine how it is used and for what purposes. However, it seems implausible that settler states will ever be willing to fully accommodate the interests of indigenous communities. Thus, tribal communities must be able to collect their own data or simply deal with the limits imposed by the settler state. For reasons already suggested, this simply has not been possible in the recent past. Data collection operations require a degree of expertise and, more importantly, financial resources beyond the means of most native communities. However, there are reasons this might change in the foreseeable future.

Growing access to the internet and the spread of mobile phone technology are two developments that tribal communities might be able to harness for data collection purposes. In many countries, mobile phone services cost less and provide better coverage than existing landlines. In some locations, the cost of the phone and the electricity to power it is a barrier to the use of this technology. Nonetheless, as a consequence of mobile phones, indigenous people are better connected to one another than at anytime in the past. Tribal governments and others wishing to obtain information from native people have an opportunity to use or develop applications that allow responses to be made on even the simplest and most inexpensive 'flip phones'. Literacy, of course, also may impede this approach, but it still presents an opportunity for indigenous people to obtain and control information that has not existed in the past.

Internet access represents a profoundly important tool for indigenous people and their communities to manage and share information, although access may be too costly in some places. However, once again, mobile phone technology can extend the reach of the internet. Furthermore, for those communities that have the internet within reach, it is a powerful tool for soliciting information from community members and for managing other sources of locally generated information. Even when an entire community lacks network access, it might be possible for local leaders to bridge this gap by creating shared access points in local schools, public libraries or kiosks in government offices. Developing the skills and talent needed to exploit technology is an urgent challenge that must be met.

Concluding comments: data sovereignty in a postcolonial world

As long as settler states surround indigenous communities, it may make little sense to talk about a fully postcolonial world. In fact, UNDRIP defines indigeneity in its relationship to colonial contact. Nonetheless, thinking of postcolonialism as a continuum instead of a simple binary condition does make it possible to think about how native people might claim greater control of data connected to them. This is especially critical in a world where information is monetised and made increasingly important and increasingly valuable. So, what features would enhance the data sovereignty of indigenous people?

1. Perhaps the most significant feature of decolonised data would be the power of indigenous people to determine who should be counted among them—that is, indigenous communities should be empowered to determine who belongs among them and who should be excluded for the purposes of data collection. Historically, settler states have made this determination, but settler states have vested interests that may or likely may not coincide with the interests of native people.

2. The content of decolonised indigenous data must reflect the interests, values and priorities of native people. This is a statement that is much easier to make than to realise. Indigenous communities are seldom of one mind about any given issue and what one segment of the community deems important and valuable may be less important and less valuable to another faction of the community. Nonetheless, to the extent that there are core values that transcend narrower interests, these certainly must guide decisions that shape the content of indigenous data. Data that put individuals or the community at risk of personal or financial harm, for example, must be scrutinised carefully in terms of their value and utility, and handled accordingly.

3. Similar to the preceding point, tribal communities must not only dictate the content of data collected about them, they must also have the power to determine who has access to these data. This measure may seem redolent of censorship, but all governments and all communities possess data that are inappropriate for widespread disclosure. In the United States, financial transactions are usually

considered private and immune to disclosure. Even the Government of the United States exercises a great deal of discretion over the data it collects, withholding some data from public access while disclosing others. For indigenous communities to have a degree of sovereignty over the data pertaining to them, they must act with the same authority.

It is one matter to make these points but another to bring them to fulfilment. Nonetheless, there are two mechanisms that may facilitate greater control over indigenous data. One is essential and the other is less essential but useful nonetheless. Expertise in the production and management of data of all types is absolutely essential. The ability to conduct surveys and censuses, manage and process administrative data and carry out qualitative fieldwork is essential for a community wishing to create and control its own data. Likewise, technical skills related to managing archives and websites, along with the networks and hardware necessary for these activities, are also essential. Historically, indigenous communities have been profoundly lacking in these capabilities; however, the cost and diffusion of this knowledge have declined dramatically in recent years, making it accessible to a wide variety of settings.

A second mechanism involves institutional oversight of research and data collection in indigenous communities. In the United States, universities and other organisations engaged in the collection of data have established IRBs to ensure ethical practices in research projects. These boards were established in the wake of highly controversial ethical breaches connected with academic research. However, some American Indian tribes have also established these boards whenever a research project is proposed to involve the tribe. As tribal people become more sophisticated about the importance and value of research in their communities, this may be one vehicle to prevent the exploitation of local knowledge, and to protect intellectual property such as that sought after by ethno-botanists.

These are but two measures that will enhance the sovereign control that indigenous people can wield over data and especially knowledge connected with indigeneity. There are a growing number of scholars addressing these issues, not least in the present volume, and particularly in regard to the deployment of research in indigenous communities (Smith 1999; Wilson 2009; Kovach 2010; Walter & Andersen 2013;

Lambert 2014). This small but growing literature promises to align academic research with the interests of native communities. Once this knowledge is produced, it is incumbent on native communities to exercise sovereignty over these data to which they are so richly entitled.

References

Bureau of Indian Affairs (BIA) (2013). *Brief overview, Office of Federal Acknowledgement*, 12 November, BIA, Washington, DC, bia.gov/cs/groups/xofa/documents/text/idc1-024417.pdf.

Clifford J (2013). *Returns: becoming indigenous in the 21st century*, Harvard University Press, Cambridge, Mass.

Harmon A (2010). Tribe wins fight to limit research of its DNA. *The New York Times*, 10 April 2010, nytimes.com/2010/04/22/us/22dna.html.

Helft M & Barboza D (2010). Google shuts China site in dispute over censorship. *The New York Times*, [Technology], 22 March 2010, nytimes.com/2010/03/23/technology/23google.html.

Kovach M (2010). *Indigenous methodologies: characteristics, conversations, and contexts*, University of Toronto Press, Toronto.

Kymlicka W (1995). *Multicultural citizenship: a liberal theory of minority rights*, Oxford University Press, New York.

Lambert L (2014). *Research for indigenous survival: indigenous research methodologies in the behavioral sciences*, University of Nebraska Press for the Salish Kootenai College Press, Lincoln, Nebr.

Lerma M (2014). *Indigenous sovereignty in the 21st century: knowledge for the indigenous spring*, Florida Academic Press, Gainesville, Fla.

Liebler CA & Zacher M (2013). American Indians without tribes in the 21st century. *Ethnic and Racial Studies* 36:1910–34.

Smith LT (1999). *Decolonizing methodologies*, Zed Books, New York.

United Nations (UN) (2004). *The concept of indigenous peoples*, Workshop on data collection and disaggregation for indigenous peoples, United Nations Permanent Forum on Indigenous Issues, New York, 19–21 January 2004.

Walter M & Andersen C (2013). *Indigenous statistics: a quantitative research methodology*, Left Coast Press, Walnut Creek, CA.

Wilson S (2009). *Research is ceremony: indigenous research methods*, Fernwood Publishing, Black Point, Nova Scotia.

4

Colonialism's and postcolonialism's fellow traveller: the collection, use and misuse of data on indigenous people

Ian Pool

'Data sovereignty' → 'data suzerainty' → 'data sovereignty'

Data sovereignty (DSov) is a somewhat narrow twenty-first-century concept from commercial law relating to the protection of digitalised individual, governmental and corporate information, and also to the safeguarding of the national security apparatus from nefarious actions. This chapter, using Aotearoa/New Zealand as a case study, extrapolates from this idea in several ways. DSov is defined here in a much broader way to include the notion of the supremacy of systems of data collection and use. It is essential to recognise that, before contact with imperial powers, indigenous peoples had their own vibrant, meaningful bodies of data, over which they had DSov. Art is one form of data storage—from cave paintings to the Benin bronzes in Berlin's ethnological museum. They show a chronological shift from African motifs to Portuguese soldiers after contact. The anonymous reviewer of this chapter pointed to another powerful example: the totem poles, which are data banks, of the tribes on the north-west coast of

North America. *Whakapapa* (systematic information on genealogies) is an emblematic Aotearoa example of a culturally embedded data source to which I will return, as it has reappeared in the twenty-first-century data systems of Aotearoa's tribes (*iwi*).

Once colonialism occurred, however, indigenous peoples' data systems were replaced, at least in the public discourse, with those of the imperial metropoles and their settler colonists. The settlers' system thus gained data suzerainty (DSuz). This situation persisted into the postcolonial era, especially for those peoples who became 'indigenous minorities' in the territories over which they once ruled. For these people, internal colonialism was a reality of daily existence, even in nation-states that were avowedly liberal and relatively egalitarian; most typically, in the most benign polities, the needs of the politically and demographically hegemonic cultural groups will still prevail and, by accident or by design, indigenous people will not be consulted or their views will be ignored. The classical examples are infrastructure development or mining, which may be beneficial for the majority, but counter to the needs and wishes of an indigenous group; a road of 'national importance' may run the risk of destroying an indigenous burial site. Most extreme were systems such as South Africa's apartheid, where a minority malignly collected and used data on the majority to control their movements and daily lives. In post-apartheid South Africa, this has had perverse consequences: in a society riven by inequality that is still primarily a function of ethnicity, data on ethnic groups cannot be collected and thus analyses of health and other social inequalities are very difficult.[1] Parastatal corporations—whose 'gold standard' is the East India Company (1765–1859) (Dalrymple 2015)—also exerted DSuz. Finally, before formal annexation, information becomes imperialism's 'fellow traveller', exemplified by hearings in Britain's House of Lords on precolonial New Zealand (*British Parliamentary Papers* 1838: vol. xxi).

I want, however, to recognise that the imposition of external data systems in both the colonial and the postcolonial eras is not restricted to settler societies, but occurs, as I will show, even in 'independent' postcolonial nations. It is a very significant issue whose import has not been sufficiently recognised. For either situation, when the colonising

---

1   Meeting, Statistical Bureau, Pretoria, May 2014; Meeting, Department of Demography, Cape Town University, June 2014.

powers achieved DSuz over existing data systems, this was more than merely the displacement of one system by another. Instead, this process was reinforced—one might say strongly reinforced, in an attempt to expunge indigenous peoples' data from the public record—by the demonisation of native culture and technology. In the colonial era, indigenous peoples were seen as lesser 'races', at an inferior stage of social evolution, as evidenced in the eyes of Victorians by technology and data systems despite having data systems that allowed them to organise complex social and economic structures. In Aotearoa/New Zealand, Māori were seen as 'Stone Age savages' despite trading the length and breadth of the country. To colonists, by definition, any datasets that they themselves had not introduced and imposed were inferior, and thus of no utility for public policy analysis, dialogue and implementation.

Nevertheless, over the colonial period, many indigenous peoples nurtured culturally embedded data systems, with precolonial, typically precontact, provenance, but these rested virtually outside the purview of hegemonic majorities other than the social anthropologists and other researchers among them. Of course, the 'natives' were also frequently encouraged, or instructed, to resurrect some aspects of their culture to amuse tourists or visiting celebrities. The most common examples were dances or songs that constitute a form of memory bank for data, yet indigenous people were discouraged from applying these same data to illuminate issues arising in the public policy arena.

The majority population's imposition of DSuz—achieved by demonising indigenous people and denigrating the validity of their data systems—has had long-term consequences, which still affect the development of indigenous peoples' data systems today. Later sections of this chapter will address this problem. Taking an Aotearoa/New Zealand case study, I explore the backstory for twenty-first-century DSov issues facing indigenous peoples. For them, DSov is not merely a technical problem contingent on state-of-the-art computing; constraints on the generation of data systems by indigenous peoples are epistemological—a function of the unique history of data collection and use, and the wider historical context, in countries in which each indigenous group resides. The New Zealand case and similar backstories have left methodological chasms between indigenous peoples and the wider populations surrounding them. Other chapters in this book try to bridge this canyon and simultaneously address how the DSov of indigenous peoples can be protected.

Until recently, indigenous peoples' data needs have been mainly confined to social and cultural rather than commercial sectors, but as more indigenous groups establish corporations, business interests come into play. Even in the social sectors, well-developed state data systems—those on which some DSov debates focus—were foisted on 'precursor peoples' (Belich 2009:180), first by their colonisers and then by successor regimes. That said, ongoing development strategies require good knowledge bases, both for indigenous peoples and for the nation-states in which they live.

Once datasets are created, however, other DSov questions emerge (Scroggie 2013), as is true across the Western world (Venkatraman 2014). Conventionally, 'data sovereignty is the concept that information which has been converted and stored in binary digital form is subject to the laws of the country in which it is located' (see Snipp, this volume). Countries develop different regulatory instruments to enforce this narrowly defined form of DSov, but mainly for: 1) business and related financial demands, and 2) state and other security issues. This has been compounded by the *Uniting and Strengthening America by Providing Appropriate Tools Required to Intercept and Obstruct Terrorism Act of 2001* (*USA PATRIOT Act*), the impacts of which spill into other jurisdictions. 'Clouds' seem especially difficult to protect (Young 2014).

For citizens in market economies, including indigenous people, personal data (for example, information on credit cards) are exported to, and stored in, foreign jurisdictions. The notion of DSov also invokes property rights and other values, which vary enormously between cultures. For example, Aotearoa's *Native Lands Act* (1865) trampled on these differences, eroding Māori wellbeing and embittering Māori–Pakeha (non-Māori) relations. In 1870, the Minister of Justice of the day made a statement that demonstrates superbly the sort of mindset Victorian colonists brought to evaluating Māori culture and its instruments such as data systems. He argued that the Land Act's function was 'to bring the vast bulk of lands ... within the reach of colonisation'—that is, it was imperative that land be made available for settlers by displacing Māori. He continued:

The other great object was the detribalisation of the Māoris—to destroy, if it were possible, the spirit of communism which ran through the whole of their institutions … It was hoped that by the individualisation of titles to land … they would lose their communistic character. (Reproduced in Statistics NZ 1990: 414)

DSov is 'not often talked about in New Zealand' (Bennett 2013). Instead, New Zealanders focus more on free-trade agreements and protection of intellectual property, including, inter alia, knowledge about natural capital (for example, plants with possible medicinal qualities). These issues interpenetrate with those on cultural capital, both demanding guardianship (*katiakitanga*) and DSov. Nationally, concerns revolve around controls and interventions that might be exerted over nation-states—or, by extrapolation, over subpopulations—by powerful multinational corporations using extraterritorial tribunals biased towards corporate interests (Kelsey 2015). Conversely, globalisation's advocates have contrary concerns: 'All kinds of laws and regulations are conspiring to force managed service providers to manage data within the local jurisdictions of multiple countries' (Vizard 2014).

In the remainder of this chapter, I first examine how contact and colonialism accidentally submerged—or intentionally expunged— indigenous peoples' extant epistemologies. This has profound implications for the acceptability of twenty-first-century indigenous peoples' data strategies—some with roots in the precontact period, some that adapt conventional techniques and others that hybridise these two. I am not a historicist, but here I am arguing that history has left very strong imprints on some contemporary data problems, especially those for which the ideational context is a key element in their genesis. Second, I review the processes for data collection and analysis over different phases of precolonialism, colonialism and postcolonialism. Finally, given these histories, what are the DSov implications of emerging methods and the information they produce: in sum, who controls what?

The historical context: demonising indigenous peoples

Indigenous peoples have felt the force of colonialism's footprint: the past half-millennium's Euro-North American imperialism bequeathed us systematic denigration of intellectual infrastructures existing before contact and/or colonial control. Unfortunately, much of colonial history focuses on Euro-American expansion and the implantation of Western institutions, thereby implicitly endorsing Victorian imperialist notions of technical, governmental, administrative and moral superiority. Despite contrary historical evidence, these assumptions remained unchallenged until the mid-twentieth century, only to be reinvigorated by twenty-first-century revisionists (for example, Ferguson 2007).

Missionaries endorsed Britain's 'civilising mission' in Aotearoa. Literate, often diligent and compassionate people, they chronicled the conversion of Māori—an alternative to 'fatal impact' (see below) (Belich 1996:156). Subsequent writers often uncritically reify missionary accounts, although conventional history has been more even-handed. Most historians are selective, using English-language sources, but Jennings's (2011) research on 2,000 French Marian documents shows how biased are more commonly used accounts. These well-travelled, Māori-speaking brothers reported a low incidence of cannibalism, whereas for some other writers, it was a widespread 'practice' (Moon 2008).

For their colonising mission, imperialists imported data methodologies, smugly assuming that epistemologies other than Euro-North American ones were inferior. This view still haunts the wider society's acceptance of information systems now being generated by indigenous scholars. Today, many indigenous peoples challenge this, but they must fight powerful demons implanted, in Aotearoa's case, from first contact (1642)—which labelled Māori as 'murderers' and Australasians as 'opposite-footers' (antipodeans)—or from the first continuous interaction (1769). Victorians exaggerated, and even invented, lurid accounts of native life both before and after contact—myth-building that has uncritically fed into the writings of revisionists, who today are framing the prejudices of public officials who must evaluate and use indigenous peoples' data systems. To justify the subjugation of indigenous peoples, they were rated as 'noble savages', at best, 'untrustworthy sub-human brutes', at worst, lacking intricate social and economic systems and mores (Wright 2008). Comments on indigenous people were often self-contradictory, even within the one commentary—for example, they could argue that native population decline was determined both endogenously (their own fault) and exogenously ('fatal impacts' due to contact with 'superior peoples').

Aotearoa was not unique. In the Americas, Spanish explorers, 'pilgrim fathers' and postcolonial American writers alike denigrated the sophisticated agricultural and urban systems of Native America, yet plundered their food, perpetrated ethnic cleansing and re-demonised them in Hollywood westerns.

> In 1867, Francis Parkman, America's popular historian … wrote 'The Indians melted away not because civilization destroyed them, but because their own ferocity and intractable indolence made it impossible that they could exist in its presence.' (Wright 2008: 62)

To Spanish theologians:

> The bleeding of the New World became an act of charity … The Indians were used as beasts of burden because they could carry a greater weight than the delicate llama, and this proved that they were indeed beasts of burden. (Galeano 1973: 52–3)

Philosopher David Hume 'declined to recognize the "degraded men" of the New World as fellow humans' (Galeano 1973: 41). But let us remember that the English also denigrated their Celtic subjects: *Water Babies* author, the Reverend Charles Kingsley, called the recently famine-decimated Irish 'human chimpanzees', adding the mantra oft-repeated across the Empire: 'I believe there are not only more of them than of old, but they are happier, better, more comfortably fed under our rule than they ever were' (cited in Hechter 1975: xvvi–ii).

In Aotearoa, Dr Newman wrote solid, scientific papers on Pakeha longevity, but on Māori, he turned rabid polemicist (1882: 175–7):

> I have made it clear that the Māoris were a disappearing race before we came here … The disappearance of the race is scarcely subject for much regret. They are dying out in a quick and easy way and being replaced by a superior race.

Reverend Wohlers, citing the 'groveling animalism' of Māori, concluded (1881: 132): 'I can positively say that the coming of the Europeans has nothing to do with the dying out of the race … [who] had outlived their time.'

Victorian epistemologies were underpinned by racial theories. 'Polygenism' saw humanity divided into groups that were racially distinct—with European superiority a given (Belich 1986: 323 ff., 1996: 125–6). Paradoxically, Charles Darwin's work reinforced that mindset, appearing 'to offer an evolutionary justification for European colonialism' (Paxman 2011: 122). Anthropology and psychology spent decades looking for racial and eugenic differences between peoples, arguing in the late-nineteenth century that, facing contact with superior civilisations, natives lost the will to reproduce or adopted social pathologies that had a 'fatal impact'—a perspective that seemed oblivious to the role of childhood survival in population replacement. The 'clash of cultures' paradigm, elaborated by interwar Oceanic anthropologists (for example, Rivers 1922; Pitt-Rivers 1923; cf. Pool 1977: 75–9), persisted in Australia until after World War II (Price 1949) and also in New Zealand, even though 'impact' had not been 'fatal' for Māori—they survived as a people (Belich 1996: Ch. 7). Indeed, by World War II, rapid Māori growth deeply concerned neo-eugenicist H. (not K.) Sinclair (1944). Finally, after the war, 'modernisation' paradigms replenished more blatantly racist frameworks, seeing America as the prototypical modern, liberal, democratic marker—an iconic paper being 'Making men modern' (Inkeles 1969). 'Take-off'—highly desired in Rostow's schema (1960: 4–16)—required social engineering that 'shocked the traditional society and hastened its undoing' (1960: 6).

Unfortunately, flawed ideas die slowly, so this undercurrent persists: Australia's twenty-first-century 'history warriors',[2] led by Keith Windschuttle and inspired by America's 'neocons', revitalised racism. Windschuttle virulently attacked New Zealand ethno-historian Anne

---

2   The movement was a reaction to eminent anthropologist 'Bill' Stanner, who lamented that Aborigines had been virtually ignored and Australia's history presented positively. One of the more extreme ideas of the 'John Howard intellectuals'—so named by Australia's former prime minister—was that settlers counterattacked Aborigines because of their unprovoked violence towards colonists. 'History warriors' also deny the repression and killing of Tasmanian Aborigines (Windschuttle 2002; cf. Attwood 2005).

Salmond's (1997) use of early Māori sources, recorded in tribal 'books'.[3] These were not reliable, Windschuttle argued, because Māori were barbarians:

> At the time of contact with European explorers, the Māori were engaged in continual tribal warfare. One of [the] prizes was the killing and eating of opposing warriors. Cannibalism was rife throughout Māori communities, and, since they had exterminated all large animals[4] and birds, human flesh constituted a major source of protein in the Māori diet. (Windschuttle 1997: 275)

Aotearoa's revisionists are more 'tabloid historians', lacking Australia's political impacts. Nevertheless, 'tabloidists' often draw uncritically on Victorian myth-building whereby Māori adopted, or inherited from prehistory, every social pathology except drug addiction. Presumably, opiates—the lifeline of middle-class ladies and aristocratic bohemians—were far too refined for 'brutish' Māori. 'Tabloidism' has, however, had two long-term negative effects. First, by focusing on the ephemeral, there is a major gap in the knowledge of the everyday social and economic lives of 'precursor peoples', of indigenously driven activities that continued after contact, often into the colonial era and beyond. Second, it has helped feed spurious ideas into the race relations discourse, and this affects how policymakers and politicians view ideas, including data systems, developed by Māori. Comments can be coded, such as those by former minister Michael Bassett (2003) that the 'poor should stop breeding'; openly prejudiced, such as Don Brash (2004), leader of the opposition National Party, attacking the privileges of Māori; or wrong, such as current Prime Minister, John Key, asserting against all historical evidence (2014) that 'New Zealand is one of the few countries that [was] settled peacefully'.

---

3   Māori oral history was documented by the middle of the nineteenth century by *iwi* (tribes), *hapū* (subtribes) and *whānau* (wider families) across Aotearoa and protected since as *taonga* (treasures). By about 1850, Māori alphabetisation levels exceeded those of Pakeha, yet the elders who preserved oral records were still alive and had been trained in specialised schools of advanced learning. The significance of oral traditions was confirmed by Judith Binney (2009:74): 'By the 1840s, orality—the recall and narration of history from memory—was being mediated by access to literacy for Māori men and women.' A great strength of Anne Salmond's work is that she is one of the rare Pakeha scholars who can read these 'books'. Māori scholar Bruce Biggs, in collaboration with scholars from other *iwi*, similarly used these records in his classic study, *Māori marriage* (1960).
4   Tiny bats were Aotearoa's only land mammals; by contrast, sea mammals were abundant, but were not made extinct by Māori, whereas Pakeha extractive industries severely reduced numbers.

At the time of editing this chapter, Brash published another comment that is highly apposite, on the issue of water rights. Appealing to the Treaty of Waitangi (1840), New Zealand's foundation constitutional document signed by chiefs from all over Aotearoa, Māori have called for consultation about allocation of water and comanagement with some local authorities. Brash (2016) sees this instead as a bid for water ownership, arguing:

> [T]o suggest that Governor Hobson saw himself, on behalf of Queen Victoria, entering into a partnership with a number of chiefs, many of whom could neither read nor write, has to be a total nonsense, Lord Cooke [a New Zealand judge, and expert on Waitangi, on the Privy Council] notwithstanding.

Brash's argument misstates the treaty signing process and therefore the understandings of signatories as to what they were signing: there were two versions, both very short, one in Māori and one in English. While there is controversy about the translation into Māori, any 'unalphabetised' chief would still have been versed in a powerful oral tradition, so would have had no difficulty understanding the Māori version, and would have assumed it to reflect accurately what was in the English version.

Empire building, postcolonialism, internal colonialism and data

Conventional historians have documented the 'displacement' of indigenous populations by conquest or 'swamping' (outnumbering by settlers) during different phases of empire building (Belich 1996: 249, 2009: 21, 180–2). To displace and control indigenous people, imperialists required data—colonialism's almost universal fellow traveller. The *Oxford English Dictionary* defines 'colonialism' as 'the policy or practice of acquiring … control over another country, occupying it with settlers, and exploiting it'. But, for indigenous peoples who are minorities, such controls have continued to the present through postcolonialism, neocolonialism and internal colonialism.

Independence also does not end the imposition of exotic data systems—neither for minority precursor peoples confronting demographically and politically hegemonic majorities nor for inhabitants of 'newly independent countries'.[5] If they are minorities, indigenous people live in postcolonial countries using data systems inherited from the former colonial power and primarily suiting the needs of the majority's elites, often drawn from the former metropole. Hopefully, as more and more indigenous people enter government and private sector management roles, they gain some say in the collection and use of data. But another issue in the twenty-first century is that data become more complex as Europeans and non-Europeans of other origins immigrate to a country, with their own needs, generating bewildering data definition problems.[6]

Indigenous minorities are still subject to 'internal colonialism', even in the twenty-first century (defined by Pool 2015). The position of indigenous peoples has parallels with the problems faced by fully independent postcolonial territories, which, in establishing data systems, will have been advised by international agencies. While advisers act neutrally in standardising data content, they still favour conventions of Euro-American provenance; in effect, this is neocolonialism in another guise. This is not hyperbole—for example, globally recommended national accounts conventions distort statistical series by failing to address the informal and subsistence sectors and nonremunerated family workforces, inter alia, underestimating women's contribution to the economy (Waring 1988). The new (post-2004) national transfer accounts methodologies show how flawed the resulting data have been: intrafamily transfers, many of which are nonmonetised, operate across all social sectors, outrunning interfamily (public, charity) transfers. If intrafamily transfers are undocumented, this significantly undercounts the real economy's transactions, even in highly developed countries, but particularly where principles of family obligation (*whanaungatanga*) are important—say, when parents, not a bank, help their children buy a house or provide afterschool care.

---

5   Indigenous minorities inhabit many countries and are treated with varying degrees of justice and equality. My chapter focuses on Australasia and North America, making side references to Latin America and elsewhere.

6   For example: the first Croatians in New Zealand were 'Austro-Hungarians', but became Yugoslavs, then Croatians; many groups of European origin have seen similar shifts. Today, 14 per cent of New Zealand's population is Māori; 10 per cent are Asians; another 8 per cent are from the Pacific; plus others from Africa, the Middle East and Latin America; in total, 39 per cent identify with a non-European ethnic group. Clearly, ethnic data collection is very complex in such a situation.

Moreover, some indigenous people engage in economic transactions outside the monetised economy—a theme elaborated in Australian work on hybrid economies (Altman & May 2011; Russell 2011).

Processes of data collection

Imperialists did not enter data deserts, but the existing systems they encountered typically did not fit their world view. Even today, non-Aborigines fail to understand the 'indicators' Aborigines exploit to 'manage' remote outback Australia (Taylor 2008). Most extant standard methodologies across the world date from the Victorians, who were fascinated by science, with a passion for 'moral statistics', eclectic in compass and, as a by-product, counting natives they encountered. Although driven by benign curiosity, some applied metrics to pseudo-science. By contrast, Thomson's *The story of New Zealand* (1859: v.2, annexes) represents the best of this genre, vesting today's scholars with useful and relatively 'robust' data.

Our data paradigms survive from the development of state registration and censuses—remembering that parish records, underpinning property rights, begat vital registration. The first British Registrar-General, Dr William Farr, promoted the 'healthy districts' movement—bucolic England (or temperate-climate colonies) versus evil cities (Lewis-Faning 1930)—so mortality statistics were prioritised. Contact and colonialism exposed precursor peoples to new data systems, ranging from counts that had almost no manifest, immediate impact—although downstream usage may have had major effects—through to imposed collections that involved disruptions and even coercion, with negative implications. At their best, colonial enumerations produced administrative data, providing us with some insight into the lives of ordinary indigenous people. Combined with other data sources, they ensure that 'historical demography is possible despite the scarcity of the sacrosanct forms of demographic data cherished by demographers' (Cordell 2010: 22). Moreover, demography's unconventional techniques applied to historical and other deficient data allow researchers to build skeletal estimates—of population growth, life tables (using indirect estimation), gross reproduction rates and similar basic information—with some likelihood that they represent real trends (Pool 2015). In this context, historical analysis is not an academic luxury, as is evident from the highly applied research contributing to New Zealand's Waitangi Tribunals.

But colonial administrations also used data to control the 'natives'— the 'colonial order and the creation of knowledge' (Ittmann et al. 2010). Counting permitted macro-level *classification*, including by caste and race, manifested in Aotearoa by a focus on 'half-castes', awkwardly categorised as 'living as Māori' or 'living as Pakeha' (Kukutai 2011, 2012). *Classification* underpinned *social engineering*, typically at a meso (community) or micro (family) level, often enforced by coercion (for example, in British Central Africa, burning the huts of subsistence-economy families unable to pay cash hut taxes, to force the men into indentured labour). The 'need for labor in a variety of forms shaped the [macro-]demographic agendas of colonial regimes', leading 'colonial states to try to alter the demographic regimes of African populations' (Cordell et al. 2010: 8).

Indigenous peoples and data sovereignty

The de-valorisation of precontact eras also relates to data modalities, even those being generated today. Indigenous groups are attempting to reform the 'colonial order's' knowledge systems, developing new 'unconventional techniques' of data collection and analysis, often grounded in their own cultural heritage. For example, *iwi* (tribal) registers in Aotearoa repackage data systems that go back at least to the first Māori arrivals (say, AD 1250), using *whakapapa*'s oral knowledge base (genealogies)—resonant of parish registers used in demography's family reconstitution techniques. *Whakapapa* trace modern individuals to a distinguished ancestor and also link them with different *hapū* (subtribes), *iwi* and *marae* (sacred central area of a village). These data were not just fundamental to Māori cultural organisation; the socio-spatial connectedness of *whakapapa* was also instrumental for economic relationships governed by *utu* (commonly translated as revenge, more correctly reciprocity).[7] Precontact Māori had highly developed, nonmonetised trading systems that extended

---

7   I thank ethno-historian Anne Salmond for generously making available to me unpublished manuscripts on nineteenth-century Māori ontology being prepared for a Marsden Research Grant.

the length of New Zealand, often involving *whakapapa*-determined reciprocal obligations; their social and economic worlds were intimately integrated (Firth 1959). Importantly, today, *whakapapa* 'drill down' more deeply into that complex nexus than do modern methodologies other than specially commissioned, highly costly surveys. Nonetheless, like surveys, *whakapapa* have error properties: 'only certain lines of descent from key ancestors to living individuals and important marriage ties between ancestors at different generational levels are remembered and passed on' (Sissons et al. 1987: 149–50).

Indigenous minorities asserting their rights as actors in democratic societies exploit existing data systems. Negotiations with hegemonic groups need systems that are reconcilable with extant wider datasets for the population as a whole, becoming most critical when litigation occurs or entitlements are sought. To 'drill deep' for their own purposes, indigenous peoples may have to tailor their own methodologies, the specifications of which will be dictated by their specific needs. But residual attitudes, shaped by history, affect the way the wider society and the polity view data generated by indigenous peoples. Attacks on Waitangi Tribunal proceedings, which identify Crown failures to meet Treaty of Waitangi obligations, hinging on what was written there (in two different languages), show how deeply these prejudices may run.

To complicate matters, DSov invokes different levels of aggregation. Individually, if credit card details are lodged in another country, individuals risk losing sovereignty. At a meso-level, indigenous groups—*whānau* (wider family), *hapū* or *iwi* in Aotearoa—can legitimately claim DSov over their collective data, yet, in this day of data 'hoovering', the possibility of these collectivities losing real DSov exists, and can be exploited against the interests of indigenous groups: knowledge of the natural resources they rightfully control is a good example. At a macro-level, there is territory-wide DSov, when indigenous rights may not be safeguarded: if, under trade treaties, nations have not protected sovereign rights (or the rights of subgroups such as trade unions or *iwi*), international practice allows foreign countries or corporations to take offending parties to tribunals outside the jurisdiction in which indigenous peoples are domiciled.

DSov practices vary between jurisdictions. But conventional usage is tangential to the wider problems facing indigenous peoples, for in this context it relates to regulating flows of digital data on Māori (or other indigenous peoples) to foreign jurisdictions. At present, public records data are restricted to digitalised—and anonymised—contemporary data in New Zealand, and their historical equivalents will be available on public record only as tabulations. This is, however, merely one dimension of DSov, which opens up major intellectual property questions, not just for digitalised data. If hardcopy historical data are converted into portable formats (for example, photo-image) then that process allows their transfer offshore. As noted already, by the 1850s, many Māori *hapū* had written down *whakapapa* and other important cultural information. To date, their use has been restricted to *hapū* themselves and specialists (see Note 3) able to read Māori of that era. But one does not have to be a futurologist to see these data converted into photo-images, exported and translated. Lest this seems histrionic—much ado about nothing—some *hapū* 'books' contain information that has scientific or other properties, sovereignty and pecuniary values, all of which are disputed in cross-national trade negotiations under way at present (such as for the Trans-Pacific Partnership). The emotional and financial costs involved in the return of shrunken tattooed heads or meeting-house carvings and other items of cultural value to *iwi* in New Zealand are a portent of what might be involved. Moreover, such intellectual property could pass not just to other countries, but also into corporate hands outside public control; *haka* and *moko* (tattoo) designs have already.

Towards a conclusion: opportunities, challenges, problems

Indigenous peoples have a real window of opportunity, with no historical precedent, to achieve data sovereignty—an opportunity available because of the fortunate coincidence of a number of factors, some of which I have not covered above. First, there is clearly a desire on their part to take sovereignty over data, to protect their own rights; as individuals, all citizens want this, but here I am referring to indigenous peoples as collectivities, as identifiable subgroups (for example, *iwi*). Second, indigenous people have the intellectual and technical resources in their human capital to formulate and exploit such datasets (see, for example, FNIGC, Hudson et al., Hudson, Jansen, Yap & Yu, this volume).

There are, however, challenges. The first is to win acceptance from their own people. But more difficult will be gaining validity in the wider community, entailing overcoming the residual imprints of historical demonisation and, for innovative methodologies, prejudices about the universal, technical superiority of Euro-American data systems. This is rendered more difficult today because data are a prime commodity in litigation as well as in research and scholarship.

Finally, there are exogenous problems. Hanging over the generation and use of knowledge is the spectre of data 'hoovering' by territorial and extraterritorial agencies and thus loss of DSov. Looking at a frontal view of a friend's house in the Cotswolds or checking an address seems a harmless use of Google. But what if those 'data' had greater economic, political or cultural significance or if my intentions were evil? What if uplifted data are patented or new parties gain DSuz over indigenous peoples' property rights without the knowledge of their original *kaitiaki*? And what if any new uses are malign or generate profits?

Indigenous peoples saw their DSov accede to DSuz under colonial and postcolonial regimes. They are on the cusp of regaining DSov for use in their own jurisdictions. It would be tragic if this metamorphosed instead into neo-DSuz under transnational corporate rule beyond the control of indigenous peoples or the polity in which they live.

References

Altman J & May K (2011). Poverty alleviation in remote Indigenous Australia. In Minnerup G & Solberg P (eds), *First world, first nations: internal colonialism and Indigenous self-determination in northern Europe and Australia*, Sussex Academic Press, Eastbourne, UK.

Attwood B (2005). *Telling the truth about Aboriginal history*, Allen & Unwin, Sydney.

Bassett M (2003). Poor should stop breeding. *Dominion Post*, 30 September 2003.

Belich J (1986). *The New Zealand Wars and the Victorian interpretation of racial conflict*, Auckland University Press, Auckland.

Belich J (1996). *Making peoples: a history of the New Zealanders from first Polynesian settlement to the end of the 19th century*, Allen Lane Penguin, Auckland.

Belich J (2009). *Replenishing the earth: the settler revolution and the rise of the Anglo-world*, Oxford University Press, Oxford.

Bennett B (2013). *Data sovereignty in NZ*, billbennett.co.nz/2013/07/05/data-sovereignty-in-new-zealand/.

Biggs B (1960). *Māori marriage*, Reed for the Polynesian Society, Wellington.

Binney J (2009). History and memory: the wood of the whau tree, 1766–2005. In Byrnes G (ed.), *The new Oxford history of New Zealand*, Oxford University Press, Melbourne.

Brash D (2004). Nationhood, an address by Don Brash, leader of the National Party to the Orewa Rotary Club, Orewa, 27 January 2004.

Brash D (2016). Act of Parliament made water ownership clear. *NZ Herald*, 26 April 2016.

British Parliamentary Papers (1838), vol. xxi.

Cordell D (2010). African historical demography in the postmodern and postcolonial eras. In Ittmann K, Cordell D & Maddox G (eds), *The demographics of empire: the colonial order and the creation of knowledge*, Ohio University Press, Athens, OH.

Cordell D, Ittmann K and Maddox G (2010). Counting subjects: demography and empire. In Ittmann K, Cordell D and Maddox G (eds), *The demographics of empire: the colonial order and the creation of knowledge*, Ohio University Press, Athens, OH.

Dalrymple W (2015). The East India Company: the original corporate raiders. *The Guardian*, 4 March 2015, theguardian.com/world/2015/mar/04/east-india-company-original-corporate-raiders.

Ferguson N (2007). *Empire*, Penguin, London.

Firth R (1959). *Economics of the New Zealand Māori*, 2nd edn, Government Printer, Wellington.

Galeano E (1973). *Open veins of Latin America: five centuries of the pillage of a continent*, [English translation], Monthly Review Press, New York.

Hechter M (1975). *Internal colonialism: the Celtic fringe in British national development*, Routledge & Kegan Paul, London.

Inkeles A (1969). Making men modern: on the causes and consequences of individual change in six developing countries. *American Journal of Sociology* 75(2):208–25.

Ittmann K, Cordell D & Maddox G (eds) (2010). *The demographics of empire: the colonial order and the creation of knowledge*, Ohio University Press, Athens, OH.

Jennings W (2011). The debate over 'kai tangata' (Māori cannibalism): New Zealand perspectives from the correspondence of the Marists. *Journal of the Polynesian Society* 120(2):129–47.

Kelsey J (2015). TPPA leak: Jacobi misleads about protections for NZ, itsourfuture.org.nz/tppa-leak-jacobi-misleads-about-protections-for-nz/.

Key J (2014). Radio interview, Te Hiku station, 20 November 2014, cited at stuff.co.nz/national/politics.

Kukutai T (2011). Māori demography in Aotearoa New Zealand fifty years on. *New Zealand Population Review* 37:45–64, Special Edition Festschrift to D Ian Pool (eds Kukutai T & Jackson N).

Kukutai T (2012). Quantum Māori, Māori quantum: state constructions of Māori identities in the census, 1857/8–2006. In McClean R, Patterson B & Swain D (eds), *Counting stories, moving ethnicities: studies from Aotearoa New Zealand*, Faculty of Arts and Social Sciences, University of Waikato, Hamilton.

Lewis-Faning E (1930). A survey of the mortality in Dr Farr's 63 healthy districts of England and Wales during the period 1851–1925. *Journal of Hygiene* [London] 30(2):121–53.

Moon P (2008). *This horrid practice: the myth and reality of traditional Māori cannibalism*, Penguin, Auckland.

Newman A (1882). A study of the causes leading to the extinction of the Māori. *Transactions and Proceedings of the New Zealand Institute* 14:59–77.

Paxman J (2011). *Empire: what ruling the world did to the British*, Viking, London.

Pitt-Rivers G [Henry Lane-Fox] (1923). *The clash of cultures and the contact of races: an anthropological and psychological study of racial adaptation, with special reference to the depopulation of the Pacific*, Routledge & Sons Ltd, London.

Pool I (1977). *The Māori population of New Zealand, 1769–1971*, Auckland University Press, Auckland.

Pool I (2015). *Colonisation and development in New Zealand between 1769 and 1900: the 'seeds of Rangiatea'*, Springer, Cham, Switzerland.

Price A G (1949). *White settlers and native peoples*, Georgian House, Melbourne.

Rivers WHR (1922). The psychological factor. In Rivers WHR (ed.), *Essays on the depopulation of Melanesia*, Cambridge University Press, Cambridge.

Rostow W (1960). *The stages of economic growth: a non-communist manifesto*, Cambridge University Press, Cambridge.

Russell S (2011). *The hybrid economy topic guide*, Centre for Aboriginal Economic Policy Research, The Australian National University, Canberra, caepr.anu.edu.au/others/Other-1306975222.php.

Salmond A (1997). *Between two worlds: early exchanges between Māori and Europeans*, Viking, Auckland.

Scroggie C (2013). The clouded issue of data sovereignty, *ABC Technology and Games*, 1 October 2013, abc.net.au/technology/articles/2013/10/01/3859628.htm.

Sinclair H (1944). *Population: New Zealand's problem*, Gordon & Gotch, Dunedin.

Sissons J, Wi Hongi W & Hohepa P (1987). *The Puriri trees are laughing: a political history of the Ngapuhi in the inland Bay of Islands*, Polynesian Society, Auckland.

Statistics NZ (1990). *NZ official year book*, Statistics NZ, Wellington.

Taylor J (2008). Indigenous peoples and indicators of well-being: Australian perspectives on United Nations global frameworks. *Social Indicators Research* 87:111–26.

Thomson AS (1859). *The story of New Zealand: past and present, savage and civilized*, 2 vols, John Murray, London.

Venkatraman A (2014). Cloud providers rush to build European datacentres over data sovereignty, *Computer Weekly.com*, 27 October 2014, computerweekly.com/news/2240233331/Cloud-providers-rush -to-build-European-datacentres-over-data-sovereignty.

Vizard M (2014). Rising to the data sovereignty challenge, *MSPmentor*, 11 December 2014.

Waring M (1988). *If women counted: a new feminist economics*, Macmillan, London.

Windschuttle K (1997). *Killing history: how literary critics and social theorists are murdering our past*, Macleay Press, Sydney [republished by Free Press, New York].

Windschuttle K (2002). *The fabrication of Australian history. Volume 1: van Diemen's Land, 1803–47*, Macleay Press, Sydney.

Wohlers J (1881). On the conversion and civilization of the Māoris of the South Island of New Zealand, *Transactions and Proceedings of the New Zealand Institute* 14:123–34.

Wright R (2008). *What is America? A short history of the new world order*, Text Publishing, Melbourne.

Young B (2014). Data protection fears vs US cloud market, *Information Week*, 5 February, informationweek.com/government/ cloud-computing/data-protection-fears-vs-us-cloud-market/d/d-id/1234862.

Part 2: Critiques of official statistics

5

Data politics and Indigenous representation in Australian statistics

Maggie Walter

Introduction

Accepting the philosophical premise that numbers exist, as per Quine (1948), is ontologically different to accepting that numbers have a fixed reality. This differential is the essence of the reality of numbers as they are applied to indigenous populations. In First World colonised nations such as Australia, Aotearoa/New Zealand, Canada and the United States, the question is not just 'are these numbers real', but also 'how are these numbers deployed and whom do they serve'. The reality query is not of the numbers themselves but of what they purport to portray.

Numbers, configured as population or population sample data, are not neutral entities. Rather, social and population statistics are better understood as human artefacts, imbued with meaning. And, in their current configurations, the meanings reflected in statistics are primarily drawn from the dominant social norms, values and racial hierarchy of the society in which they are created. As such, in colonising nation-states, statistics applied to indigenous peoples have a raced reality that is perpetuated and normalised through their creation and re-creation

(Walter 2010; Walter & Andersen 2013). The numerical format of these statistics and their seemingly neutral presentation, however, elide their social, cultural and racial dimensions. In a seemingly unbroken circle, dominant social norms, values and racial understandings determine statistical construction and interpretations, which then shape perceptions of data needs and purpose, which then determine statistical construction and interpretation, and so on. Just as important is that the accepted persona of statistics on indigenous people operates to conceal what is excluded: the culture, interests, perspectives and alternative narratives of those they purport to represent—indigenous peoples.

This chapter investigates how Australia's racial terrain permeates statistics on Indigenous Australians. I examine the shape and context of these statistics as currently 'done' in Australia (Walter & Andersen 2013) and also the absences—how they are 'not done'. Within this, I interrogate the construction and dissemination of the contemporary Australian statistical Indigene and its wider social and cultural contexts and consequences. The chapter also challenges researchers to consider how reversing the analytical lens to generate data conceptualised through an Indigenous methodological framework might alter the narrative, concepts, discourse and, ultimately, policy directions of Indigenous Australia.

Five-D data and the statistical Indigene

If you Google the term 'Indigenous statistics', the list that comes back in a millisecond is a depressingly predictable one. The first 10 entries are associated with eight different entities presented from 10 slightly different perspectives. But all focus in one way or another on statistical representations of the dire, and longstanding, socioeconomic and health inequities between Aboriginal and Torres Strait Islander peoples and non-Indigenous Australian people. I summarise these as the five 'Ds' of data on Indigenous people (5D data): disparity, deprivation, disadvantage, dysfunction and difference. For example, the Australian Human Rights Commission (humanrights.gov.au) uses statistical data to highlight overall inequality between Indigenous Australians and the rest of the population; the Australian Bureau of Statistics (abs.gov.au) entries look at homelessness and education disparities; the Australian Institute of Health and Welfare (aihw.gov.au) discusses the overrepresentation of Indigenous people in the numbers of deaths from preventable causes; creativespirits.info takes a more original approach and uses the data to map out the depressing average Aboriginal Australian's life; while australianstogether.org.au looks at the direction of the 'Closing the Gap' policy and determines there is a long way to go. And so it goes. There is, seemingly, no shortage of data on, or data usage to compile portrayals of, Aboriginal and Torres Strait Islander inequality.

If you are interested in data on contemporary Aboriginal social phenomena that are not directly related to the five Ds, your search will likely be less productive. For example, Ting et al. (2015), in their examination of the division of household labour, found that not only did Aboriginal and Torres Strait Islander women do less housework per week than a non-Indigenous Australian-born sample, but also the division of labour was more egalitarian in Indigenous Australian households. The problem for the researchers was that the Aboriginal and Torres Strait Islander sample in their dataset—the Household Income and Labour Dynamics in Australia (HILDA) survey—is small and groups Aboriginal and Torres Strait Islander households into one base category. The authors concede, based on these limitations, that despite their tantalising findings, their results cannot reliably tell us anything about how Aboriginal and Torres Strait Islander households do domestic labour.

This seemingly minor issue exposes the positionality of Aboriginal and Torres Strait Islander people within the statistical terrain of our contemporary nation-state. The problem is that there is a plethora of easily accessible 5D data. Attempting to move outside this trope of the statistical Indigene is to find yourself in a data desert. There are no existing datasets available for researchers wanting to further investigate their findings on household division of labour. The Longitudinal Study of Indigenous Children has some questions on household functioning in relation to children but none about how family life is lived. The National Aboriginal and Torres Strait Islander Social Survey, as it is currently constructed, is focused almost completely on indicators of socioeconomic, lifestyle, health and neighbourhood non-wellbeing, and the Census of Population and Housing, the other major source of data on Indigenous Australians, contains data on homeownership and occupation but not household functioning.

The crucial point is that the nation-state's data collection topic priorities for its Indigenous and non-Indigenous peoples differ dramatically. This critique is not to undermine the necessity of the continued collection of data on socioeconomic and demographic disparities; the deep-seated and whole-of-colonisation period presence of inequality in the life outcomes and chances for Aboriginal and Torres Strait Islander peoples marks the obvious importance of these. Rather, the critique is of the non-existence of other data for Indigenous people— the kinds of data that are regarded as critical to collect on the majority population.

These data absences raise critical questions. Why, for example, did the federal government initiators and funders of the (very expensive) HILDA survey project, and the research consortium that conducts the project, not feel it necessary to generate an Indigenous sample that was large enough to yield robust statistics regarding their separate circumstances? In the early 2000s, the very wide range of household, income and labour fields, including data on household division of labour, collected in the HILDA survey were considered so important by policymakers that a large-scale national longitudinal study was established to collect and collate data on them. Yet, it seems there is no similar urgency, or perhaps even interest, in gathering such data about Indigenous Australians. This question leads to a second. Why is understanding Aboriginal peoples through anything but the lens of a social problem seemingly un-thought of and perhaps unthinkable within our major statistical institutions? It is through the unravelling of these conundrums that the racialised politics of contemporary data collection in Australia can be understood.

5D data and the deficit data/problematic people correlation

Current Australian practices in regard to the collection of data on Indigenous people are the cloned descendants of the data imperatives of colonisation. In what I refer to as the deficit data/problematic people (DD/PP) correlation, processes of enumeration have long been used to correlate the highly observable societal Aboriginal and Torres Strait Islander inequality with the concept of racial unfitness. This situation is not unique to Australia. As Tuhiwai Smith (1999) argues, in an argument that resonates around the colonised indigenous world, numbers rationalise our dispossession, marginalisation and even our right to be indigenous. The heritage and ubiquity of these statistics, everywhere, allow the reality of the indigenous peoples they depict to go largely unchallenged in public and political discourse.

The DD/PP correlation's basic premise is that racial inequality and racially aligned social and cultural differences are directly connected. Many Indigenous and other researchers would agree with some aspects of that premise. What they strongly disagree with is the direction of the relationship. In the DD/PP correlation, the problematic people are the ones who, through their behaviour and their choices, are ultimately responsible for their own inequality. The power of the DD/PP correlation is such that it still works in contemporary times as a mechanism for disenfranchising and dispossessing. Echoes of this discourse are clearly evident in the rationales of both the federal and Western Australian Governments for why Aboriginal communities should be closed rather than supported. The Premier of Western Australia, Colin Barnett, is cited as repeatedly drawing a direct link between the necessity of community closures in the Kimberley region and the problems of violence and suicide experienced in some (but certainly not all) of these communities (ABC 2014). Ditto for the Northern Territory Emergency Response, and the list could go on.

The concept of the DD/PP correlation fits within the theoretical frameworks aligned with the sociology of new racism. Predominantly emerging from the United States, theories of new racism attempt to explain how contemporary African American/white American relations have not changed substantially despite the fact that racism per se is now almost universally regarded as socially, culturally and politically unacceptable. Researchers such as Bobo (1997) and Kinder and Sears (1981) argue that the continuation of racism can be explained by the replacement of discredited ideas of racial biological inferiority with rationales of non-white cultural and moral inferiority. These moral and cultural racial differences, just like old-fashioned notions of biological inferiority, are then problematised as the cause of and explanation for socioeconomic disparity. Under this new reasoning, Bonilla-Silva (2010) argues that it is now possible for claims for non-white inferiority to be made simultaneously with claims of non-racism—or what he refers to as racism without racists. Bonilla-Silva takes these ideas further, arguing that the 'new' morally and culturally pejorative interpretation of racial differences is structurally, not only individually, situated, and that the embeddedness of these ideas in the institutions and functions of the state may be even more powerful than old-fashioned racism. Under the individual and systemic promulgation of this discourse, race-based inequality is undisturbed within an almost hegemonic argument that (individual) racism is an anachronism.

Race relations that emerge from colonising settler states, however, add a complexity to the black or brown/white binary of theories of new racism that are strong in the United States. In nations like Australia, the primary race relations locus is between the majority European population, especially the dominant Anglo-heritage group and its historical and contemporaneously dominant instruments of state, and the first peoples of Australia. The act and practice of colonisation, historically and through its current day realities, saturate this relationship. It is colonisation that pervasively frames Australian racial/social hierarchies. In turn, these hierarchies are supported and rationalised by racialised discourses that circulate through the dominant society, defining and positioning the Indigenous peoples they have dispossessed and from whose lands and resources the now-settler nations draw their wealth and identity (Walter 2014). As I have argued elsewhere (Walter 2010; Walter & Andersen 2013), these discourses draw on the projected 5D data depictions of Aboriginal and Torres Strait Islander people as their evidentiary base. Statistical portrayals of Aboriginal and Torres Strait Islander people sit at the centre of how they are understood by the dominant settler society. They also frame the lived realities and the socially, politically and culturally framed understandings of the Australian nation-state's relationship with 'its' Indigenous population.

This racialised 'politics of the data', therefore, has powerful consequences in the determination, and practice, of the nation-state/Indigenous population relationship. In the absence of other portrayals, stereotype-enhancing data pictures of Aboriginal 'deficits' and 'inadequacies' are all the more glaringly visible. 5D data provide an infinitely variable circular rationale for Aboriginal and Torres Strait Islander inequality, to the convenient exclusion of other less palatable explanations. More insidiously, they provide a virtuous veil to draw over the use and misuse of the power of the nation-state in its ongoing interactions with Australian Indigenous peoples—being cruel to be kind as it attempts to 'help' those who, obviously as per the 5D data, are incapable of helping themselves. The silencing of Indigenous voices within this discourse can also be justified through the presentation of the state/Indigenous relationship as akin to that between a stern but caring parent and a wayward child.

Academic research is not immune from the lure of the DD/PP correlation, which in turn adds a scholarly legitimation to the picture of Indigenous people as unfit and blameworthy. Weatherburn's (2014) analysis of arrest, incarceration, socioeconomic and other statistics relating to Australian Indigenous people, for example, concludes that the primary reason for the heavy overrepresentation of Indigenous people in incarceration is widespread criminality among Australian Indigenous peoples. The growth in this overrepresentation, he argues, can be explained by the change in the relative rates of Indigenous and non-Indigenous involvement in serious crime. Uncritically reiterating the correlation mantra that the cause and the remedy for inequality (in this case, the over-incarceration of Indigenous people) can be found within those people themselves, Weatherburn posits data on poor parenting, poor school performance, early school leaving, unemployment and drug and alcohol abuse as the social correlations of offending and, therefore, its causes. But these phenomena are not social facts in and of themselves; they do not just exist. They are the predictable outcomes of longstanding social, cultural and racial inequality that is the signature product of colonising settler states (see, for example, Aotearoa/New Zealand, Canada and Hawai'i for a near mirror image of these inequalities and social outcome phenomena). Moreover, the classic 'correlation equals causation' error is made by Weatherburn, as it is in much of the DD/PP correlation interpretations. It is not that these things—that is, poverty, low educational attainment, unemployment and so on—'cause' offending, but that offending, overrepresentation *and* these indicators are part of the same landscape of inequality.

How 5D data construct the dominant discourse on indigeneity

The numerical form of statistics is a primary contributor to normalisation of the DD/PP correlation. Statistical analytical processes rely on the conversion of social and cultural phenomena, or measurements of social and cultural phenomena, to assigned numerical values. This transference allows examinations of relationships between objects to be represented in numerical form. It is here that the mental shift occurs. Indigenous statistics—these representations of phenomena such as relationship to the labour market, experience of high mortality and morbidity and housing positioning—in numerical form acquire within this conversion process a mantle of impartiality, if not full objectivity. Indigenous socio-structural realities are transmuted into neutral data points. Once social phenomena are perceived as 'data', it is an easy step to regard these data points as social facts—a dispassionate representation of Aboriginal and Torres Strait Islander reality.

Positioned as objective descriptors, these particular numbers operate now, as they have always done, as mechanisms of unequal power relations. They define who and what Indigenous people are. They also define what we cannot be. The Indigene remains the object, caught in a numbered bind, forever viewed through the straitjacketing lens of deficit (Walter & Andersen 2013). As such, relentless measurement, re-measurement and comparison of our invidious positioning within Australian society, to the exclusion of other investigations, reify and cement these 5D portrayals. The advent of big data, with its tendency to further distance lived social and cultural realities from their database embodiment, has only exacerbated the pejorative power of numbers to further marginalise and dispossess.

When the only Aborigine you know is the 5D statistical Aborigine

The DD/PP correlation's grip on how the settler majority population, policymakers and statistical agencies 'know' Indigenous people is exacerbated by the intense disjuncture between black and white lives. Regardless of the fact that a predominantly urban Aboriginal population lives alongside the predominantly urban non-Aboriginal population, Aboriginal lives remain out of sight and mind—spatially, politically, socially and culturally absent from non-Indigenous Australia. The limited data available indicate very clearly that Indigenous and non-Indigenous Australians occupy different social and spatial realms; we live in different places even when living next to each other (Atkinson et al. 2010). Aboriginal people are largely invisible, as people and as peoples, in conceptions of everyday Australian life except as pejorative (statistically informed) stereotypes. This invisibility extends to the nation-state's concept of itself and the business of state, except, reluctantly, as a seemingly unresolvable 'equity issue'. Political and spatial marginalisation also insidiously support the perception of Indigenous peoples as remote outsiders, just another minority group, rather than Australia's first nations. It is therefore unimportant, from within a majority Australian identity perspective, to know much about Aboriginal Australia.

This lack of knowledge fosters the building of non-Indigenous to Indigenous relations around pejorative stereotypes and this can be heard through the patter of almost thoughtless denigration and casual disrespect of Aboriginal and Torres Strait Islander people, culture and society that pervades our society's conversations. As an Aboriginal person with pale skin, I hear this conversation everywhere—on public transport, at social gatherings and also in the university classroom. The widely held notions of Aboriginal responsibility for their own disparate socioeconomic position and a simultaneous but contradictory belief system about Aboriginal over-entitlement, which are doggedly resistant to the overwhelming evidence to the contrary, are repeated ad nauseum every day, between conversationalists who would (and do) take umbrage at any suggestion that such talk is founded on racism. Academic claims such as that Aboriginal culture is violent (see Weatherburn 2014) or that the deprived living conditions of many families in remote communities are culturally related (see Sutton 2005) just reflect and support this normalised terrain of disdain.

The almost complete absence of Aboriginal and Torres Strait Islander people within the life orbits of non-Indigenous Australia supports rather than restricts discourses of disregard. 5D data allow the non-Indigenous majority population to be assured in their knowledge of Aboriginal and Torres Strait Islander people regardless of the fact that they are unlikely to know any Aboriginal or Torres Strait Islander people. This is borne out by results from a battery of questions on attitudes to Aboriginal issues I asked in the nationally representative 2007 Australian Survey of Social Attitudes (AuSSA) (n = 2,699). Responses from the 34 survey participants who identified as Aboriginal or Torres Strait Islander were removed from the sample for analysis.

The answers revealed that a modest to bare majority disagreed that equal treatment is now a reality (58 per cent), that injustices are all in the past (51 per cent) and that Aboriginal identity goes beyond traditional lifestyles (57 per cent). A similar proportion agreed with Aboriginal cultural autonomy (53 per cent). The responses to the restorative justice items—agreement that extra government assistance because of ongoing disadvantage is warranted (45 per cent) and disagreement that Aboriginal land rights are unfair to other Australians (33 per cent)—did not find majority support.

Table 5.1 OLS regression variable description and coefficients predicting 'attitudes to Aboriginal issues' scores

Variable		β	%
Constant		0.255	
Age	18–34 years	0.087	18.8
	35–49 years	0.033	29.3
	50–64 years#		31.0
	50–64 years	0.115	20.8
Gender	Male	−0.155**	52.6
	Female		47.4
Education	< Year 12	−0.622***	20.2
	Year 12	−0.481***	10.8
	Trade/technical	−0.673***	16.7
	Certificate/diploma	−0.480***	28.0
	Bachelor degree or above		24.3
Occupation	Manager	−0.111	14.9
	Professional		22.1
	Technical/trade	−0.139	13.8
	Community/personal service worker	−0.212*	9.6
	Clerical/administration	−0.175*	17.6
	Sales*	−0.199*	8.3
	Machinery operator/driver	−0.145	5.0
	Labourer**	−0.249**	8.6
Location	Capital city	0.242***	59.4
	Other urban	0.155*	8.2
	Rural		32.5

Variable		β	%
Respondent individual income	$0–15,599	0.088	26.0
	$15,600–36,399	0.031	27.2
	$36,400–77,900	–0.083	32.9
	$78,000 +		14.0
Ancestry	Euro-Australian	0.180˙	93.7
	Non–Euro-Australian		6.3
Social proximity	Mix regularly with Aboriginal people on a day-to-day basis		9.1
	Know Aboriginal people but do not mix regularly with them	0.012	44.6
	Do not know any Aboriginal people personally	0.030	45.9
Adj. R²			0.111

˙ $p < 0.05$

˙˙ $p < 0.01$

˙˙˙ $p < 0.000$

\# Collinearity diagnostics do not indicate multicollinearity between 'Education' and 'Occupation' variables.

Source: Adapted from Walter (2012).

This first set of responses suggests there is awareness, albeit very incomplete, within broader non-Indigenous Australian society that racial inequality is a contemporary reality for Aboriginal and Torres Strait Islander people. Explaining why this awareness does not translate into majority support for remedial action can be explained by both the prevalence of 5D data and the associated DD/PP correlation. There is no need to redress inequality if you can rationalise the cause of that inequality not within wider society, but within the people who experience it. This supposition is supported by findings from the set of social proximity questions asked in the same AuSSA. The results find more than 90 per cent of respondents do not interact with Aboriginal people regularly and more than half do not know any Aboriginal people (Walter 2012). An ordinary least-squares (OLS) multiple regression with 'Attitudes towards Aboriginal issues' constructed from a single-scale variable from the six statements[1] as the dependent variable finds that a number of sociodemographic factors influence non-Indigenous Australians' attitudes. As displayed in Table 5.1, in line with the

---

1   Principle component analysis: Eigenvalue 2.70, 45 per cent of variance; Cronbach's alpha 0.75.

literature on the topic (see Goot & Watson 2001; Bean et al. 2001; Pedersen et al. 2004; Goot & Rowse 2007; Walter & Mooney 2007), gender, education level, residential location, ancestry and occupation are all independently associated with non-Indigenous Australians' attitudes to Aboriginal issues (for a full discussion, see Walter 2012).

The association that is my focus here is the social proximity variable—more particularly, it is the lack of a statistically significant independent association between attitudes *towards* Aboriginal issues and the level of interaction by non-Indigenous respondents *with* Aboriginal people. My theoretical explanation for this result is that few non-Indigenous people know Aboriginal people and that knowing, or lack of knowing, is not associated with attitudes. Therefore, in light of this lack of social proximity, it must be that dominant public discourses *about* Aboriginal people are the major informer of non-Indigenous attitudes (Walter 2012). In terms of this chapter, 5D data are central to the construction of these discourses and the impact of 5D data on attitudes operates independently of Aboriginal and Torres Strait Islander people.

Disrupting the paradigm of Indigenous statistics

Let's return to our original proposition that for Indigenous statistical data the question is not merely 'are these numbers real', but also 'how are these numbers deployed', 'what do they purport to portray' and 'whom do they serve?' Our earlier discussion has established that the numbers are deployed in very limited ways and, while they purport to portray Indigenous reality, what they actually portray is primarily a picture of Indigenous deficit, contrasted with the (normal) non-Indigenous majority. Such numbers reinforce dominant discourses about Indigenous peoples and, in so doing, they support the status quo of the subordinate Indigene position within the nation-state. Disrupting this limited and limiting paradigm therefore requires that the established tropes of data on Indigenous people be disturbed, ontologically and epistemologically.

Disturbing and disrupting the dominant paradigm of these data is more difficult than might be imagined. Their unquestioned default position is founded on embedded ways of seeing the world, and these world views are what shape their discursive reality. The primary problematic is that the Indigenous ways of seeing the world are not doing the shaping. Let me explain. As elaborated in my co-authored book *Indigenous statistics* (Walter & Andersen 2013), the theoretical frame of social positioning within Indigenous statistics draws on the concepts of social space and habitus from the work of Pierre Bourdieu (1984). Bourdieu used the concept of an individual's or group's position in three-dimensional social space (consisting of social, cultural and economic capital positions) to explain how people from similar positions tend to share a similar world view.

This shared view, especially among groups with the highest levels of social, cultural and economic capital, leads to a 'synthetic unity' (Bourdieu 1984)—a presumption that their world view is *the* world view. For 5D data, the key change is to add race capital to Bourdieu's group—a four-dimensional not three-dimensional social space. We argue that a similar positioning along the continuum of race, social, cultural and economic capital is a shared constitutive element of the world view of those who control the commissioning, analysis and interpretation of Indigenous data—a predominantly Euro-Australian and middle-class group. It is the world view of this group that shapes how Indigenous statistics are understood and 'done'.

As cultural theorists Hofstede and Hofstede (2005) argue, similar groups of people are mentally programmed with 'software of the mind' to produce similar constructs, which they form into logical, affective and behavioural models. Thus, this shared habitus of the primary creators of data on Indigenous Australians and their lifelong positioning as Euro-Australian middle-class people shape (subconsciously mostly) the production of data on Indigenous Australians and their subsequent portrayal, thereby confining and/or prescribing how these data are 'done'. As evidenced in the previous section, the majority of these controllers of such data, like the majority of the non-Indigenous population, are unlikely to personally know any Aboriginal people. Rather, the only Indigene they are likely to be familiar with is the portrayal drawn from 5D data. The contrasting (and distant) four-dimensional social space position of the object of the data (Indigenous peoples) reinforces the uncontested 'synthetic unity' (Bourdieu 1984) of dominant perspectives.

The central point is that dominant discourses of a society, not statistical methods, determine social data meanings. As Zuberi and Bonilla-Silva (2008) argue, claims of objective methodology allow dominant settler society questions to be perceived—largely unchallenged within the institutions and entities that pose them—as the only questions. The reality of these numerical data points, however, emerges not from mathematically supported computational techniques but from the social, racial and cultural standpoints of their creators. The power and the politics of the data are embedded in the 'who' of who has the power to make the assumptive determinations—to determine: what is the problematic, what it is that requires investigation, which objects to interrogate and which variables and variable relationships to test (see also Morphy, this volume). In the terrain of Indigenous Australian statistical data initiation, this 'who' among which these powers remain is most definitively not Aboriginal and Torres Strait Islander people.

Research constructed from statistics and data imagined from Indigenous ways of seeing the world will, by definition, change the terrain of Indigenous statistics. Yet it is important to stress that arguments around Indigenous methodological conceptual and practical distinctiveness are not to say: 1) that such statistics are in opposition to those emerging from the Western habitus, or 2) that differences from Western-framed statistics are what make Indigenous-framed statistics Indigenous. Neither are statistical techniques nor the ways of measuring per se what delineate 5D data from Indigenous-framed data. Rather, as argued in Walter and Andersen (2013), the Indigenous position in four-dimensional social space in a particular society makes apparent the gaps in current frameworks and in existing categories, concepts and conceptualisations of Indigenous data. In changing the 'who' of who has the power to make the assumptive determinations that shape data practices, the terrain of what is the problematic, what needs to be measured, how it is measured and very often who is doing the measuring is also changed (see also Lovett, this volume). Altering the paradigm of statistics on Indigenous people is critical if the statistical 'recognition gap' is to be addressed. As per Taylor (2008) and Kukutai and Walter (2015), the 'recognition gap' is the ongoing propensity for our official statistics agencies to misrecognise the social and cultural phenomena that are important to the wellbeing of Indigenous peoples. Expanding the 'recognition space' between Indigenous and non-Indigenous understandings allows us to speak back to the state in the language of statistical evidence that they both understand and culturally respect, reframing the narratives about us.

A case study

One way to disrupt established tropes surrounding Indigenous statistics is to reverse the presumed direction of the DD/PP correlation with place. In so doing, not only would Indigenous world views be incorporated into the assumptive determinations of what the problematic is and how it should be investigated, but also non-Indigenous Australians would become the sometimes difficult to comprehend 'them' and their social structural positioning would become the research object. To demonstrate this, I use a research example that takes the Indigenous perspective as its epistemic starting point. In so doing, it disrupts the trope of statistical production regarding Indigenous people and demonstrates an alternative Indigenous numbers paradigm. Yes, the numbers are real and their deployment bridges an ontological gap—providing a space for a discourse of Aboriginal perspectives on Indigenous *and* non-Indigenous social and cultural values, norms and life circumstances. It is this reality that these numbers purport to portray.

The research was conducted in 2014–16 by colleagues and myself. The project, 'Telling it Like it Is',[2] was undertaken in partnership with Larrakia Nation, the organisation representing the traditional owners of the country where Darwin now stands and where Aboriginal people make up about 10 per cent of the total population. Our research rationale was that the unevenness of race relations has meant that Aboriginal people are rarely asked their views on Australian values, Australian society and their own place within it. This project's aim was to redress this gap across multiple platforms. Initial results from the interviews of 40 respondents demonstrated a severe disconnect between Aboriginal and non-Aboriginal lives, lifestyles and values in Darwin. Respondents described how Indigenous and non-Indigenous people occupy different social worlds, with most social interaction being transactional rather than relational. Life disconnects were described in terms of the uncomfortableness of being Aboriginal in public spaces such as shopping centres, frequently feeling judged and feeling they did not belong. Value disconnects centred on what

---

2 'Telling it Like it Is' is an Australian Research Council (ARC) funded research project conducted by Habibis, Walter and Elder. ARC Linkage Project 130100622. See also Habibis et al. (2016).

was perceived as the Western core value of material success versus central Aboriginal obligations of family and culture. Although respondents understood material benefits, they also saw the price many non-Indigenous people pay—stress, long working hours, with accumulation of material goods and career progression as the measures of personal success—as too high.

Results from the interview phase shaped the development of a stratified sample survey of over 400 Aboriginal people. Survey data were collected face to face by an Aboriginal survey team from the Darwin area. The results confirmed the qualitative findings as being representative of Aboriginal peoples' views in the Darwin area. The survey data also revealed a deep lack of trust of the Euro-Australian–dominated institutions and governance bodies and a resentment of their refusal to recognise, in any meaningful way, Aboriginal, and particularly Larrakia, sovereignty of their own land. Disturbingly, for a majority of the respondents, regardless of their socioeconomic positioning, negative racialised encounters with non-Indigenous residents of Darwin remain an everyday, even normalised, experience (Walter 2016).

Conclusion

Alternative-paradigm Indigenous statistics cannot but disrupt the status quo of Indigenous data production: 5D data and the DD/PP correlation. But challenging long-established practices is likely to also disturb the ontological and epistemic security of those for whom the current way of creating such data is the norm. The alternative-paradigm results may also be hard to hear and potentially hard to understand for the wider non-Aboriginal audience. Nonetheless, such Indigenous-framed numbers are powerful and, by virtue of their framing of the ontological realities of Aboriginal life from an Aboriginal perspective, political. Most significantly—statistically significantly—the paradigm will reverse the hitherto one-way track of how Australia's racial terrain permeates Indigenous statistics.

References

Atkinson R, Taylor E & Walter M (2010). Burying indigeneity: the spatial construction of reality and Aboriginal Australia. *Social and Legal Studies* 19(3):311–30.

Australian Broadcasting Corporation (ABC) (2014). Colin Barnett: closing WA's remote Aboriginal communities will cause great distress but he has no choice. *The World Today*, ABC National Radio, 13 November 2014.

Bean C, Gow D & McAllister I (2001). *Australian election study: user's guide for the machine-readable data file: SSDA study no. 1048*, Social Science Data Archive, The Australian National University, Canberra.

Bobo L (1997). Race, public opinion, and the social sphere. *The Public Opinion Quarterly* 61(1):1–15.

Bonilla-Silva E (2010). *Racism without racists: colour-blind racism and the persistence of racial inequality in the United States*, 3rd edn, Rowman & Littlefield, Lanham, Md.

Bourdieu P (1984). *Distinction: a social critique of the judgment of taste*, Routledge, London.

Goot M & Rowse T (2007). *Divided nation: Indigenous affairs and the imagined public*, Melbourne University Press, Melbourne.

Goot M & Watson I (2001). One Nation's electoral support: where does it come from, what makes it different and how does it fit? *Australian Journal of Politics and History* 47(2):159–91.

Habibis D, Taylor P, Walter M & Elder C (2016). Repositioning the racial gaze: Aboriginal perspectives on race, race relations and governance. *Social Inclusion* 4(1):57–67, doi:10.17645/si.v4i1.492.

Hofstede G & Hofstede GJ (2005). *Cultures and organizations: software of the mind*, 2nd edn, McGraw-Hill, New York.

Kinder DR & Sears DO (1981). Prejudice and politics: symbolic racism versus racial threats to the good life. *Journal of Personality and Social Psychology* 40(3):414–31.

Kukutai T & Walter M (2015). Recognition and indigenising official statistics: reflections from Aotearoa New Zealand and Australia. *Statistical Journal of the IAOS* 31(2):317–26.

Pedersen A, Beven J, Walker I & Griffiths B (2004). Attitudes towards Indigenous Australians: the role of empathy and guilt. *Journal of Community & Applied Social Psychology* 14:233–59.

Quine WVO (1948). *On what there is. Review of metaphysics*, reprinted in his *From a logical point of view (1953)*, Harvard University Press, Cambridge, Mass.

Sutton P (2005). The politicisation of disease and the disease of politicisation: causal theories and the Indigenous health differential, paper presented at 8th National Rural Health Conference, Central to health: sustaining wellbeing in remote and rural Australia, Alice Springs, NT, 10–13 March 2005.

Taylor J (2008). Indigenous peoples and indicators of wellbeing: Australian perspectives on United Nations global frameworks, *Social Indicators Research* 87(1):111–26.

Ting S, Perales F & Baxter J (2015). Gender, ethnicity and the division of household labour within heterosexual couples in Australia. *Journal of Sociology* (April):1–18.

Tuhiwai Smith L (1999). *Decolonizing methodologies, research and indigenous peoples*, Zed Books, London & New York.

Walter M (2006). Using the power of the data within Indigenous research practice. *Australian Aboriginal Studies* (2):27–34.

Walter M (2010). The politics of the data: how the statistical indigene is constructed. *International Journal of Critical Indigenous Studies* 3(2):45–56.

Walter M (2012). Keeping our distance: non-Indigenous/Aboriginal relations. In Pietsch J & Aarons H (eds), *Australia: identity, fear and governance in the 21st century*, ANU E Press, Canberra.

Walter M (2014). The race bind: denying Aboriginal rights in Australia. In Green J (ed.), *Indivisible: indigenous human rights*, Fernwood Publishing, Winnipeg.

Walter M (2016). Social exclusion/inclusion for urban Aboriginal and Torres Strait Islander people, *Social Inclusion* 4(1):68–76.

Walter M & Andersen C (2013). *Indigenous statistics: a quantitative methodology*, Left Coast Press, Walnut Creek, CA.

Walter M & Mooney G (2007). Employment and welfare. In Carson B, Dunbar T, Chenhall R & Bailie R (eds), *Social determinants of Indigenous health*, Allen & Unwin, Sydney.

Weatherburn D (2014). *Arresting incarceration: pathways out of Indigenous imprisonment*, Aboriginal Studies Press, Canberra.

Zuberi T & Bonilla-Silva E (2008). *White logic, white methods: racism and methodology*, Rowman & Littlefield, Lanham, Md.

6

Indigenising demographic categories: a prolegomenon to indigenous data sovereignty

Frances Morphy[1]

> We should recognize that quantification facilitates a peculiarly modern ontology, in which the real easily becomes coextensive with the measurable. (Espeland & Stevens 2008: 432)

> Reference to 'reality' is a commonplace among both producers and users of statistics. This 'reality' is understood to be self-evident: statistics must 'reflect reality' or 'approximate reality' as closely as possible. (Desroisières 2001: 339)

Introduction

Is engagement with quantification inevitable for indigenous peoples who seek sovereignty over data that describe them? A radical response would be to resist the hegemony of quantification and reject quantitative social science, and demography in particular, as a 'way of knowing'—about anything. The least radical would be simply to

---

1   The author acknowledges and thanks the Center for Advanced Studies in the Behavioral Sciences at Stanford University, where she was a 2015–16 Research Affiliate. The final draft of this chapter was completed there.

accept the status quo and continue to allow others to frame indigenous identities and futures—to accept what I have elsewhere termed 'enforced commensurability' (Morphy 2007a: 40). But the ubiquity of quantification as a technology of power (see Scott 1998; Anderson 2006), at the state level and now increasingly on the world stage (see Espeland & Stevens 2008; Davis et al. 2012; Davis, this volume), seems to make engagement a strategic imperative if people are to act for themselves rather than merely be acted on.

If indigenous people accept, as a pragmatic middle course, that they should engage with and refashion this technology of power to their own ends, it is necessary to understand precisely what this entails, both as an ontological and as a logistical project. In pressing for more active participation in, even control of, the framing and collection of quantitative data that describe them, the world's indigenous peoples are faced with a complex double bind, for this engagement entails negotiating the 'peculiarly modern ontology' in which the measurable is coextensive with the real—a proposition that is at serious odds with many indigenous ontologies and epistemologies.[2] It involves appropriating a technology of Global Northern modernity and refashioning it as a defence for alternative indigenous modernities founded on very different ontologies and on primarily qualitative systems of value—and evaluation. In the process, indigenous ontologies will inevitably become entangled in the ontology of the quantifiable. Managing the consequences of such an ontological shift is one of the major challenges facing indigenous people as they define their own futures.

As an illustrative example, in a recent article in *Arena*, Codding et al. (2015) deploy the technology of quantification to make a persuasive argument for the value of mosaic burning practices to the Western Australian (WA) economy. They put some dollar figures on the contribution of Martu people in the desert country of WA to 'ecosystems service' through this practice. The article makes the argument that removing Martu from their small remote communities, so that they can no longer make this contribution, will be more expensive in the long run for the WA Government than supporting them to live on their country.

---

2   It is also at serious odds with many intellectual traditions of the West, including those with a strong tradition of qualitative research such as anthropology.

Making Martu burning practices 'real' entails re-categorising them so that they become visible to the technologies of quantification. In re-categorising mosaic burning in quantifiable terms, the authors are countering former prime minister Tony Abbott's comment that living in remote communities is merely a 'lifestyle choice'. They choose this strategy because state and Commonwealth governments—deaf to qualitative discourse about the social value of 'connection to country'—are more likely to take note of such quantitative evidence. Yet this framing of Martu burning practices as a quantifiable 'ecosystems service', while mounted by others in defence of the Martu way of life, is not how most Martu themselves would frame it.[3] Should they later decide to do so, they are the ones who will need to work to reframe their own cultural practices as quantifiable.

There are two major aspects to data sovereignty. If a transfer of responsibility for the framing of data is to occur, power relations need to change. Davis et al. (2012: 89) suggest that institutions of power could focus on 'empowering *actors who are governed by indicators*—for example by giving them access to the expertise they need to contest decisions based upon indicators' (emphasis in the original). I will not address this aspect of data sovereignty in detail, since it is the topic of other chapters in this volume (see, in particular, the contributions by Smith, Snipp and FNIGC), but I note that, as the Martu example shows, quantitative work is expensive, time-consuming and logistically complex, in addition to requiring very specific kinds of expertise.[4] Transfer of power will need to be accompanied by institution building, and transfers of expert knowledge and considerable quantities of money.

In the remainder of this chapter, I focus on the second, less often discussed, epistemological aspect of data sovereignty. Davis et al. (2012: 89) suggest that 'institutions of power might support or subsidise the production of competing indicators, and refrain from promulgating indicators themselves'. I call this sovereignty over

---

3   A point to which this group of authors pays detailed and careful attention in their writing for an academic audience (see, for example, Bliege Bird et al. 2008, 2012; Codding et al. 2014).

4   Rendering Martu practice as quantifiable has required years of meticulous research by a team of environmental anthropologists who have employed a range of sophisticated statistical techniques in the process of quantifying the data (see, for example, Bliege Bird et al. 2008, 2012; Codding et al. 2014).

the process of categorisation. It is not just a question of contesting decisions based on indicators preordained by others; it also involves the assertion of sovereignty over the choice of indicators.

In what follows, I begin by sketching what appear to me to be crucial aspects of the technology of quantification that indigenous peoples need to bear in mind to make informed judgements about how to refashion (or subvert) it. I then move to consider challenges that indigenous peoples face in their efforts to achieve epistemological sovereignty over the data that define them. The first is to challenge the 'reality' (or normativity) of preordained systems of categorisation. In addressing this question, I will pay particular attention to the culturally inflected categorisations that frame conventional demographic inquiry and show how these distort or render invisible potential alternative, indigenous categorisations.

The second challenge is how, then, to determine the nature of the data to be collected—including how to set about 'naming' the indicators that measure indigenous realities. Space precludes any detailed consideration of these issues, which I have begun to explore in a series of publications deriving from population-related research undertaken on behalf of the peoples of the Fitzroy Valley in Western Australia (Morphy 2010a) and the eastern Yolngu clans of north-east Arnhem Land in the Northern Territory (Morphy 2007b, 2010b, 2012).

'Data' and 'indicators'

It is important to distinguish between data and the use of data to create indicators. Davis et al. draw the contrast between data per se—for example, on numbers of people between the ages of zero and 14, between 15 and 64 and 65-plus—and the aggregation of such data in a particular way:

> [F]or instance, by dividing the sum of the first and third figures by the figure for the number of people in the 15 to 64 group. If that number is then labeled a 'dependency ratio,' and the same calculation is made for other units or other times, the collection of processed data is capable of being used for the purposes of … comparisons of 'dependency' and qualifies as an indicator. (2012: 74)

This example serves at once to make the distinction between the two and to illuminate pervasive Global North categorisations in demography, at the level of both data and indicators. The Global North assumption that data on chronological age can be used to construct a valid index of 'dependency' rests on several other assumptions: first, that chronological age ranges are a proxy for (indicators for) degrees of economic engagement; second, that a 'normal' economy is one in which capacity to earn money is the primary source of acquiring the means to live. In a Global North economy, this is, broadly speaking, the case: capacity to earn is the basis of participation in the economy and it resides with people in the 15–64 age group; those aged under 15 (who are in compulsory education) and those over 65 (who are in retirement) are 'dependants'. The acceptance of this indicator as a measure of some kind of universal socioeconomic 'truth' leads then to the idea of the 'demographic dividend' in populations where people of 'working age' substantially outnumber their 'dependants'.

Now imagine a society where capacity to produce food through foraging (or subsistence horticulture) is almost as significant as money earned through wages and welfare transfers,[5] where the 'good' of compulsory schooling (particularly if children have to attend boarding schools to receive it) offsets the time that 'school-age' children can spend in honing their knowledge of their environment and their productive skills—a process that begins as soon as they are effectively mobile. In this society, those 'over 65' are respected elders on whose lifetime of accumulated wisdom and knowledge everyone else depends. In such a society, school-age children are already active economic players and elders, far from being 'dependants', are the reservoirs of productive

---

5   Bliege Bird et al. (2012) collected data on Martu foraging in the summer months of 2006 (January to April) and in the transitional and winter months (April to August) in 2009. They calculate that in summer, per capita consumption of 'bush foods' averaged 29.13 per cent, ranging from 16 per cent to 41 per cent, of daily caloric intake. In the second period, when allocation of time to foraging is generally higher, mean bush food consumption represented 49 per cent of daily caloric intake. Martu live in a desert environment. In the tropical north, working with Kuninjku people, Altman (1987) made a major study of foraging at Mumeka outstation in 1979–80, and participated in a follow-up study in 2002–03 (see Altman 2011). Altman reports that in 1979–80, based on an analysis of foraging over 269 days, 46 per cent of Mumeka's energy needs and 81 per cent of their protein came from bush foods (2011: 124). In 2002–03, although foraging produced a smaller proportion of the total intake, 'the quantum harvested was of a similar magnitude' (Altman 2011: 129). In many parts of more 'settled' Australia, such as on the south coast of New South Wales, foraging remains an important source of food for Aboriginal people (see Gray & Altman 2006).

knowledge on which an important part of the economy depends.[6] For such a society, 'dependency' is a more complex phenomenon than in the Global North—it is not a one-way relationship—and chronological age is not necessarily a good indicator of dependency.

A 'dependency ratio' may be judged by the members of such a society as something important to calculate for their own purposes—or maybe not. If it is, what kinds of data might illuminate it? Accepting demography's 'off the peg' ratio is almost certainly not the answer. So there are two levels, not one, at which an indigenous demography needs to pay attention to the collection of data for its own purposes: what indicators will be useful for its defined purposes and what data will be used to construct them?

Characteristics of indicators

In the next section, I move to consider what lies behind the framing of data, but it is worth first considering some characteristics of indicators. Davis et al. (2012) identify four, which I discuss in turn below.

Indicators name things

Naming asserts the claim that the phenomenon measured by the indicator exists (is 'real'): 'The indicator represents an assertion of power to produce knowledge and to define or shape the way the world is understood' (Davis et al. 2012: 76). Thus, indicators are never neutral and 'objective'; they depend on culturally specific categorisations that determine what it is 'significant' to measure. And, if they are dictated 'from above', the power of definition rests there. To claim 'naming rights', indigenous peoples need to replace indicators that have been constructed according to hegemonic categories and motivated by Global North normative assumptions with indicators that reflect their own local understandings of their social world.

---

6   See Kukutai & Taylor (2012: 18) for further commentary on the problems of using chronological age to construct indicators.

Indicators compare and rank

The ordinal structure of indicators enables comparison and ranking, and this exerts pressure for 'improvement' as measured by the indicator (Davis et al. 2012: 76). Encapsulated indigenous minorities within settler states constantly find themselves being compared, as a 'population', with the 'mainstream population'—and found wanting. They have 'gaps' that need to be 'closed', and improvement is defined in terms of the indicators that measure the gaps. The homogeneity of indicators at the national level is justified in terms of the 'problem of comparability'. In Australia (although perhaps not in Aotearoa/New Zealand; see Bishop's chapter, in this volume), this is a hermeneutic circle that seems completely resistant to external pressures for change and to the introduction of heterogeneous measures. It is a manifestation of enforced commensurability.

To break this hermeneutic circle, it is necessary first to interrogate the objects of comparison. In Australia, the 'Indigenous population' is a construct defined in terms of its opposition to the 'non-Indigenous population'. This definition may have some relevance at the national level, but it is of limited utility to particular Indigenous organisations, groups or people (I will call these 'polities' for the sake of brevity) intent on forging their own set of comparators.[7] Indigenous demographies are most likely to be local or, at most, regional in their scope, and the first task is to define the relevant group with which comparisons are to be drawn (see Snipp, this volume). This is far from an easy matter and in some instances may involve contestation over identity and over the boundaries of the group (see Rodriguez-Lonebear, this volume). It may entail creating boundaries where none existed before. These groups, too, will in most cases inevitably be relational constructs because encapsulated indigenous polities in postcolonial societies are linked in complex ways to both other indigenous polities and the encapsulating society.[8]

---

7   I intend 'polity' to encompass more than the 'post-classical' 'families of polity' identified by Sutton (2003). The groupings he describes are most typical of regions of Australia where dispossession, displacement, disease and frontier violence have taken their heaviest toll. In 'very remote' Australia, such as in the Yolngu region of north-east Arnhem Land, forms of social organisation that are more similar to local precolonial forms have persisted; for a relevant discussion, see Morphy (2013).

8   See Axelsson & Sköld (2011) for a range of examples.

The second task is to define what is to be compared, and the answer, most often, is not likely to be direct comparison with the 'mainstream' population. In constructing their own indicators, indigenous polities need to attend to their own values, social structures and aspirations. The comparator more likely to be of interest is some wished-for set of conditions for their own polity. The relevant comparisons will therefore be across the same polity over time rather than between polities or 'subpopulations'. And each set of such indicators for comparison, far from being homogeneous with other such sets, is likely to be unique to the polity in question because of particularities of culture, locale and defined purpose.

There are also likely to be commonalities of value, of structural factors and of aspirations between indigenous polities, and this possibility will be worth exploring. Indigenous polities can learn from each other as they go about the task of building their own sets of indicators. More 'homogeneous' sets of indicators may emerge from such processes, but the important point is that this is not the initial goal. In indigenous demography, it is heterogeneity—the identification of difference and the measurement of that difference in its own terms—that is the primary goal.

A final, additional point can be made about this aspect of indicators. In the world of the Global North, change (aka 'development' or 'improvement') seems to be constantly desired, as if there was some perfect future state to which all of humanity should be jointly aspiring. However, an indigenous perspective might allow for the possibility that 'improvement' is not always necessary; sustaining something of value that already exists may be equally (or more) important.

Indicators simplify complex phenomena

As Davis et al. put it: 'Simplification, or reductionism, is central to the appeal (and probably the impact) of indicators' (2012: 76). In the next section, I will examine how categorisation is used as a tool of simplification with respect to complex phenomena such as the 'family' and the 'household'. Here I give one example from the Australian Census in which, in both 2001 and 2006, Indigenous people were faced with a question in which 'traditional beliefs' were listed as an option for religious affiliation. In 2001, I observed that at a Yolngu community in north-east Arnhem Land:[9]

> Q. 16 (What is your religion?) generated much debate; people wanted to mark more than one box ... As one interviewee put it: 'My beliefs are traditional, but my religion is [Christian denomination]'. ...

> There is no explicit indication that it is permissible to mark two boxes for this question. [One of the local Yolngu paid enumerators] E1's solution was to mark only 'Traditional Beliefs', often declaring as he did so, 'Yolngu [Indigenous] comes before Balanda [non-Indigenous], so we'll put Traditional Beliefs'. Most interviewees agreed to this. The other enumerators sometimes marked both [Christian denomination] and 'Traditional Beliefs', and sometimes only one or the other, depending presumably on what the interviewee's response was. (Morphy 2002: 46)

As with many simplifications, relevant complexity is masked by inadequate categorisation. In both 2001 and 2006, the logistics of the census in north-east Arnhem Land were nightmarish for the organisers and collectors because the regional population was constantly on the move between funerals (see Morphy 2002, 2007c). The size, complexity and importance of Yolngu funerals are directly attributable to aspects of 'traditional beliefs' combined with the importance of extended kin networks, and indeed there has been an intensification of mortuary ritual activity in response to the contemporary conditions of Yolngu life (see Morphy & Morphy 2008, 2011). Yet many if not most Yolngu are also Christians. Because of the lumping of 'traditional beliefs' into the same category as religions such as Christianity, the prevalence of the former is consistently underreported. This feeds into a narrative about the inevitable demise of such belief systems in the face of encroaching modernity and masks their continuing—while changing—significance in contemporary Yolngu lives.

---

9   A feature of the 'Indigenous enumeration strategy' employed in remote Indigenous communities, where levels of literacy in English are typically low, is that the census form is administered by interview unless people opt to fill in their own form.

Indicators implicitly evaluate

This characteristic of indicators has particular relevance to Indigenous lives in Australia today. Indicators do not just shape the way the world is understood, but also contain embedded value judgements:

> Indicators often have embedded in them ... a much further-reaching theory—which some might call an ideology—of what a good society is ... Often the theory or policy idea is not spelled out at all in the indicator but remains implicit. (Davis et al. 2012: 77)

In the 'good society' envisaged by successive Australian governments, Aboriginal people will be healthy, well educated and employed in the mainstream workforce. Full stop. The Closing the Gap indicators (as at 2011: see NIRA Working Group 2011), numbering 27 in all, are divided into three sets to measure health performance, education performance and employment performance. Anything that might be considered distinctively Indigenous—apart from 'disadvantage'—is studiously and deliberately ignored.[10]

In challenging such an ideology of the good society, an indigenous polity is once again faced with a complex task: the need to articulate its own vision of a good society and devise the indicators that are relevant to it. As a useful heuristic exercise, Indigenous Australian polities might want to examine the categorical assumptions that lie behind the framing of the Closing the Gap indicators, and reframe them (those that are considered relevant) according to a different set of categorisations. They might also consider the silences in the indicators: what are the missing categories? These are the kinds of questions to which I now turn.

Conventional demographic categories and their silences

Let us assume for the moment that the goal of any sovereign indigenous demography is first to define what a particular indigenous polity sees as a 'good society' or a 'good way of life' for its members and, second,

---

10   As Kukutai & Taylor note: 'The aim is not to give expression and substance to indigenous difference, but simply to compare those aspects of it that the State feels it wants to influence' (2012: 16).

to devise indicators that quantify its components so that change can be monitored over time.[11] Conventional demographic categories reflect mostly implicit assumptions about what is 'good' or 'normal'; making these assumptions explicit is the first step to deconstructing them and constructing new categories with which to replace them.

In the demographic tradition of the Global North, national population surveys are founded on a basic categorisation of socio-spatial units as bounded containers (see Adams & Kasakoff 2004; Morphy 2007c). The prototypical 'family' is the two-generational 'couple (heterosexual) family' consisting of parents and their children; the prototypical 'household' consists of a nuclear family and is contained within a single dwelling. Social space stops at the boundaries of the dwelling: agglomerations of dwellings are defined spatially as 'statistical areas' and the like, and then grouped into ever larger spatial units, up to the boundaries of the nation-state.

Degrees of variation from the prototype are acknowledged, but these reflect the kinds of variation found commonly in settler state societies. So, in Australia, 'lone-parent' families exist as a variant of the family, as do 'three-generational (but only three) families', and the presence of 'other relatives' is allowed for. Households (defined in terms of commensality) may consist of more than one 'family' and may contain 'unrelated' people as well. Finally, a dwelling may contain more than one 'household'.

From a Yolngu point of view, this system of categorisation contains many important silences. The following crucial building blocks of Yolngu sociality, and of their socioeconomic life, are made invisible: a kin-based social universe, in which everyone calls everyone else by a kin term, and extended kin networks. Yolngu dwellings are not bounded containers, but rather anchoring points for a multigenerational subset of an extended family; often only a small core of people are permanent residents of the dwelling—other kin come and go over time.[12]

Moving beyond the level of the dwelling, the silences deepen. Where is the household (if defined in terms of commensality) that encompasses more than one dwelling? Where are the clusters of dwellings that

---

11   For examples of this process in action, see Hudson, and Yap and Yu, in this volume.
12   For a detailed analysis, see Morphy (2007b, 2010b, 2012).

together anchor larger subsets of an extended family? Where are the homelands communities, in which everybody, ultimately, is related to everybody else in some way, and which function as a single 'household' when it comes to the distribution of meat from large game such as turtles and dugong? Where are the patrilineal landowning clans? Where are the kin links with the people of the surrounding communities?

These are the social silences, and silence matters (see also Pool, this volume). In the Yolngu case, as in many indigenous societies, higher-level units of kin-based social grouping are crucial to an understanding of social formations and of the values that underlie Indigenous views of the 'good' society. Yet Global North demographic categories literally make these invisible, as when, in the Data Processing Unit in Melbourne in 2006, the data coders dismembered Yolngu extended family households and reconstituted them as separate nuclear families (see Morphy 2007d: 107–9).

The deepest silences, however, are spatial; this speaks directly to the rights-based agendas of many indigenous polities. In Global North demography, there is a characteristic silence—an absence of indicators—concerning the nature and extent of connection to (or, in many cases, severance from) place. For indigenous peoples, this is surely the one factor that uniquely distinguishes them from encapsulating settler populations. These are fundamentally emplaced peoples, whose very identities are constituted through their autochthonous connection to particular places. In contrast, settler populations come from somewhere else. Whatever meaning-making they undertake to forge connections to the new places they colonise, these meanings are not founded in a sense of autochthony.

Yolngu communities are not just placed arbitrarily in the landscape. Elsewhere (Morphy 2010b), I have detailed the Yolngu clan-based system of landownership and shown how contemporary homelands settlements in north-east Arnhem Land are strategically placed within clan estates. The 1970s homelands movement in this region was in part a reaction to the advent of mining near Yirrkala, the mission settlement to which people from the surrounding clan estates had been drawn from the 1930s on. There was a desire to indicate to the wider Australian society that Yolngu country was not just 'empty wilderness' ripe for settler exploitation, but an inhabited—and owned and cared for—

landscape. For many Indigenous polities, indicators that make place visible as a foundation of valued sociality are likely to be of paramount importance. Yet conventional demographic inquiry is almost always silent on the matter of place; instead, it deals in arbitrarily divisible space. In Australia, space is divided into statistical areas (levels one through four, defined in terms of population size). The resulting lines on the map bear no relation to anything social—or socio-spatial.

Conclusion: the complications of visibility

Indigenous demographies would seek to make visible the formerly invisible, to give 'reality' to significantly different ways of being in the world. Their efficacy would be gauged in the first instance by their usefulness to the indigenous polities that devise and own them: do such demographies allow them to articulate what they value and plan in a measurable way for a desired future? But they would also highlight clearly, perhaps often for the first time, substantive differences that need to be acknowledged and accepted by settler states if they are to formulate policy that supports rather than undermines the self-defined goals of encapsulated indigenous peoples.

In one important respect this makes indigenous demography a double-edged sword, for substantive difference may result from incommensurable systems of value. Once difference is explicitly articulated, what of the right to remain different, even when a valued difference violates the norms of the more powerful encapsulating society? A clear case in point in Australia, where polygamy is officially illegal, concerns the polygynous unions that exist, albeit in modified form, in many Australian Aboriginal societies (see Morphy 2013), including among Yolngu people.

Currently such arrangements are barely visible to the state. Most Yolngu marriages are unregistered, being classified as 'tribal' marriage arrangements. Polygynous family formations are largely invisible in the census and other surveys because typically a man's wives live in separate (usually contiguous) dwellings and, as we have seen, 'households' by definition do not extend beyond the boundaries of a dwelling. The Yolngu appear to have, as a result, rather a lot of 'households' with female heads. Currently, in the matter of widows' pensions, there is tacit acceptance among local Centrelink staff that all of a man's widows should receive a pension on his death, but would such arrangements survive the official 'outing' of polygyny on to a wider stage? Yolngu need to think carefully about the possible consequences of a Yolngu demography that makes polygyny more visible. Creating an indigenous demography entails a double ontological shift: the indigenous self must appraise not only its own sense of what is real and valued, but also what is real to and valued by the encapsulating other.

References

Adams JW & Kasakoff AB (2004). Spillovers, subdivisions and flows: questioning the usefulness of the 'bounded container' as the dominant spatial metaphor in demography. In Szreter S, Sholkamy H and Dharmalingam A (eds), *Categories and contexts: anthropological and historical studies in critical demography*, Oxford University Press, Oxford.

Altman JC (1987). *Hunter-gatherers today: an Aboriginal economy in north Australia*, Australian Institute of Aboriginal Studies, Canberra.

Altman JC (2011). From Kunnanj, Fish Creek, to Mumeka, Mann River: hunter-gatherer tradition and transformation in Western Arnhem Land 1948–2009. In Thomas M & Neale M (eds), *Exploring the legacy of the 1948 Arnhem Land Expedition*, ANU E Press, Canberra.

Anderson B (2006). *Imagined communities*, rev. edn, Verso, London.

Axelsson P & Sköld P (eds) (2011). *Indigenous people and demography: the complex relation between identity and statistics*, Berghahn Books, Oxford.

Bliege Bird R, Bird DW, Codding BF, Parker CH & Jones JH (2008). The 'fire stick farming' hypothesis: Australian Aboriginal foraging strategies, biodiversity, and anthropogenic fire mosaics. *Proceedings of the National Academy of Sciences* 105(39):14796–801.

Bliege Bird R, Codding BF, Kauhanen PG & Bird DW (2012). Aboriginal hunting buffers climate-driven fire-size variability in Australia's spinifex grasslands. *Proceedings of the National Academy of Sciences* 109(26):10287–92.

Codding BF, Bird DW & Bliege Bird R (2015). The real cost of closing remote communities: doing the sums on the contribution made by traditional Aboriginal economies. *Arena* 135:5–6.

Codding BF, Bliege Bird R, Kauhanen PG & Bird DW (2014). Conservation or co-evolution? Intermediate levels of Aboriginal burning and hunting have positive effects on kangaroo populations in Western Australia. *Human Ecology* 42:659–69.

Davis KE, Kingsbury B & Merry SE (2012). Indicators as a technology of global governance. *Law & Society Review* 46(1):71–104.

Desroisières A (2001). How real are statistics? Four possible attitudes. *Social Research* 68(2):339–55.

Espeland WN & Stevens ML (2008). A sociology of quantification. *European Journal of Sociology* 49(3):401–36, doi:10.1017/S0003975609000150.

Gray MC & Altman JC (2006). The economic value of harvesting wild resources to the Indigenous community of the Wallis Lake catchment, NSW. *Family Matters* 75:10–19.

Kukutai T & Taylor J (2012). Postcolonial profiling of indigenous populations: limitations and responses in Australia and New Zealand. *Espace Populations Sociétés* 2011(1):13–27.

Morphy F (2002). When systems collide: the 2001 census at a Northern Territory outstation. In Martin DF, Morphy F, Sanders WF and Taylor J (eds), *Making sense of the census: observations of the 2001 enumeration in remote Aboriginal Australia*, CAEPR Research Monograph 22, ANU E Press, Canberra.

Morphy F (2007a). Performing law: the Yolngu of Blue Mud Bay meet the native title process. In Smith BR & Morphy F (eds), *The social effects of native title: recognition, translation, coexistence*, CAEPR Research Monograph 27, ANU E Press, Canberra.

Morphy F (2007b). Uncontained subjects: 'population' and 'household' in remote Aboriginal Australia. *Journal of Population Research* 24(2):163–84.

Morphy F (2007c). Mobility and its consequences: the 2006 enumeration in the north-east Arnhem Land region. In Morphy F (ed.), *Agency, contingency and census process: observations of the 2006 Indigenous enumeration strategy in remote Aboriginal Australia*, CAEPR Research Monograph 28, ANU E Press, Canberra.

Morphy F (2007d). The transformation of input into output: at the Melbourne Data Processing Centre. In Morphy F (ed.), *Agency, contingency and census process: observations of the 2006 Indigenous enumeration strategy in remote Aboriginal Australia*, CAEPR Research Monograph 28, ANU E Press, Canberra.

Morphy F (2010a). *Population, people and place: the Fitzroy Valley population project*, Working Paper 70, Centre for Aboriginal Economic Policy Research, The Australian National University, Canberra.

Morphy F (2010b). (Im)mobility: regional population structures in Aboriginal Australia. *Australian Journal of Social Issues* 45(3):363–82.

Morphy F (2012). *The Yolngu in place: designing a population survey for north east Arnhem Land*, Working Paper Series, Agreements, Treaties and Negotiated Settlements Project, University of Melbourne, Melbourne.

Morphy F (2013). Making them fit: the Australian national census and Aboriginal family forms. In Calder G and Beaman L (eds), *Polygamy's rights and wrongs: perspectives on harm, family and law*, UBC Press, Vancouver.

Morphy F & Morphy H (2008). Afterword: demography and destiny. In Glaskin K, Tonkinson M, Musharbash Y & Burbank V (eds), *Mortality, mourning and mortuary practices in Indigenous Australia*, Ashgate, Aldershot, UK.

Morphy F & Morphy H (2011). 'Soon we will be spending all our time at funerals': Yolngu mortuary rituals in an epoch of constant change. In Howell S and Talle A (eds), *Returns to the field: multitemporal research and contemporary anthropology*, Indiana University Press, Bloomington.

National Indigenous Reform Agreement (NIRA) Working Group (2011). *Review of the National Indigenous Reform Agreement performance framework, final report, November 2011*, Council of Australian Governments, Canberra, coag.gov.au/sites/default/files/Final%20 Report%20-%20Review%20of%20the%20National%20 Indigenous%20Reform%20Agreement%20Performance%20 Framework_0.pdf.

Peterson N (2006). Culture. In Hunter BH (ed.), *Assessing the evidence on Indigenous socioeconomic outcomes: a focus on the 2002 NATSISS*, CAEPR Research Monograph 26, ANU E Press, Canberra.

Scott JC (1998). *Seeing like a state: how certain schemes to improve the human condition have failed*, Yale University Press, New Haven, Conn.

Sutton P (2003). *Native title in Australia: an ethnographic perspective*, Cambridge University Press, Cambridge.

7

Governing data and data for governance: the everyday practice of Indigenous sovereignty

Diane E Smith

Not everything that can be counted counts,
And not everything that counts can be counted.

— Albert Einstein (according to the available data)

Introduction

The right of indigenous peoples to pursue development and cultural agendas in keeping with their self-determined aspirations and needs has been asserted by the United Nations Declaration on the Rights of Indigenous Peoples (UNDRIP). The reluctance of nation-states to recognise self-determination, let alone sovereignty, among the indigenous polities within their borders has been the subject of both critical commentary and advocacy. However, it is only recently that attention has been given to the kinds of internal expertise and institutions that are needed to mobilise the exercise of such rights by indigenous peoples. The argument of this chapter is accordingly twofold. First, that the foundation stone for translating indigenous rights into everyday practice now—as opposed to remaining an intangible future goal—is the collective ability of indigenous nations, communities and groups to self-govern, to make informed and internally accountable decisions about their current priorities and future direction. Second, for such effective self-governance to occur, indigenous peoples need access to a range of culturally relevant and accurate information about themselves; they need data they can trust.

A particular catalyst for much recent innovation by indigenous peoples in both these areas has been the imperative to decolonise the governance arrangements and the colonial data archives that have been externally created for and about indigenous peoples. As a consequence, a common set of interrelated questions is being considered by indigenous peoples across Canada, Australia, New Zealand and the United States (CANZUS), in spite of their having distinctive cultural traditions, histories and legal rights. These influential questions include:

- Who exactly is the collective 'self' in the *self*-determined and *self*-governing indigenous polity?
- Who are the intergenerational members of such polities on whose behalf data are to be collected and used?
- What kind of collective identity do indigenous people want to shape for themselves, now and into the future?
- What kinds of development—social, cultural and economic—will be pursued, and who should benefit from it?
- What role should indigenous culture play in collective decisions and solutions about these matters?
- What kinds of data will best support informed decision-making and effective solutions about these matters?
- And, importantly, who should have the authority to govern data on indigenous peoples—to collect, validate, interpret, own and use it?

These questions are considered here primarily through the lens of 'governance', meaning the institutions, relationships, processes and structures by which the collective will of a nation, clan, group or community is mobilised into sustained, organised action (Dodson & Smith 2003; Smith 2005). Neither governance arrangements nor social collectivities are static; they are dynamic entities that may be modified and reconfigured according to changing conditions and needs. But for changes in governance and collective identity to be considered legitimate and so be supported by group members, 'knowledgeable agents' (Giddens 1984: 199) are needed who are able to mobilise consensus and consent among those members. For that to occur, timely access to relevant information about current circumstances, options and likely future outcomes is an influential precondition for arriving at condoned action.

It is not surprising then that data collection *for* exercising effective governance and the effective governance *of* data are emerging as twin capabilities fundamental to underwriting the daily exercise of indigenous self-determination and sovereignty for the social good. These entwined issues are examined in the remainder of this chapter. But first it is useful to understand more about the *common* conditions that have invigorated conversations and initiatives among indigenous peoples about data sovereignty in the four CANZUS countries.

From *datum nullius* to data sovereignty

The governance of data—that is, who has the power and authority to make rules and decisions about the design, interpretation, validation, ownership, access to and use of data—has emerged as a site of contestation between indigenous peoples and the colonial settler states within which they reside. A particularly salient concern is the concept of 'data', which is itself a socially constructed field with epistemologically diverse underpinnings and corresponding issues of validity, relevance, application and dissemination (see, for example, Agrawal 1995; Smith 1991ab, 1994; Smylie & Anderson 2006).

At their most basic, data are simply attributes or properties that represent a series of observations, measurements or facts that are suitable for communication and application (Ellis & Levy 2012; Bruhn 2014). Data constitute a point-in-time intervention into a flow of information or behaviour—an attempt to inject certainty and meaning into uncertainty. As such, data can be useful for generalising from a particular sample to a wider population or category set, for testing hypotheses, for choosing between options and determining the relationship between particular variables. However, when derived from ethnocentric criteria and definitions, data can also impose erroneous causal connections and simplify social complexity, thereby freezing what may be fluid formations in the real world. In their unadorned quantitative form, data are hard-pressed to cope with social and cultural intangibles.

'Data' should also be conceptually distinguished from 'information', which results when people attribute meaning and values to data in a particular context. In intercultural contexts, seemingly objective data and their interpretation as information can become misguided political, policy and ideological instruments. For that reason, both data and information may have limited validity or usefulness when externally imposed as constructions of indigenous behaviours and social formations.

Efforts to permanently settle and control mobile indigenous peoples have been a perennial project of colonial and contemporary nation-states in all four CANZUS countries. Indigenous families were frequently forcibly relocated from their lands, separated from each other and centralised into artificial communities. Their collective rights and self-constructed categories of social organisation were reshaped by colonial frameworks resting on the Western principles and primacy of individual citizenship and assimilation. The scope of the colonial paradigm of *'nullius'* has been more broadly applied beyond the legal fiction of *terra nullius*. It has also purported equivalent fictions about indigenous governance and knowledge systems.

Colonial governments deployed strategies to standardise and simplify the indigenous 'social hieroglyph into a legible and administratively more convenient format' (Scott 1999: 3). Indigenous 'peoples' were enumerated into 'populations' (Taylor 2009); their domestic arrangements and wellbeing were constrained within quantitative datasets and indicators that reflected colonial preoccupations and values. For example, in Australia, the Indigenous logic of family structures, shared parenting and kin relations disappeared under the overwhelming weight of national census statistical analyses (Smith 1991a, 1994; Daly & Smith 1996). Indigenous economies were relegated to a precapitalist category positioned outside so-called mainstream indicators of what constituted 'economically active work', employment and unemployment and productive development (Smith 1991b).

In a similar vein, Indigenous modes of governance across Australia were variously portrayed in colonial discourse as a form of *gubernare nullius*—that is, empty, invisible and unknowable—frozen in an underdeveloped 'primitive' stage of social evolution. From such a standpoint, they were pathologised as being hopelessly dysfunctional and corrupted by kin relationality (Smith 2008). Indigenous knowledge systems in turn were treated as *datum nullius*—a blank slate on which could be constructed the edifice of a distorting 'colonial archive' (Nakata 2007; see also Pool, this volume).

In all four countries, similar *nullius* fictions contributed to the imposition of Western modes of democratic governance, the disruption of indigenous leadership networks and the belittling of indigenous systems of authority and knowledge. Collective institutions of governance were overridden and transformed into legal corporations where indigenous governing traditions, roles and responsibilities were curtailed and externally regulated. New categories and institutions of governance—of boards, executives, councillors, voting, representation, democracy and so on—were inserted into the daily fabric of indigenous peoples' lives.

Today, these tools continue to facilitate the neoliberal control and management of indigenous peoples' lives by nation-state governments. It is hardly surprising, then, that there has been a common move by indigenous groups and their leaders over recent decades to reassert their self-determined modes of governance and their self-identified aspirations. However, as indigenous groups begin to replace outsiders' agendas with their own, they are often confronted with the daunting reality that their contemporary governance arrangements have been significantly eroded and that they lack the relevant data on which to make informed decisions and take action.

Over 25 years ago in Australia, the Royal Commission into Aboriginal Deaths in Custody (RCIADIC 1991) recommended that:

> When social indicators are to be used to monitor and/or evaluate policies and programs concerning Aboriginal people, their informed views should be incorporated into the development, interpretation and use of the indicators, to ensure that they adequately reflect Aboriginal perceptions and aspirations. (RCIADIC 1991: Recommendation 2:53)

> In the development of future national censuses and other data collection activity covering Aboriginal people, the Australian Bureau of Statistics and other agencies … ensure that full account is taken of the Aboriginal perspective. (RCIADIC 1991: Recommendation 2:63).

> Commonwealth, State and Territory Governments provide access to all government archival records pertaining to the family and community histories of Aboriginal people. (RCIADIC 1991: Recommendation 2:79)

These were groundbreaking recommendations and were asserted in different contexts by indigenous leaders and organisations in each of the CANZUS countries. However, it has become increasingly clear that the process of rebuilding or strengthening indigenous governance is closely aligned with the need to also reassert indigenous peoples' control and interpretation into the colonial data archives, and to produce alternative sources of data that are fit for their contemporary purposes.

It is in this historical context that the concept of data sovereignty has emerged to describe the ability of indigenous peoples to practice self-rule and self-governance when it comes to data and the opening of data, and their capacity to gather and manage data for their own purposes and use.

The indigenous governance challenge

The international experience of former UN Special Rapporteur on Indigenous Rights James Anaya (Smith 2012) led him to identify three eras in the fight by indigenous peoples for self-determination, with each era having its own discrete governance challenges. These are:

1. the prerecognition era of colonisation with its denial of indigenous sovereign governance
2. the battle for rights and recognition in which indigenous governance solutions focused on political priorities
3. the post–UN Declaration era of governance implementation.

Over the past 40 years, in each of the four CANZUS jurisdictions, a transition has been occurring from the rights battle to the governance and development challenge. Which is not to say that the rights battle has been won, but rather that the progress made on the rights agenda has led directly to a critical issue—one captured in Patrick Dodson's comments to an international conference on indigenous peoples (see Smith 2012: 11):

> The challenge for traditional owners, like the Yawuru, is how do we, as a people, leverage our native title rights so as to promote our own resilience and reliable prosperity in the modern world.

Arguably, this is the challenge of governance performance and effectiveness—a challenge that has turned out to be a very different task from that of fighting for rights.

Successfully achieving a treaty or land claim, negotiating a resource agreement or implementing an economic initiative invariably requires indigenous people to reassess and restructure their existing governance arrangements. This is because what worked to get them through negotiations is not necessarily what will work to implement the conditions of resulting agreements, claims and treaties. Furthermore, success propels people from thinking about past grievances to thinking about future priorities and how to achieve them.

In addition, there is now an entire generation of young indigenous people whose careers and involvement in indigenous affairs have taken place in the post–land rights, post-treaty and post-settlement environment. Not only does this give them a different viewpoint on history and what is possible, but also they are impatient for strong indigenous governance, for sound decision-making and informed action that will translate the promise of rights into tangible outcomes. From these varied indigenous viewpoints, the collection, ownership, analysis and strategic use of a range of robust data are increasingly recognised as being fundamental to building resilient governance capable of delivering outcomes.

Data *for* governance

Effective governance, whether for a small group or a large nation, means being capable of leadership and stewardship, future-oriented planning, problem solving, evaluating outcomes, developing strategies and taking remedial action. To support that suite of governance capabilities, many indigenous groups and their governing bodies are choosing to produce, interpret and manage their own information systems and databases (Smith 2002, 2005; Taylor 2005; Taylor et al. 2014). In an age of information overload, this can be a daunting governance task in itself.

As part of designing the methodological and conceptual framework for the conduct of the Australian Indigenous Community Governance (ICG) Research Project, I identified several key dimensions and influential components of indigenous modes of governance—both internal and external (Smith 2005: 23–4). Each of these dimensions is associated with a range of governing capabilities, institutions, structures and practices that can be strengthened and adapted through considered interventions (Dodson & Smith 2003). For that to happen successfully, various kinds of data and information will be needed about each dimension (Table 7.1).

Table 7.1 Data for building and evaluating indigenous governance arrangements

Dimensions of governance	Some key items of information/data needed
Cultural geography and legitimacy	The culturally valued layers and aggregations of social relations and territorial organisation forming the bases of group ownership of land and related identities.
Power and authority	Sources, scope, composition, social boundaries and distribution, networks, checks and balances, accountability, transmission, modes and standards of exercise.
Leadership/governors	Pathways, selection, monitoring, accountability, roles and responsibilities, standards of conduct, hierarchies, succession, capacity-building of leaders and decision-makers (male and female).
Decision-making	Processes, mechanisms and rules for, forms of, consensus orientations, implementation of, free prior informed consent, social organisation and subsidiarity of.
Institutional bases	Standards, measures, structures, purposes, goals, capacities, policies, actions and outcomes, transparency, compliance, organisational bases and structure for.
Strategic direction	Planning, priorities, strategies for short and long-term risk management.
Participation and voice	Group membership, demographic characteristics, extent of participation and involvement in decision-making, elections and voting, communication with members/citizens, dispute resolution.
Accountability	Rules and norms, mechanisms and procedures for internal and external controls over corruption and rent-seeking behaviour.

Dimensions of governance	Some key items of information/data needed
Resource governance	Cultural, human, natural, economic, technological, financial and other resources and assets that indigenous people need, have access to or control over. Availability, use and impacts of resources.
Governance of (nation-state) governments	Institutions, structures, values and capacities, powers, policy and service delivery, funding mechanisms, accountability mechanisms, communication and negotiation with.
Governance environment	Web of relationships with external parties, wider operating environment, stakeholder analyses, fiscal flows and funding, impact of wider regional, state and national environment, markets.
Capacity development	Skills, expertise, knowledge, information, abilities to build governance, capability gaps between government rhetoric and on-the-ground reality about what works.
Governance self-evaluation	Standards and measures by which governance 'success' is defined from indigenous and other perspectives, influential factors, meaningful criteria and principles for assessing effective and legitimate indigenous governance.

Source: The author.

Prioritising data for governance: where to start

A challenge in indigenous governance more generally is that often it is the case that everything needs work, which sometimes means that little gets done. So what kind of data *will* support indigenous peoples' purposes of evaluating and strengthening their governing arrangements? Is there a way to think about priority areas for data collection and analysis that would: 1) begin to implement data sovereignty, 2) provide a data foundation on which to build, and 3) move people further down the road towards self-governance based on robust information?

Strengthening and rebuilding governance is a journey. All the issues cannot be addressed at once, and there are no perfect 'good governance' solutions. Rebuilding governance might require immediate substantial changes or small progressive ones. Someone has to lead the way, but it is also critical to keep the nation and community members fully informed, with a voice in decisions. The process of data collection may challenge existing vested interests within a community and in the wider external environment. So being inclusive, transparent and consultative promotes credibility and participation in the process. Whatever the initial impetus, data strategies will be more effective and sustainable if the governance problems and solutions are identified by the group or organisation itself.

Governance is about relationships. As a consequence of colonial interventions and violence across the CANZUS countries, one of the very first issues that arises when indigenous people discuss the kind of governance they have or want is the configuration of their own *collective cultural identity and internal relationships*: Who is the '*self*' in their particular mode of *self*-determination? Who is, and is not, a member? Is the '*self*' differently constituted at different societal levels? On whose behalf are leaders and representative organisations governing? These questions go to the heart of self-determined legitimate solutions for governance. To answer them, people often seek out information about their particular cultural geographies and group membership.

Usually such information is not to be found in mainstream data collections and institutions (such as university libraries, government archives, national censuses, sample surveys). Those invariably operate at the level of Western enumeration concepts and categories. Such datasets are rarely available at the level of indigenous culturally based polities (such as nations, governments, regions, communities, local groups, clans and extended families).

Accordingly, a priority data area for governance is to get some hard *demographic* facts about group membership and relationships that are also linked to landownership. That can include finding out about such things as: what matters to members about their governance as well as their concerns and suggestions; what they think can be done about it; how many members are attending annual general meetings or are involved in selecting or electing leaders; and how many young people are involved in decision-making processes. Such data will reveal a lot about the future demands on governance and services.

Another critical area for early data collection and analysis is *governance performance*. For example, are decisions and risk assessments routinely informed by relevant sound data? Have decisions over the past year been implemented? What are the leadership strengths and gaps? These data will give a better idea of governance effectiveness and future needs. Today, indigenous nations and their organisations are increasingly using computerised systems to keep records of decisions made, allocate responsibility for follow-up action, track outcomes, report back to their governing bodies and deal with any problems.

Data for *financial planning and accountability* will help a nation or community to understand their overall financial situation as reported, ask the right questions so members can know the true state of their collective finances and make more informed decisions about financial priorities and development options. However, it is important for complex financial and business information to be pulled together into accessible formats for presentation to governing bodies and members.

A cornerstone of collective resilience in times of crisis and rapid change is strong governance built on knowing what you have and using it well. This means having information about the *strengths*, *assets*, *resources* and *expertise* a nation, community or organisation already has and can bring to bear. Everyone in a group has skills, abilities, knowledge and experience that can be drawn on to strengthen governance and reinforce a shared commitment to rebuilding. An early data collection priority therefore is to document a group's existing infrastructure, technology, funding sources and base, human and cultural capital and natural assets.

While most data are informative, not all data will be fit for indigenous peoples' purposes of assessing and (re)building their governance. On the contrary, when an indigenous governance agenda is imposed from the outside, data needs and the bases for interpretation are also effectively imposed from the outside. This can seriously undermine indigenous self-evaluation of governance and the design of self-determined solutions. From this perspective, poor data quality and analyses arguably contribute to poor governance. By contrast, robust culturally informed data used in relevant contexts can serve as a foundation to support more effective and legitimate indigenous governance.

This suggests the possibility of creating a self-reinforcing system—a 'virtuous' cycle—in which improving the relevance, validity and applicability of data enhances governance, which in turn improves capability for a range of governance responsibilities, including that of collecting and governing data.

Culture-smart information

In every society there are cultural determinants of what constitutes leadership, decision-making, representation, group membership, participation, legitimacy and accountability. And different behaviours, standards and measures may apply. Serious problems arise when supposedly objective statistics do not adequately reflect these differences. Exacerbating that limitation is the tendency to dismiss as unimportant those processes and behaviours which we do not know how to measure by standard methods. The result is a tyranny of the measureable, which confers power and legitimacy on the thing that is measured. So the production of data for and about governance immediately raises issues of relative power—that is, whose voice is given priority in determining the meaning, validity and values attached to data (see Morphy, this volume)?

Just as governance is a culturally based concept, so, too, are the criteria, indicators and measures used to generate systems of data and information. Hence, in Indigenous Australia, not all information is freely available to everyone within a group. There are influential gender and age dimensions and associated rules around certain restricted forms of information, who owns and can reproduce and authorise information and who has access to it and for what purposes. There is also a hierarchy of value given to different fields of information and knowledge, with certain kinds constituting 'inalienable possessions' passed on from one generation to the next. Information about high-value things (be they land, sites, names, body designs, songs, stories, knowledge, ritual practices or paraphernalia) becomes imbued with the intrinsic and ineffable identities of their owners, accreted with history, and acts as a repository of collective memories and identities.

As a consequence, authority over particular kinds of indigenous information is distributed across interdependent social layers and polities, establishing a culturally based subsidiarity of information and knowledge. Often particular people and subgroups are charged with the transfer of specific areas of knowledge from one generation to another. Such information and things constitute what Radin (1982) and Moustakas (1989: 1185) refer to as rights in cultural 'property for grouphood'. This complex knowledge economy has implications for the collection, digitisation and dissemination of indigenous knowledge (see Nakata & Langton 2006; Nakata et al. 2008). Furthermore, assessments by indigenous people of the legitimacy of their leaders and governance are sometimes closely linked to their ability to protect and maintain these valued heartlands of cultural information.

These culturally based conditions and practices do not negate the importance of quantitative data for governance performance. Indigenous groups want governance that not only is culturally legitimate, but also has the practical capacity to deliver outcomes. Furthermore, to facilitate free, prior informed consent, people need accurate and relevant information. And local levels of governance require 'the development of local-level data collection, management and reporting systems' (Smith 2002: 18). These various goals depend on having collection, access and use procedures and policies for the governance of both qualitative and quantitative data, supported by technical skills and infrastructure. From this perspective, then, data system priorities and standards should be driven by the strategic priorities of indigenous communities and nations, rather than imposed from the outside via nation-state policies and agendas.

To govern for the future, indigenous people are looking for what I would call 'culture-smart' data—that is, information that can be produced locally, captures local social units, conditions, priorities and concerns and is culturally informed and meaningful. These kinds of data build on existing indigenous capabilities and knowledge, have direct practical application and represent collective identities, rights and priorities. Culture-smart data have greater potential to mobilise support and a mandate from group members, to boost accountability and legitimacy and to improve the quality of actual service delivery— all of which are fundamental ingredients in the practical exercise of sovereignty.

Governance *of* data and information

The ownership of, access to and control over the use of data are governance issues (Nakata & Langton 2006; Bruhn 2014). Contrary to contemporary Western conceptualisations of corporate governance and 'big data' management systems, indigenous peoples' governance or stewardship of data is not simply about the data. It is about the *people* who provide and govern an asset that happens to be data. From this perspective, arrangements for the governance of data tend to be assessed by indigenous peoples according to whether they satisfy the spirit and intent of reproducing their culturally based systems of knowledge, alongside delivering on their planning, service-delivery and development aspirations.

Critical functions of governance therefore are the collection and analysis of relevant packages of information that can be communicated effectively to governing bodies, leaders, group members, organisations and external stakeholders. Strong governance creates checks and balances to ensure that data collection supports the priorities of a group or organisation, implements agreed standards for data quality control and works to ensure data are available in a timely way. Ineffective governance of data can lead to uninformed decision-making, low participation by membership, project failures, loss of reputation and credibility and missed development opportunities.

The clear conclusion is that nations, communities and organisations need practically effective governance arrangements to collect and convert relevant and meaningful information into sensible advice and options. Unfortunately, many indigenous groups lack the economies of scale and human capital needed to underwrite the governance of big data systems, especially where data are of varied quality and reliability.

Therefore, to deliver on the promise of culture-smart and relevant information systems, indigenous governance arrangements need to be designed and implemented under a framework of principles and practices that:

- Sets and enforces agreed standards, culturally informed definitions and classification systems for data production, ownership, analysis and administration.

- Develops and enforces agreed rules, policies and processes around access, dissemination, monitoring, management and review of data, including what kinds of data will *not* be collected or will have restricted access.

- Identifies and publicises clear cultural rules and protocols with respect to indigenous intellectual property rights, which outline the consents required to access and use high-value cultural information that has been collated.

- Sets out a management structure for data that clarifies the roles, responsibilities and accountabilities of people charged with collecting, analysing, maintaining and communicating data. This includes leaders, executive committees, managers and community members.

- Puts in place user-friendly technologies and infrastructure and member-focused data platforms that include building the capabilities of members to access, interpret, use and maintain their own data.

- Ensures governance arrangements for repatriating and protecting indigenous data property rights are based on the principle of self-determination.

When such data governance is in place, indigenous communities and nations will have a more reliable foundation on which to make sound decisions about their overall goals and objectives; what kind of life they want to build; what assets they have or require; what things they want to retain, protect or change; the kind of development they want to promote or reject; and what actions they need to take to achieve those goals (see also FNIGC, Hudson et al., Hudson, Jansen, Yap & Yu, this volume).

Conclusion

The concept of data sovereignty has emerged as a particularly salient one for indigenous nations and groups whose sovereignty has been diminished and whose representation within colonial archives has often been maligned. It is a concept that alludes to the promise that self-determination can be put into practical effect by indigenous people gathering data that are fit for their own purposes. It also implies having not only a recognised right, but also the local mandate and capacity to produce more meaningful, culture-smart information.

Sovereignty includes being able to design rules for the restriction and opening of data. Open data in the context of indigenous peoples is a double-edged sword. On the one hand, open data could be used to inform development, allocate resources and set a future vision—and to influence wider public opinion and debates. On the other hand, opening up data may be accompanied by concern about protecting indigenous cultural information, rights and intellectual property (see Pool, this volume). Importantly, data sovereignty means taking on a significant responsibility to collect and maintain data that reinforce/ restrict particular collective identities and assist in delivering real improvements in people's circumstances. From this perspective, indigenous governance of data assets is about stewardship for both present and future generations.

Finally, in light of the rapid spread of internet technologies and the globalisation of access (legal and illegal) to information, we must consider the extent to which data sovereignty is facing additional, significant new challenges. Everything seems to be becoming, in one way or another, public data; even the strongest encryptions and firewalls cannot protect modern data systems. But this phenomenon is dependent on certain technologies. Perhaps the next challenge in this arena is for indigenous people to identify whether there are ways to use their own technologies and institutions to protect confidential data—for example, by keeping certain culturally valued or personal data in the form of oral tradition or producing data using indigenous languages. Long-term data protection for indigenous peoples may directly depend on the preservation and transmission of their technologies of language, art and semiotics and the extremely narrow distribution of the knowledge necessary to use those technologies. The narrowness of such distribution perhaps makes this a fragile kind of protection—but, at the very least, as a consequence of considering and making informed decisions about such data challenges, indigenous peoples are effectively *acting* in sovereign ways. In other words, the very act of designing workable ways of governing data for contemporary purposes, and producing indigenous data representations of collective identity, contributes to constructing self-determination as a current practice rather than an ephemeral future goal.

References

Agrawal A (1995). Dismantling the divide between indigenous and scientific knowledge. *Development and Change* 26(3):413–59.

Bruhn J (2014). Identifying useful approaches to the governance of indigenous data. *The International Indigenous Policy Journal* 5(2):1–32.

Daly A & Smith DE (1996). The contemporary economic status of Indigenous Australian families. *The Australian Journal of Social Issues* 31(4):354–75.

de Alcantara CH (1998). Uses and abuses of the concept of governance. *International Social Science Journal* 155:105–13.

Dodson M & Smith DE (2003). *Good governance for sustainable development: strategic issues and principles for Indigenous Australian communities*, CAEPR Discussion Paper No. 250, Centre for Aboriginal Economic Policy Research, The Australian National University, Canberra.

Ellis T & Levy Y (2012). *Data sources for scholarly research: towards a guide for novice researchers*, Graduate School of Computer and Information Sciences, Nova Southeastern University, Fort Lauderdale, Fla., proceedings.informingscience.org/InSITE2012/InSITE12p405-416Ellis0114.pdf.

Giddens A (1984). *The constitution of society*, Polity Press, Cambridge.

Moustakas J (1989). Group rights in cultural property: justifying strict inalienability. *Cornell Law Review* 74:1179–227.

Nakata M (2007). *Disciplining the savages: savaging the disciplines*, Aboriginal Studies Press, Canberra.

Nakata M & Langton M (eds) (2006). *Australian Indigenous knowledge and libraries*, University of Technology, Sydney EPress, Sydney.

Nakata M, Nakata V, Gardiner G & McKeough J (2008). Indigenous digital collections: an early look at the organisation and culture interface. *Australian Academic & Research Libraries* 39(4):223–36.

Radin MJ (1982). Property for personhood. *Stanford Law Review* 34:957–1015.

Royal Commission into Aboriginal Deaths in Custody (RCIADIC) (1991). *Royal Commission into Aboriginal Deaths in Custody (RCIADIC) national report: overview and recommendations*, Commissioner Elliott Johnson, Australian Government Publishing Service, Canberra.

Scott JC (1999). *Seeing like a state: how certain schemes to improve the human condition have failed*, Yale University Press, New Haven, Conn.

Smith DE (1991a). The cultural appropriateness of existing survey questions and concepts. In Altman JC (ed.), *A national survey of Indigenous Australians: options and implications*, CAEPR Research Monograph No. 3, Centre for Aboriginal Economic Policy Research, The Australian National University, Canberra.

Smith DE (1991b). *Towards an Aboriginal household expenditure survey: conceptual, methodological and cultural issues*, CAEPR Discussion Paper No. 10, Centre for Aboriginal Economic Policy Research, The Australian National University, Canberra.

Smith DE (1994). *The cross-cultural validity of labour force statistics about Indigenous Australians*, CAEPR Discussion Paper No. 69, Centre for Aboriginal Economic Policy Research, The Australian National University, Canberra.

Smith DE (2002). *Jurisdictional devolution: towards an effective model for Indigenous community self-determination*, CAEPR Discussion Paper No. 233, Centre for Aboriginal Economic Policy Research, The Australian National University, Canberra.

Smith DE (2005). *Researching Australian Indigenous governance: a methodological and conceptual framework*, CAEPR Working Paper No. 29, Centre for Aboriginal Economic Policy Research, The Australian National University, Canberra.

Smith DE (2008). Cultures of governance and the governance of culture: transforming and containing Indigenous institutions in western Arnhem Land. In Hunt J, Smith DE, Garling S & Sanders W (eds), *Contested governance: culture, power and institutions in Indigenous Australia*, CAEPR Research Monograph No. 29, Centre for Aboriginal Economic Policy Research, The Australian National University, Canberra.

Smith DE (2012). *Common roots, common futures: different pathways to self-determination. An international conversation, conference report*, The University of Arizona, Tucson, 20–22 February 2012.

Smylie J & Anderson M (2006). Understanding the health of indigenous peoples in Canada: key methodological and conceptual challenges. *Canadian Medical Association Journal* 175(6):602–5.

Taylor J (2005). Capacity building for Indigenous governance: social indicators for Indigenous governance, Paper prepared for the ICG Research Project workshop with WA and Australian governments, Centre for Aboriginal Economic Policy Research, The Australian National University, Canberra.

Taylor J (2009). Indigenous demography and public policy in Australia: population or peoples? *Journal of Population Research* 26:115–30.

Taylor J, Doran B, Parriman M & Yu E (2014). Statistics for community governance: the Yawuru Indigenous population survey, Western Australia. *The International Indigenous Policy Journal* 5(2):1–31.

Part 3: Data sovereignty in practice

8

Pathways to First Nations' data and information sovereignty

First Nations Information Governance Centre (FNIGC)[1]

Introduction

In 1994, the Government of Canada launched three major national longitudinal health surveys that excluded First Nations people even though, at that time, the greatest data gap existed for First Nations people living 'on reserve'. The federal government eventually moved to address this deficiency with a new supplemental survey, subsequently named the First Nations and Inuit Regional Health Survey (RHS), to collect data on reserve. To try to ensure the success of the new survey, a group of First Nations representatives came together from coast to coast, formulated the RHS Steering Committee and took over the project and resources from the Canadian Government. The RHS project created space in the Canadian research environment in which to progress rapidly towards data jurisdiction and it helped secure the environment for data and information sovereignty that fundamentally changed the way that research on and with First Nations was conducted in Canada.

1   The original version of this chapter was presented on behalf of the FNIGC by Ceal Tournier (Chairperson of the FNIGC) at the Academy of the Social Sciences in Australia workshop 'Indigenous data sovereignty: current practice and future needs', Canberra, 9–10 July 2015.

This chapter outlines the steps taken by First Nations, and the First Nations Indigenous Governance Centre (FNIGC) on their behalf, towards giving expression and practical meaning to the concept of indigenous data sovereignty in Canada. It begins by explaining the preconditions for this development in the decades of dubious research practices in regard to indigenous peoples. It then traces the origins of the RHS, before examining the construction of ideas and principles of data ownership, control, access and possession that are now a registered trademark (OCAP®: 'ownership, control, access and possession') of the FNIGC (AFN 2007). Finally, the mechanisms that give practical expression to OCAP® are detailed.

A gift from the people

In the world view of First Nations, the conduct of the Regional Health Survey (RHS) in 1997 was by them and for them, and the processes and principles of OCAP® that stemmed from it came from 'the people'. Rooted in self-determination and inherent rights, within the context of data and information management, the cultural framework of the RHS was the foundation from which many tools, documents, theories and mechanisms regarding data sovereignty emerged and matured.

The success of the work on this survey—past, present and into the future—is directly attributed to the support, investment and vigilance of First Nations people at the grassroots and leadership levels. Without this, no success would ever have been achieved and no foundational principles would have been developed to challenge the status quo in research, data collection, data holdings and stewardship. This body of thought, along with the obligation to ensure its integrity in appropriate contextual applications, was entrusted to a regionally representative steering committee, which transitioned over time to become the FNIGC. This work has had a transformational impact on the status quo, the credit for which needs to remain with *the people*.

This trust obligation requires the FNIGC to ensure that the products that come from the work of *the people* are attributed rightfully back to the people in a manner that is recognisable and attached to its initial formulation. It is for this reason that appropriate citation in the written world is credited back to *the people* through reference to the mandated custodians of this endeavour, the FNIGC. It is also why sanction is sought from, and given by, the FNIGC to the veracity and application of these principles and processes in third-party documents and applications. It is because of the strength of the First Nations' teachings and the support and encouragement given by the people that this work was accomplished. The work, therefore, must be appropriately recognised and attributed.

Data: a renewable resource

First Nations recognise that information is a resource that has value and that First Nations' information has value to First Nations. In a practical sense, information can be used to advise policy and decision-making, it enhances understanding of a particular area of study and it can be used to leverage funding for specific purposes. For example, information about the health conditions of First Nations allows them to identify particular risks and to target programs to mitigate those risks. First Nations' information also has value to the extent that it is a representation of the knowledge, status and conditions of a community.

First Nations' information also has value to non-natives. In the context of research, information can lead to academic prestige and advancement. It can also be used by the Crown to influence its policy and decision-making vis-a-vis First Nations. First Nations' information also has financial value to entities such as pharmaceutical companies, resource development companies and others. To put it more succinctly, the problems with the use of First Nations' information stem from who is in control—and thus what gets done, how it is done and who knows about it. The question of whose interests are served is central. And, of course, there is a clear advantage for those who collect and control data and information over those who provide the data and seek to benefit from that contribution. As aptly expressed by Ceal Tournier, Chair of the FNIGC, 'he who controls the data controls the gold' (Tournier 2002).

First Nations themselves are the only ones who have the knowledge and authority to balance the potential benefits and harms associated with the collection and use of their information. There is no law or concept in Western society that recognises inherent community rights and interests in data and information. First Nations' principles of

OCAP® arose in this context. As a more general expression of OCAP®, First Nations own their information; therefore, First Nations govern their information in the same way that jurisdiction is exercised over First Nations' lands.

When First Nations' information is viewed as a resource, with value to both First Nations and non–First Nations, it is easier to see that the governance of that resource is part of a First Nation's inherent right. Inherent right, as it relates to First Nations, implies having the requisite jurisdictional authorities to enact laws and implement governing structures, institutions and processes along with institutional capacities to formulate policies, to design, deliver and evaluate programs, as well as to develop financial, technical and human resource capacities. First Nations' governance and self-governance also imply jurisdictional authorities and institutional capacities in respect of research and information (FNIGC 2003: 4–5). First Nations' citizens and leaders acknowledge and act on the premise that information needs defending and protecting; just as we protect our lands, our forests, our animals and our fish, we need to protect our data, which are an extremely valuable renewable resource.

The need for First Nations' data jurisdiction

In hindsight, it is clear that the stage was set for the developments that resulted in the FNIGC taking complete control of the first RHS and developing OCAP®. Quite simply, First Nations people and their communities recognised that they had been subjects of dubious research practices for decades. While the phrase 'we've been researched to death' has been said too many times to cite, there is more to this than just a view about the volume of research, as it also derives from recurring grievances about research and researchers over the years. The American Indian Law Center has catalogued an extensive list of such complaints and these provide the backdrop from which OCAP® emerges (AILC 1999).

To paraphrase from this source, First Nations have been the subject of too much irrelevant research, with the majority of research projects initiated by, paid for and carried out by non-indigenous people from universities, government and industry. Accordingly, researchers have tended to select subjects of personal or academic interest, or of interest to the larger society, and have often not been interested in First Nations' priorities. In this way, they have frequently pre-empted meaningful community involvement by presenting completed research designs, often already funded, for community approval rather than collaborating from the start. For their part, governments gather administrative and other data on First Nations often without their knowledge or consent and both they and researchers analyse, interpret and report First Nations' data, often without consent, approval, review or input by First Nations representatives.

Part of the problem here is the fact that research funding is largely controlled by a few external agents and is generally not accessible to community groups and First Nations organisations, with the result that researchers have profited professionally and economically from First Nations research without employing local people or compensating research subjects; they have often treated First Nations as merely a source of data and have pressured community authorities and individuals to support or consent to a project because it is 'good for the community' rather than asking community members what kinds of projects might serve their needs. In this way, individuals have felt pressured to participate in studies or other data-gathering processes because community authorities have consented or are involved. They have been persuaded to participate in research without fully understanding risks to health and safety or the potential application or misapplication of research outcomes. First Nations have been led to believe that participation in research projects is necessary to maintain their right to services.

On the matter of informed consent, researchers have not explained their studies in a language or manner to fully ensure this and they have treated First Nations researchers as informants, rather than colleagues, and have appropriated or failed to acknowledge some of their work. Research results are often not returned to the community or, if they are, they are returned in a form or language that is inaccessible. Although community elders consider certain researchers unworthy to speak the community's truths, researchers rely primarily on peers and funding agencies to confer their speaking rights. Even where good rapport has been built, members of a research team can often be replaced with people who are not known or trusted by the community members.

Other issues of research integrity include the observation that researchers have not respected individual or community confidentiality to the same degree that they would for non–First Nations people and that they often disrespect the basic human dignity of participants or their religious, spiritual or cultural beliefs. As examples of this, they have collected First Nations' genetic material for purposes that are demeaning to the dignity of First Nations communities and individuals and have gathered information on dissident indigenous groups that has later been used against them by repressive regimes (for example, in South America). Researchers have also disregarded cultural taboos and secrecy by publicising (and sometimes profiting from) sensitive cultural information. They have also presented cultural information out of context and drawn inaccurate conclusions. Human remains and cultural property have been taken for storage, display in museums or sale, and information made available by researchers has been distorted, appropriated and treated as a commodity. For example, First Nations legends and stories have been used for movies, books and toys, while spiritual practices and ceremonies have been adapted and often marketed to practitioners of New Age spirituality. Researchers, particularly from government and industry, have collected information about traditional remedies—sometimes under false pretences—in a search for medicines to be patented and used for commercial gain and they have used leftover portions of blood samples for secondary research without consent. Finally, researchers have recklessly sensationalised problems among First Nations, without regard for the impact on communities or their social and political interests. Their research tends to focus on problems without looking at the positive and it often portrays First Nations people as solely poor, sick, dependent, violent and child-like. Not surprisingly, given this catalogue of complaint, the benefits of research to First Nations individuals and communities are frequently unclear.

Examples abound of the misuse and abuse of First Nations' information and many of those who stimulated the articulation of OCAP® are drawn from the field of community health information. An infamous example is provided by the Nuuchah-nulth First Nation 'Bad Blood' research. Between 1982 and 1985, University of British Columbia (UBC) researcher Dr Richard (Ryk) Ward took 883 vials of blood from the Nuuchah-nulth people under the guise of a $330,000 Health Canada–funded study of arthritis among the nation. In 1986, Ward left UBC and moved to the University of Utah and then to Oxford University, taking the blood samples with him, collecting research grants and furthering his own academic career. He subsequently published over 200 research reports based on the blood samples in areas as diverse as HIV/AIDS and population genetics. Ward even used the blood samples to support his theories about migration across the Bering Strait, entirely disrespecting and undermining the Nuuchah-nulth traditional beliefs about Creation (Wiwchar 2004).

Another example involves the misuse of community health information of the Havasupai Tribe in Arizona. In the early 1990s, the tribe approved a diabetes study including genetic analysis by Arizona State University researchers. Without consent, the data were subsequently used for published research on in-breeding, anthropological migration patterns and schizophrenia (Rubin 2004). Likewise, in the 1970s, the Barrow Alcohol Study on alcoholism in an Alaskan community released its unfavourable findings at a press conference at the researchers' university in Philadelphia. Not only did this lead to internal stigmatisation by people from Barrow and nearby Alaskan communities, it also resulted in the devaluation of the municipality's Standard & Poor's bond rating to the economic detriment of the entire community (Kaufman & Ramarao 2005).

An equally troubling example of the Canadian Government's management of First Nations' information is the Non-Insured Health Benefits (NIHB) database controlled by Health Canada. NIHB holds an enormous amount of information about First Nations beneficiaries' use of health services and goods such as prescription drugs, medical transportation, dental care and medical devices. In 2001, Health Canada began releasing comprehensive pharmacy claims data to Brogan Inc., a health consulting and analysis firm that then offered the NIHB data for sale to pharmaceutical companies for their own research use. Health Canada removed personally identifying information from the data that were given to Brogan, but community identifiers remained. First Nations were not advised that their health data were being given to private companies or being sold to pharmaceutical companies until 2007. In 2007, Health Canada, having already agreed to extend Brogan's access to NIHB data for an additional five years, advised the Assembly of First Nations and provided a copy of the agreement. The rationale provided by Health Canada for disclosing the data was that personally identifying information had been removed and there were no longer any privacy interests attached, and that Health Canada felt that if Brogan made an 'Access to Information Act' request, the pharmaceutical use information would have to be disclosed anyway. Those involved in the Brogan disclosure had no concept whatsoever that First Nations would have an interest in such commercial use of their data. In 2010, Brogan amalgamated with IMS Health, a global company that provides information, services and technology to the health care industry. According to the IMS/Brogan website, NIHB data continue to be provided to the global company, available for sale to IMS clients (IMS Health Inc. 2014).

Government officials, researchers and corporations may or may not understand, support or even be aware of the aspirations of First Nations. They may not prioritise these and may even be at odds with community interests. Nonetheless, these other 'users' of First Nations' data are often seen as unbiased experts, endorsed by others with power, able to speak with authority about First Nations realities.

It was in this environment in 1995 that First Nations representatives from each region of Canada found themselves called to Ottawa to discuss the opportunity of helping the Medical Services Branch (MSB) of Health Canada (now First Nations & Inuit Health Branch) to implement a national health survey on First Nations reserves. At this time, the issue of First Nations jurisdiction over all matters including ownership of information was at the forefront of First Nations' political thinking. Innocuous as that invitation may have appeared, it led to a positioning by the First Nations caucus that established RHS as the new *red standard* approach to conducting survey work in First Nations communities (AFN & FNIGC 2007: v). The RHS thereby became the first national survey to be fully owned, controlled and stewarded by First Nations. Nothing like it had ever been successfully completed anywhere in the world. Concepts such as full ownership of data and intellectual property by First Nations, First Nations stewardship of data and government access through a limited licence to use were to become essential elements of the original RHS and they form the backbone of the OCAP® principles as they exist today.

The vehicle: the First Nations Regional Health Survey (RHS)

In 1996, the Assembly of First Nations (AFN) Chiefs Committee on Health (CCOH) mandated that a First Nations health survey be implemented every four years across Canada. This mandate came as a result of activities that began in 1994, when three major national longitudinal surveys were launched by the federal government, which specifically excluded First Nations living on reserve and in northern First Nations communities. These decisions subsequently led MSB to extend the aforementioned invitation.

The first RHS took place in 1997. The survey was implemented to address First Nations and Inuit health and wellbeing issues while acknowledging the need for First Nations to control their own health information. The survey design sought to balance First Nations content with content from comparable Canadian surveys while remaining culturally and scientifically valid. Community participation in all aspects of design, collection and analysis assisted in communicating both the need for and the relevance of the RHS to every First Nation in Canada. Space was made in the survey design to allow for region-specific inquiry or enhancement. The groundwork for future development and capacity in information governance was being laid but, most importantly, it ensured that the data were beneficial and relevant to the local community. Governance and accountability mechanisms were developed and implemented.

Although the resulting data were invaluable, helping to generate program resources in several key public and community health areas, First Nations were acutely aware of the opportunity to utilise the RHS as a vehicle to move the benchmark ahead in favour of First Nations' data jurisdiction and ensure the continued forward momentum of sovereignty over data, information, knowledge and stories. It was from the work of the RHS that the concepts inherent to data jurisdiction were articulated.

The fuel: OCAP®

OCAP® has been described as a 'political response to colonialism and the role of knowledge production in reproducing colonial relations' (Espey 2002: 6). Much of the impetus for OCAP® can be linked to the sorry history of research involving First Nations people in Canada described earlier. According to the report of the Royal Commission on Aboriginal Peoples:

> The gathering of information and its subsequent use are inherently political. In the past, Aboriginal people have not been consulted about what information should be collected, who should gather that information, who should maintain it, and who should have access to it. The information gathered may or may not have been relevant to the questions, priorities and concerns of Aboriginal peoples. Because data gathering has frequently been imposed by outside authorities, it has met with resistance in many quarters. (Canada Royal Commission on Aboriginal Peoples 1996: 498)

OCAP® is self-determination applied to collective data, information and knowledge. It is a response to being 'researched to death' and offers a way forward for First Nations research and information management. Originally known as 'access, control and ownership', the principles were named during a 1998 brainstorming session of the RHS National Steering Committee (now FNIGC). Cathryn George of the Association of Iroquois and Allied Indians is credited with arranging the original concepts into 'OCA'—a more resonant acronym with its nod to the 1990 OKA Crisis between Mohawk people and the town of Oka in Quebec. The 'P' was soon added to create OCAP® when the FNIGC recognised the importance of considering 'possession' of First Nations' data and the rights and limitations associated with it under Canadian law.

The notions inherent in OCAP® are not new. The term's salience lies in the fact that it crystallised themes advocated by First Nations for years. Inherently internalised in the context of history, treaty rights and resourcing opportunities by First Nations, OCAP® was not understood or respected in all venues of data and knowledge generation. Those who felt threatened deliberately attempted to manipulate OCAP® understanding to ensure their continued unfettered access to First Nations' data, information and resources.

These continued attempts to manipulate OCAP® definitions led not only to the supplemental descriptions published by the FNIGC, but also to the protection of the concepts through Canadian trademark law. OCAP® is also an expression of First Nations' jurisdiction over information about the First Nation. The descriptions below are useful to provide understanding of the context of the OCAP®; however, they are not a definition. OCAP® goes beyond the strict definition of each word in the acronym. It represents principles and values that are intertwined and reflective of First Nations' view of jurisdiction and collective rights. As Bonnie Healy[2] explained:

> [W]e cannot pick and choose which elements of OCAP® that will be followed. They are one. We cannot ignore 'ownership' or 'possession' any more than the Four Directions can omit the East or the North.

Nonetheless, the various components can be described as follows:

- **Ownership:** The notion of ownership refers to the relationship of a First Nations community to its cultural knowledge/data/ information. The principle states that a community or group owns information collectively in the same way that an individual owns their personal information. Ownership is distinct from stewardship. The stewardship or custodianship of data or information by an institution that is accountable to the group is a mechanism through which ownership may be maintained.

- **Control:** The aspirations and inherent rights of First Nations to maintain and regain control of all aspects of their lives and institutions extend to information and data. The principle of 'control' asserts that First Nations people, their communities and representative bodies must control how information about them is collected, used and disclosed. The element of control extends to all aspects of information management, from collection of data to the use, disclosure and ultimate destruction of data.

- **Access:** First Nations must have access to information and data about themselves and their communities, regardless of where it is held. The principle also refers to the right of First Nations

---

2   Operations Manager, Alberta FNIGC, former FNIGC board member and officer speaking at an OCAP® information session at the invitation of Aboriginal Affairs and Northern Development. FNIGC, Ottawa, 14 January 2013.

communities and organisations to manage and make decisions regarding who can access their collective information.

- **Possession:** While 'ownership' identifies the relationship between a people and their data, possession reflects the state of stewardship of data. First Nations possession puts data within First Nations' jurisdiction and, therefore, within First Nations' control. Possession is the mechanism by which to assert and protect ownership and control. First Nations generally exercise little or no control over data that are in the possession of others, particularly other governments.

The mechanics: making it all work

To give practical expression to these principles and values, the FNIGC also developed a set of governance and structural supports to ensure that data sovereignty was achieved and protected. These include the following.

Code of research ethics

The Code of Research Ethics (FNIGC 2016) (a framework that originated as part of the RHS project) has been revised to reflect the evolving needs of the FNIGC and the information governance principles of the First Nations regions participating in the RHS and other data-collection processes. The RHS Code of Research Ethics protocol for access to data is entirely logical and has been used as a template by many First Nations information governance systems. It requires approval by the national governing body[3] for access to national-level First Nations' data, while access to regional-level First Nations' data must be authorised by the regional First Nations organisations. Finally, community-level data cannot be accessed without the direct consent of the First Nation involved. This protocol respects and reflects the governance structure and unique processes that exist within the contemporary First Nations' organisational structure.

---

3   Originally, the First Nations Information Governance Committee, and now the First Nations Information Governance Centre.

Privacy impact assessments

Mindful that the survey respondents participating in the RHS share very personal and often sensitive information, the RHS has also been very vigilant in the protection of personal privacy. Independent privacy impact assessments have been conducted and updated, and policies and procedures regarding privacy and security have been implemented. The RHS continues to meet the highest standards of personal privacy protection. OCAP® is the application of the collective privacy of the First Nation.

Cultural framework

The FNIGC's RHS *Cultural framework* (FNIGC 2004), among other things, reconciles a First Nation or indigenous world view with the need to collect data and conduct research. It presents a framework from which data on the health and wellbeing of First Nations can be collected, used and presented in a manner that is meaningful to First Nations peoples and communities.

Incorporation

The RHS was 'hosted' by several organisations in its formative years. Jokingly referred to as the 'foster child of First Nations' institutions', it bounced from home to home until getting the gentle push from then national chief Phil Fontaine while he hosted at the AFN, stating, 'it's time you move out and establish the required arm's-length distance from which the RHS and FNIGC credibility cannot be challenged'. It was a timely turning point, as the FNIGC committee had recently explored the trademarking of OCAP® and it was aware that a legal entity would be required to hold that trademark 'in trust' for the First Nations of Canada. With a flood of documents, papers and presentations purporting to assert what OCAP was and was not, it was time to protect OCAP® as the tenement of the First Nations' world view of data jurisdiction and governance. Therein, on 22 April 2010, the First Nations Information Governance Committee became the First Nations Information Governance *Centre*, absorbing the committee members as directors of the board.

The FNIGC has a clear mandate to make the most of research and information that will truly benefit the health and wellbeing of First Nations. It strives to partner with entities that seek to achieve success in working with First Nations through the use of credible information and processes that respect First Nations' jurisdiction to own, protect and control how their information is collected, disclosed and published.

OCAP® certification

The FNIGC has a special role in advocacy and education involving OCAP®. Immediately on incorporation, the board pursued the trademarking of OCAP® as a protective measure against misuse, misapplication or improper interpretation of what OCAP® actually means and how it is to be applied. This requires the development of and then adherence to a trade certification process. The OCAP® certification process will be a valuable tool that can be used to establish OCAP® credentials for research projects or information management systems. The process itself will also result in the publication of more information about OCAP® standards, adding to the knowledge base for those interested in First Nations research and information management.

Conclusion: achieving indigenous data jurisdiction

In Canada, it is from the premise that First Nations are accountable to their membership for the use and management of community information that First Nations will exercise jurisdiction in relation to information governance. This authority is based on inherent and treaty rights supported by international instruments such as the United Nations Declaration on the Rights of Indigenous Peoples (UNDRIP). Internationally, indigenous political leaders, technicians and administrators must be aware of the impact that ignoring their sovereign and inherent rights over data and information will have on their citizens and territories into the future. Leaders in all sectors will need to provide direction on how information can be used to benefit the community in a manner that mitigates any harm. In addition, those responsible for outlining a plan of action will need to be well versed in their relevant constitutional and legal frameworks. In Canada, some examples include:

- **Jurisdiction:** First Nations can exercise jurisdiction through enacting privacy, OCAP® and access to information laws in their community. These laws can govern how community information may be used and under what circumstances. It can also address personal privacy concerns.

- **Policies and procedures:** These can be developed to provide direction on the protection of personal and collective privacy. They can describe what requirements are needed for data-sharing agreements or licences to use contracts. Policies may define the relationship with outside contractors and researchers, ensuring that supplementary publication is controlled and approved.

- **Repatriation:** First Nations should investigate where their information/data are held or collected and consider how they can exert governance over those data. Federal and provincial governments, universities and other organisations hold First Nations' data. Governance can be exerted ideally through repatriation of the data back to the First Nation. Where repatriation is not possible or practical, data governance agreements or data-sharing contracts can be negotiated to effectively maintain First Nations' control over their data (see Hudson et al., Hudson, and Jansen, this volume for examples of this from Aotearoa/New Zealand).

The concepts of OCAP® can be applied by indigenous peoples worldwide, although approaches may need to be modified. Every indigenous population will face opportunities, as well as challenges, as they strive to exert jurisdiction over their data and information. The most important element is to make a start. From the FNIGC's experience, this would involve gathering or inviting a representative group of concerned indigenous citizens whose *only* focus is data jurisdiction and then ensuring there are no conflicts between that objective and individual biases or conflicts. Following an examination of the operating environment, a plan of attack should be drawn up that guarantees success. This would involve utilising every tool, law, initiative and mechanism available to capture one of the most important renewable resources of modern times: data. There will be a need, as well, to examine the impacts of 'open government, open data' initiatives, and to weigh the benefits and the consequences to the local indigenous populations.

In Canada, as First Nations take control of their own data and participate in a society in which digital recordkeeping is the norm, the importance of OCAP® has grown from a set of principles and standards for the conduct of research to a path for First Nations' information governance. While it may appear that there are many barriers to OCAP® implementation, there are equally many tools that can be used to overcome those barriers. The examples contained in this chapter assure that success can and will be achieved but it must be based on the local reality, environment and construct of laws. OCAP® is a path to First Nations' information governance. By building information governance capacity, enacting our own laws, entering into data-sharing and licence-to-use contracts, creating regional data centres and repatriating our data, First Nations are getting closer to exercising full jurisdiction over our information.

References

American Indian Law Centre (AILC) (1999). *Model tribal research code: with materials for tribal regulation for research and checklist for Indian health boards*, 3rd edn, American Indian Law Centre, University of New Mexico, Albuquerque.

Assembly of First Nations (AFN) (2007). *OCAP: ownership, control, access and possession: First Nations inherent right to govern First Nations data*, Assembly of First Nations, Ottawa.

Assembly of First Nations (AFN) and First Nations Information Governance Centre (FNIGC) (2007). *First Nations longitudinal health survey (RHS) 2002/03: the people's report*, rev. 2nd edn, AFN & FNIGC, Ottawa.

Canada Royal Commission on Aboriginal Peoples (1996). *Report of the Royal Commission on Aboriginal Peoples. Volume 3: gathering strength*, Canada Group Communication, Ottawa.

Espey J (2002). *Stewardship and OCAP*, Discussion Paper, First Nations Statistical Institute, Ottawa.

(First Nations and Inuit) Regional Health Survey (RHS) Project (various years). *Minutes, resolutions and motions*, First Nations Information Governance Centre, Ottawa.

First Nations Information Governance Centre (FNIGC) (2003). *Submission of the FNIGC to the House of Commons Standing Committee on Aboriginal Affairs, Northern Development and Natural Resources on the proposed First Nations Fiscal and Statistical Management Act (Bill C-19)*, prepared by Panousos E for the FNIGC of the First Nations Centre@naho, Ottawa, June 2003.

First Nations Information Governance Centre (FNIGC) (2004). *Cultural framework*, First Nations Information Governance Centre, Ottawa.

First Nations Information Governance Centre (FNIGC) (2016). *Code of research ethics*, First Nations Information Governance Centre, Ottawa, fnigc.ca/sites/default/files/ENpdf/RHS_General/rhs-code-ofresearchethics-2007.pdf.

IMS Brogan (2016). Website. IMS Brogan, Montreal, www.imsbrogan capabilities.com.

Kaufman CE & Ramarao S (2005). Community confidentiality, consent, and the individual research process: implications for demographic research. *Population Research and Policy Review* 24(2):149–73.

Rubin P (2004). Indian givers. *Pheonix New Times*, 27 May 2004.

Tournier C (2002). Don't be on the other side of the digital divide: an overview of current health information initiatives impacting aboriginal peoples, Live address as part of the Aboriginal Health Information Symposium, Ottawa, 11–13 February 2002.

Wiwchar D (2004). Nuu-chah-nulth blood returns to west coast. *Ha-Shilth-Sa* 31(25) (16 December 2004).

9

Tribal data sovereignty: Whakatōhea rights and interests

Maui Hudson, Dickie Farrar and Lesley McLean

Introduction

The vast array of activities that tribal organisations in Aotearoa/ New Zealand are responsible for illustrates the importance of high-quality information to support their decision-making. Tribal information needs encompass a broad range of domains, types of information and processes for management. This chapter examines the growing *iwi* (tribal) interest in data and their uses in the context of one *iwi*, Te Whakatōhea, to explore how *iwi* are beginning to conceptualise their rights and interests over data in Aotearoa/ New Zealand. It is focused on the Whakatōhea Māori Trust Board and how it is collecting and becoming the steward for a range of administrative datasets, health and social service records, commercial information, historical accounts, indigenous knowledge, strategy documents and research. The tribe has recognised that robust planning will create a strong foundation for taking advantage of investment opportunities and this is based, in part, on the provision of quality information to governors to create more transparent decision-making processes. Each year the data and information needs of the tribe increase as we strive to improve our businesses and our services and to uplift our nation.

What is driving *iwi* interest in data?

Growing role of *iwi*

Māori consider themselves to be *tangata whenua*—people of the land—and, as such, tribes have always had a responsibility to look after and protect both their tribal estate and their people. Both land resources and people are necessary to sustain and grow tribal identities, histories and traditions. Despite the damaging effects of colonisation, the confiscation of land, the loss of language and the urbanisation of the population, tribes have maintained their standing as a cornerstone of cultural identity and as advocates for self-determination. The obligation to sustain culture, sustain people and sustain the land motivated the fight against the Crown to gain recognition and compensation for historical injustices. There is growing momentum around the treaty settlement process, which has led to increasing interest in the role that tribes will play in society in the post-treaty settlement phase.

Over time, tribal entities and structures have become more complex as the relationship between tribes and the Crown has evolved. Traditional leadership structures sit alongside and have become intertwined with contemporary structures comprising an intricate web of land trusts, incorporations, Māori trust boards, *runanga* (assembly or gathering), urban authorities and statutory boards. Tribal representation on an increasing number of cogovernance entities and committees—for example, Waikato River Authority,[1] Tupuna Maunga o Tamaki Makaurau Authority (Auckland Council 2016), Rangitaiki River Forum (Bay of Plenty Regional Council 2016) and the Independent Māori Statutory Board[2]—is providing a foundation for involvement in a greater number of decision-making contexts. The requirement to make robust and enduring decisions increases the need for high-quality information, and many of these entities have dedicated secretariats and/or technical advisory groups. The key features that distinguish postsettlement tribal entities from presettlement tribal entities relate to political and economic influence. Political influence increases through formal mechanisms such as co-governance arrangements,

---

1   See: waikatoriver.org.nz/.
2   See: imsb.maori.nz.

comanagement functions and relationship agreements that provide statutory support for tribal participation in policy direction and resource allocation. However, influence is also enhanced by the mere fact that settlement allows the tribe to divert a greater portion of its intellectual and economic resources towards tribal development and advocacy.

Growing economic influence

Economic influence has been enhanced through the provision of direct resources (settlement funds, first right of refusal on Crown property), which allows the tribal entities to advance their economic aspirations and partner with other players in the commercial realm. With the total value of settlements to date exceeding NZ$1 billion, this has contributed significantly to increasing tribal engagement in the economy. Over time, this has translated into increased asset bases—for example, Waikato-Tainui and Ngai Tahu, two of the earliest tribes to settle with the Crown, have turned NZ$170 million settlements into asset bases worth NZ$1.1 billion (Smellie 2014) and NZ$1.075 billion (Te Rūnanga o Ngāi Tahu 2014), respectively. They have also developed innovative mechanisms to encourage financial literacy and entrepreneurship among their tribal members. Ngāi Tahu supports financial knowledge and economic independence among its members through the Whai Rawa scheme, a hybrid between a superannuation scheme and a unit trust, in which they match savings 4:1 for children and 1:1 for adults (Te Rūnanga o Ngāi Tahu, no date). Waikato-Tainui has partnered with a business incubator to provide workshops based at *marae* (sacred central area of a village) supporting tribal members to develop businesses. The nine-part workshop series covered topics including how start-ups work, design thinking, market validation, business modelling, marketing, finance, intellectual property (IP), governance and pitching (Waikato-Tainui 2014).

The Māori economy has been valued in excess of NZ$36 billion (BERL 2011a) and a number of reports have begun assessing the contribution of Māori to regional economies (BERL 2012; TPK 2014). Māori are playing an increasingly significant role in the New Zealand economy through participation in the workforce, contribution to gross domestic product (GDP) and ownership of assets. A focus on strategies for Māori economic development at the national level

(Māori Economic Development Panel 2012), the regional level (Bay of Connections 2014) and at tribal levels has emphasised the need to extend the discourse on Māori/tribal economic development to address social and cultural underdevelopment in their communities (Smith et al. 2015). Indirect economic influence can also be exerted through resource management responsibilities and consultation mechanisms associated with economic development. Tribes are also now organised within nationally representative bodies (Te Ohu Kai Moana, iwi Chairs Forum, Federation of Māori Authorities) and engage in the formation of economic development strategies from regional to national levels as well as resource allocation policies (fisheries, aquaculture, water). To engage effectively in these activities, tribes require access to high-quality technical information as well as the intellectual resources to frame policy parameters around tribal values and indigenous world views.

Growing intellectual capital

Māori intellectual capital has grown significantly over the past 30 years, with significant improvements in Māori tertiary participation, higher-level degree completions and Māori research infrastructure. In 2013, there were over 22,000 Māori students enrolled in bachelor or higher qualifications in New Zealand institutions (Ministry of Education 2014). Māori participation in higher-level degrees has also been on the increase, with the number of Māori doctoral graduates increasing from 90 in 2001 to 311 by 2010, with a further 392 enrolled in PhD programs (NZIER 2014). The increase in Māori tertiary participation can be attributed in part to the development of Māori tertiary providers (for example, Te Whare Wananga o Aotearoa, Te Whare Wananga o Awanuiarangi, Te Wananga o Raukawa), Māori research centres within tertiary institutions and the Māori Centre of Research Excellence (Nga Pae o te Maramatanga). The increase in Māori intellectual capital has led to an employment shift from trades to professions and business as well as generating a number of Māori professional networks (for example, Māori Medical Practitioners Association, National Māori Accountants Network, The Māori Law Society, National Network of Māori Design Professionals). The increase in higher degree completions has provided intellectual capacity to direct towards Māori research, which has been facilitated by Māori-specific funding mechanisms—

for example, Rangahau Hauora Māori[3] and the Vision Mātauranga Capability Fund (Ministry of Science and Innovation 2016)—and policy settings that support Māori participation within the research sector, including collaborative investment mechanisms such as the National Science Challenges. While the policy focuses on unlocking the science and innovation potential of Māori knowledge, people and resources for New Zealand's benefit, tribal interest in research is aligned to realising their own aspirations, including the opportunities that arise from engaging with the knowledge economy through science and innovation (BERL 2011b; Harmsworth 2011; Nana et al. 2012).

Growing opportunities for indigenous knowledge

The Māori renaissance has gained momentum in Aotearoa/New Zealand over the past 40 years. Its initial focus was on Māori language, but has since spread to a range of cultural practices, art forms and areas of expertise that collectively represent their indigenous knowledge or *mātauranga Māori*. This renaissance has had at its heart the revitalisation and rejuvenation of traditional knowledge bases (Royal 2009), including not only efforts to preserve and maintain traditional resources, but also the right to advance and develop them (Gibbs 2005). Māori studies departments in universities refocused research on Māori culture and traditions towards cultural regeneration, creating opportunities for indigenous knowledge to become a part of the academy. Research to inform Waitangi Tribunal and Treaty settlement processes has provided tribes with repositories of indigenous knowledge that can be used for other purposes. However, indigenous knowledge is not just the domain of tribal entities. Networks of practitioners in traditional medicine, non-instrument navigation, cultural performance, traditional arts and cultural tattoo cross tribal boundaries and support the restoration of tribal histories and practices. Many of these practitioner organisations have interests in supporting education and training initiatives as well as research and commercial applications and have begun thinking about their role as stewards of indigenous knowledge (Boulton et al. 2014). The growing role and economic influence of *iwi* as well as the growing intellectual capital in the Māori community are creating additional opportunities to apply indigenous knowledge to a range of domains including resource management, health research and entrepreneurial activities.

---

3   Health Research Council of New Zealand: hrc.govt.nz/.

The presence of indigenous brands also speaks to the way in which indigenous knowledge is being used to inform and support commercial activities, providing greater diversity and richness of experience in the marketplace (Jones et al. 2005).

Mātauranga Māori can be defined as 'the unique Māori way of viewing the world, encompassing both traditional knowledge and culture' (Waitangi Tribunal 2011), reinforcing the view that knowledge emerges from the land, defining both our relationship with it and our responsibilities towards it. It is in the environmental space that opportunities for *mātauranga Māori* are being advanced, with the development of Māori frameworks, approaches and models to support environmental decision-making and monitoring (Awatere & Harmsworth 2014). Through the increasing range of cogovernance and comanagement relationships, tribes are asserting the importance of including indigenous knowledge as an information source in environmental decision-making (Hudson et al. 2016). Some examples of cultural indicators, monitoring frameworks and assessment tools utilising *mātauranga Māori* include the Cultural Health Index for streams and rivers, State of the Takiwa, Mauri Model, cultural indicators for wetlands and *iwi* estuarine toolkits (Nelson & Tipa 2012).

New Zealand's data future

There are a number of challenges for *iwi* in accessing good-quality data. Limitations in infrastructure and people-capacity constrain the amount and quality of the data *iwi* can collect and manage independently. Governments collect a vast amount of data about *iwi* members; however, there are limited opportunities for *iwi* to access these information sources. This is due in part to the variable quality of ethnicity data (Kukutai & Walter 2015) and the absence of *iwi* affiliation in many data sources. Using a health analogy, it could be said that *iwi* suffer from inequities in data access and inequalities in data infrastructure.

However, this picture may change with the establishment of Statistics New Zealand's Integrated Data Infrastructure (IDI) (Statistics New Zealand, no date). The IDI is a linked longitudinal dataset that currently includes economic, education, justice, health and safety, migration, tenancy and business data. It has been created to support research, analysis and policy evaluation on transitions and outcomes for people.

The IDI can be accessed by approved researchers and used within a 'five safes' framework that ensures access to micro-data is provided only if all of the following conditions can be met:

- safe people—researchers can be trusted to use data appropriately and follow procedures
- safe projects—the project has a statistical purpose and is in the public interest
- safe settings—security arrangements prevent unauthorised access to the data
- safe data—the data inherently limit the risk of disclosure
- safe output—the statistical results produced do not contain any disclosing results.

The creation of the IDI supports the government's intention to harness the economic and social power of data (New Zealand Data Futures Forum 2015ab). New Zealand's digital future is dependent on a data revolution and the expectation that data will be more abundant and ubiquitous, connecting people, places and things. It is also anticipated that the widespread use of 'big data', where data are used, reused, processed and reconfigured, will fundamentally challenge legislative frameworks around privacy and information. Definitions of 'personal information', the role of consent and individual control and principles of data minimisation and purpose limitation will come under pressure during this data revolution (New Zealand Data Futures Forum 2015b). The New Zealand Data Futures Forum suggests that data should be recognised as a strategic asset for New Zealand and that we need to develop new ways to achieve trust and privacy in an environment where institutions should manage data use rather than focus on data ownership. The four principles they proposed for safely managing and optimising the use of data are:

1. Value: New Zealand should use data to drive economic and social value and create a competitive advantage for the country.
2. Inclusion: All parts of New Zealand society should have the opportunity to benefit from data use.
3. Trust: Data management in New Zealand should build trust and confidence in our institutions.
4. Control: Individuals should have greater control over the use of their personal data (New Zealand Data Futures Forum 2015b).

The importance of data and its role in future health care have emerged from discussions with tribes being conducted as part of a research project exploring Māori views on biobanking and genomic research.[4] While the focus of the project has been primarily on the safe collection and use of human tissue, the tribes considered that the genetic data produced from human tissue must also be protected. Participants understood the increasingly complex nature and changing expectations of data use, which see personal information (genetic data, clinical records) being used in a public domain to improve services, but often to private or corporate advantage. The participants recognised that data are a strategic asset for Māori, especially as they are becoming an increasingly valuable resource. They also felt that individuals and tribes have rights to the tissue and raw data as well as interests in any research or applications of those data. The genetic data, while a blueprint for an individual, are also representative of the collective and there exist both individual and collective rights and interests in the information—a position that has led to the development of a tribal agreement on the use, storage and protection of genome-wide sequence data.[5]

Informing tribal data sovereignty

As governments look to reform the nature of relationships, rights and responsibilities relating to data between individuals, businesses and the state, there is a growing awareness that ensuring indigenous participation in the knowledge economy and a data-rich future will inevitably lead to a discussion about indigenous data sovereignty and establishing the nature of tribal rights to and interests in different sources of data. Tensions around the relative rights of individuals and collectives that have long pervaded Māori critiques of Western ethics are likely to re-emerge in the discussion about principles to underpin data use and management (Hudson et al. 2010). Issues of individual

---

4   Te Mata Ira: Culturally Informed Guidelines for Biobanking and Genomic Research is an interdisciplinary research project funded by the Health Research Council.
5   Ngati Porou Hauora have developed this agreement with Associate Professor Tony Merriman from the Department of Biochemistry at the University of Otago to store computer data at the University of Otago from the Genetics of Gout in Tairawhiti and the Genetics of Gout and co-morbidities: genes and environment research projects.

and collective consent, Māori involvement in governance mechanisms and what constitutes personal, *iwi* and state rights and interests in data will be the crux of negotiations. Tribal positions are likely to be informed by a number of areas, including cultural and indigenous intellectual property rights, indigenous research ethics and existing resource rights.

Indigenous cultural and intellectual property rights

Iwi are developing their own views about culturally appropriate management and use of data, most often in relation to their own data sources and indigenous knowledge. The Mataatua Declaration on the Cultural and Intellectual Rights of Indigenous People emerged from an international conference held in 1993 and was written in response to indigenous concerns about the exploitation of their knowledge and resources (IRI 1997). The Mataatua Declaration reaffirmed Māori rights to self-determination, recognition as the exclusive owners of their cultural and intellectual property, the importance of ensuring the first beneficiaries of indigenous knowledge are the direct indigenous descendants and that all discrimination and exploitation of indigenous peoples, indigenous knowledge and indigenous cultural and intellectual property rights must cease. These ideals have been reinforced by the United Nations Declaration on the Rights of Indigenous Peoples (UNDRIP) (UN 2007), which codifies historical indigenous grievances, contemporary challenges and sociopolitical, economic and cultural aspirations. Article 31 speaks directly to intellectual property and indigenous control over data and information:

> Article 31: Indigenous peoples have the right to maintain, control, protect and develop their cultural heritage, traditional knowledge and traditional cultural expressions, as well as the manifestations of their sciences, technologies and cultures, including human and genetic resources, seeds, medicines, knowledge of the properties of fauna and flora, oral traditions, literatures, designs, sports and traditional games and visual and performing arts. They also have the right to maintain, control, protect and develop their intellectual property over such cultural heritage, traditional knowledge, and traditional cultural expressions. (UN 2007)

Indigenous research ethics

Research also provides a context from which a number of conversations about tribal rights and responsibilities for protecting indigenous data have emerged. Frameworks for indigenous research (Smith 1997: 526; Smith 1999) and indigenous research ethics (NHMRC 2003; Ermine et al. 2004; Hudson et al. 2010) speak directly to issues of access, use of indigenous knowledge and the responsibilities of collectives in managing and protecting that information. The principles of ownership, control, access and possession (OCAP®) also inform indigenous best practice and reflect self-determination in research for aboriginal and First Nations communities in Canada (Schnarch 2004; FNIGC, this volume). 'Ownership' refers to the relationship between indigenous communities and their cultural knowledge, data or information. It asserts community ownership of information and recognises stewardship as the mechanism by which ownership is asserted. 'Control' asserts the right for indigenous communities to control all aspects of research and information management processes. 'Access' refers to the right to have access to information and data about themselves and their communities (which others hold), as well as to make decisions about access to collective information (which they hold). 'Possession' is a counterpoint to past experience of data misuse and represents a key mechanism through which ownership can be asserted and control maintained.

While the OCAP® principles have been developed for the research context, they also reflect fundamental considerations that tribes will expect to be recognised within any data-sharing environment. Affirming tribal sovereignty is a core focus of the National Congress of American Indians. Through their Policy Research Centre, they have commented on the Draft National Institutes of Health Genomic Data Sharing Policy, including the role that traditional laws and appropriate research have in informing the policy. They highlighted five overarching points that are relevant to this discussion, including:

- Tribal nations have sovereignty over research conducted on tribal lands and with tribal citizens.
- Researchers must secure active tribal approval for the collection, use and sharing of tribal data.

- There are successful models of tribally driven data sharing that serve to both protect and benefit native people.
- Research ethics need to acknowledge the importance of community consent alongside individual consent.
- Research ethics need to include protections for biological samples collected from both living and deceased human beings.[6]

Resource rights and interests

A unique aspect of the treaty environment in New Zealand is the ability to submit claims to the Waitangi Tribunal for contemporary grievances relating to any enactment, policy or practice adopted or an act done or omitted by the Crown after 21 September 1992 that breaches the Treaty of Waitangi (Chen 2012). Over 200 contemporary claims have been filed, some of which have led to significant settlements with the Crown, including:

- The *Māori Fisheries Act 1989*, *Treaty of Waitangi (Fisheries Claims) Settlement Act 1992* and *Māori Fisheries Act 2004*, which granted Māori NZ$150 million and effective control over one-third of New Zealand's commercial fishery.
- The *Māori Commercial Aquaculture Settlement Act* (2004), which granted Māori 20 per cent of the aquaculture space created after 1992, covering pre-commencement space (before 2005) and new space (2005 onwards).
- The *Crown Forests Asset Act* (1989) transferred Crown forests to state-owned enterprises while protecting the claims of Māori under the Treaty of Waitangi. The Crown Forestry Rental Trust was established to manage the annual rental fees from Crown licensed forest land until the beneficial owners have been determined. Since 1990, it has facilitated the settlement of Māori claims by providing assistance to tribes who have Crown forests within their claimant area to prepare, present and negotiate their settlements. This included the 'Treelords' settlement, which returned NZ$195.7 million of Crown forest land and NZ$223 million in accumulated rentals to seven tribes in the central North Island (NZPA 2008).

---

6   National Congress of American Indians, comments on Draft NIH Genomic Data Sharing Policy, 20 November 2013.

- Claims over radio spectrums led to the reservation of space for Māori radio stations, Māori television and the establishment of a Crown funding agency, Te Mangai Paho. The evolution of technology and commercialisation of other spectrums also resulted in NZ$5 million being provided to the Te Huarahi Tika Trust to enable Māori a right to purchase 3G radio frequency spectrum in 2000. Te Huarahi Tika Trust also supported claims for 4G spectrum, which were ultimately unsuccessful.

- The Waitangi Tribunal's WAI262 report on the flora, fauna, cultural and intellectual property claim (Waitangi Tribunal 2011), which took 21 years to complete, made a number of recommendations including the development of a treaty-compliant bioprospecting regime; however, the Crown has yet to respond.

- Māori rights and interests in relation to fresh water have been the subject of recent claims prompted in part by the partial privatisation of energy companies with hydroelectric and geothermal resources. Arguments have been made to the Waitangi Tribunal and the Supreme Court that Māori have proprietary interests in water and the government has indicated it would work towards recognition of Māori water rights on a catchment-by-catchment basis (Radio NZ 2015). Māori positions are being informed by elements of previous settlements, collaborative water reform processes (Land and Water Forum 2012) and advocacy from the Freshwater iwi Leaders Group.[7]

Settlements have often been prompted by the privatisation of Crown assets or the establishment of regulatory processes that create proprietary interests for the rights-holders (that is, fish quotas, radio spectrum). A feature of these settlements has been their pan-tribal nature, which has resulted in the creation of Māori entities to grow the settlement assets and work out appropriate distribution models (for example, Te Ohu Kai Moana, Crown Forestry Rental Trust, Te Huarahi Tika Trust).

---

7   Iwi Chairs Forum: iwichairs.maori.nz/.

Establishing tribal rights and interests in data

If the primary role of a tribe is to sustain its people by maintaining its resources and culture across generations then how do data and information support the expression of this self-determination across political, cultural and economic domains? Te Whakatōhea provides one example of how *iwi* are considering the issue of indigenous data sovereignty in the context of their information needs and development aspirations.

Whakatōhea are located in the eastern Bay of Plenty region of New Zealand and have approximately 12,000 tribal members. Their primary genealogical connections associate the *iwi* with two ancestral voyaging canoes, the Nukutere and Mataatua. Their tribal boundaries surround the township of Opotiki in the Bay of Plenty, extending eastwards from Ohiwa Harbour to Opape along the coastline, and inland to Matawai. These lands have long held an abundance of food resources, particularly seafood, and most settlements are located near the coast. Whakatōhea's history of land confiscations (*raupatu*) from the early 1800s led to a series of events involving the loss of an economic base and the destruction of social structures, both of which had a devastating impact on tribal identity, culture, economy, health and wellbeing.

The Whakatōhea Māori Trust Board was established in 1947 and recognised in legislation in 1955 when the *Māori Trust Board Act* came into effect. The board was given functions under section 24 of the Act, including to: administer Whakatōhea's assets, promote health, economic and social welfare and educational and vocational training (Walker 2007). The board is the largest employer in Opotiki, with over 90 staff across its commercial, education, health and social service activities. The board has commercial interests in forestry, dairy farming, kiwifruit and property and is the majority partner in Eastern Seafarms Limited, which holds the consent for 3,800 ha of water space. Through the Whakatōhea Fisheries Trust and Asset Holding Company, it is the mandated *iwi* organisation for the settlement of fisheries assets and, through Te Wheke Atawhai Limited, it manages a GP clinic, health and social services as well as an education unit.

What is driving Whakatōhea's interest in data?

The vision for the Whakatōhea Māori Trust Board is represented in the *whakataukī* (tribal saying) *'Ko te kai hoki i Waiaua'*, which translates as 'To be the food bowl that feeds the world'. The board has developed 50-year economic, education, environmental, social, health and cultural plans focusing on community transformation to restore Whakatōhea's *mana* (prestige/power), wellbeing and economic strength. It also has a wide portfolio of commercial interests in the horticulture, farming and property sectors that require high-quality information and expertise to support sound financial investments. The board has recognised that quality data are the foundation for robust decision-making and this is now being actively promoted across the entire range of its activities. Information is being collected through research, administrative systems and collection of historical documents. Examples of research include:

- A comprehensive *iwi* health survey, He Oranga o te rohe o te Whakatōhea Wellbeing Survey 2010, involving face-to-face interviews with 750 registered adult members of Whakatōhea living in the Opotiki district.

- An aquaculture research strategy to prepare Whakatōhea to engage in research and development as well as identify opportunities for future development of consented and (currently) nonconsented species in the 3,800 ha of marine space they manage.

- Research to better understand how Māori values inform investment decisions for collective assets so the tribe can be more transparent in the way it applies Whakatōhea values and indigenous corporate responsibility into their decision-making processes (Hudson 2014; Hudson & Farrar 2015).

- The integration of practice models grounded in *mātauranga Māori* (indigenous knowledge) has broadened the focus of professional development from technical competency into areas of cultural competency, creating a number of direct benefits (Haring et al. 2015).

Information systems support human resources, information technology, finance, quality management, asset management and communication across the board's business groups. A new customer relationship management database system is being developed to enhance operational-level access to relevant information about clients and their family. Tribal information including tribal minutes, Māori land court minutes, maps and stories dating back to the early 1800s are captured on a separate server to create a digital archive. Communication systems allow the trust board to connect with its people and share information. Significant investment has been undertaken with a revamp of the website, Facebook page, internal rebranding and promotion of events including tribal elections and updates on the treaty settlement process.

Conceptualising tribal rights and interest in data

So what does all this mean for Whakatōhea and how might data sovereignty support their development? To realise their strategic aim—'*Ki te whakarangatira i nga uri o Whakatōhea*' ('to lift our nation, and to grow and invest in the wellbeing of our people')—Whakatōhea will require access to data and information as well as information systems and the capability to operate them (Whakatōhea Māori Trust Board 2011).

Whakatōhea have already realised that improving data connectivity within their organisation across diverse activities enables better service delivery. They expect that access to government data about their tribal members would also enhance their ability to provide services to tribal members. Access to the complete range of data allows the tribe to interpret information in more positive and productive ways, providing a counterbalance to the disparity-focused reports that are regularly produced by researchers. It would also allow them to create stronger networks and opportunities for tribal members living outside the tribal boundaries and consider how best to provide services, access to skills and connections and to build capacity. Access to government-collected data will enhance their ability to participate in nation-building activities for both Whakatōhea and Aotearoa/ New Zealand. Building a stronger and more connected tribe is an important goal as 90 per cent of the tribal population lives outside their traditional lands.

Whakatōhea consider that access to government-collected data and information is a treaty right and that the tribal entity is better placed to create benefit for tribal members than government departments or research organisations. They argue that the acknowledgement of *whakapapa* (tribal genealogy) creates rights and responsibilities, including establishing a social contract for tribal entities to serve their people. Access to information is a foundation for establishing appropriate services or activities. Whakatōhea recognise the sensitivity of, and need to appropriately manage, data and have done so effectively as part of the delivery of health and social services to the wider community. Moving into the collection of data for tribal members who are not users of their health and social services prompts the question, should a consent to connect with the tribe on the tribal database translate to a consent to access government administrative data? Or, alternatively, if tribal affiliation is listed in government datasets, should tribes have access rights to de-identified data in the same way that researchers do?

Table 9.1 Data sovereignty: articulating tribal rights and interests for Whakatōhea

Rights and interests	Type
Exclusive rights	Indigenous knowledge Client relationship management data Commercial intellectual property Genetic data—tribal members and indigenous flora
Shared rights	Central government administrative data Service-level information created by tribal entities
Shared interests	Research outputs Government and agency reports Commercial activities

Source: The authors.

As shown in Table 9.1, Whakatōhea recognise the reciprocal nature of some forms of data and understand that some information will be shared and rights to other types of information could be more exclusive. From a tribal perspective, exclusive rights exist around culturally or commercially sensitive information and would include indigenous knowledge, client relationship management data, commercial intellectual property and genetic data arising from tribal members and indigenous flora. Shared rights exist around information that supports the development of funding streams or service improvements for tribal members, which might consist of service-level information relating to government-funded activities. Tribal services provide this information to government agencies but would like access to information about additional tribal members that these agencies collect. Shared interests arise from the outcomes of the use of tribal information (exclusive or shared) by ensuring that the tribe can benefit from opportunities to develop relationships or partnerships that advance their interests through research outputs, government reports or commercial activities. The tangible expression of these rights to data would be the ability to influence how data are interpreted and the types of stories that are told about the tribe.

Conclusion

Tribes have increasingly complex information needs across all sectors of society and, while they are slowly raising their internal capacity and capability to collect and manage information, they will continue to rely on partnerships with government agencies and research institutions to address all their information needs. In the digital age, the old adage 'knowledge is power' is more relevant than ever. As Aotearoa/New Zealand transitions into a new data future, tribes must ensure that they can access and utilise the new data networks and infrastructures being created to realise tribal aspirations and benefit their members. Data are becoming a tangible and potentially valuable resource and many data sources are being made available for researchers to access. As data sharing becomes a normal activity, it is important that tribes articulate the nature of their treaty rights and establish appropriate boundaries for their tribal data.

References

Auckland Council (2016). *Tūpuna Maunga o Tāmaki Makaurau Authority*, Auckland Council, Auckland, aucklandcouncil.govt.nz/en/aboutcouncil/representativesbodies/maungaauthority/Pages/home.aspx.

Awatere S & Harmsworth G (2014). *Nga Aroturukitanga tika mo nga Kaitiaki: Summary review of mātauranga Māori frameworks, approaches and culturally appropriate monitoring tools for freshwater monitoring and management*, Client Report LC1774, Landcare Research, Lincoln, NZ.

Bay of Connections (2014). *He mauri ohooho: our people, our wealth, our future—Māori economic development strategy*, Bay of Connections, Tauranga, NZ.

Bay of Plenty Regional Council (2016). *Rangitaiki River Forum*, Bay of Plenty Regional Council, Whakatāne, boprc.govt.nz/council/committees-and-meetings/rangitaiki-river-forum/.

Boulton A, Hudson M, Ahuriri Driscoll A & Stewart A (2014). Enacting Kaitiakitanga: challenges and complexities in the governance and ownership of Rongoa research information. *International Indigenous Policy Journal* 5(2), doi:10.18584/iipj.2014.5.2.1.

Business and Economic Research Limited (BERL) (2011a). *The asset base, income, expenditure and GDP of the 2010 Māori economy*, BERL, Wellington.

Business and Economic Research Limited (BERL) (2011b). *The Māori economy, science and innovation*, BERL, Wellington.

Business and Economic Research Limited (BERL) (2012). *Situational analysis: Māori contribution and position in the Bay of Connections economy—report to the Bay of Plenty Regional Council*, BERL, Wellington.

Chen M (2012). *Mai Chen: Contemporary treaty claims*, 13 September 2012, Chen Palmer: New Zealand Public and Employment Law Specialists, Wellington, chenpalmer.com/news/news-articles/mai-chen-contemporary-treaty-claims/.

Ermine E, Sinclair R & Jeffery B (2004). *The ethics of research involving indigenous peoples*, Indigenous Peoples' Health Research Centre, Saskatoon, Canada.

Gibbs M (2005). The right to development and indigenous peoples: lessons from New Zealand. *World Development* 33(8):1365–78.

Haring RC, Hudson M, Erickson L, Taualii M & Freeman B (2015). First Nations, Māori, American Indians and native Hawaiians as sovereigns: EAP with indigenous nations within nations. *Journal of Workplace Behavioral Health* 30(1–2):14–31, doi:10.1080/15555240.2015.998969.

Harmsworth G (2011). Māori perspectives on the science and innovation system. *New Zealand Science Review* 68(1):45–8.

Hudson M (2014). *Optimising the Māori in Māori economic development: how Māori values inform investment decisions for collective assets*, Case study report, Whakatōhea Māori Trust Board, Opotiki, NZ.

Hudson M & Farrar D (2015). *Optimising the Māori in Māori economic development: how Māori values inform investment decisions for collective assets*, Case study report II, Whakatōhea Māori Trust Board, Opotiki, NZ.

Hudson M, Collier K, Awatere S, Harmsworth G, Henry J, Quinn J, Death RG, Hamilton DP, Te Maru J, Watene-Rawiri E & Robb M (2016). Integrating indigenous knowledge into freshwater management: an Aotearoa/New Zealand case study. *The International Journal of Science in Society* 8(1)(March):1–14.

Hudson M, Milne M, Reynolds P, Russell K & Smith B (2010). *Te Ara Tika guidelines for Māori research ethics: a framework for researchers and ethics committee members*, Health Research Council, Auckland.

International Research Institute for Māori and Indigenous Education (IRI) (1997). Mataatua declaration on cultural and intellectual property rights of indigenous people. In Pihama L & Waerea-i-te-rangi Smith C (eds), *Cultural and intellectual property rights: economics, politics and colonisation. Volume 2*, International Research Institute for Māori and Indigenous Education, University of Auckland, Auckland.

Jones K, Gilbert K & Morrison-Briars Z (2005). *Māori branding: a report investigating market demand for Māori cultural elements*, Waka Tohu Research Project, New Zealand.

Kukutai T & Walter M (2015). Recognition and indigenising official statistics: reflections from Aotearoa New Zealand and Australia. *Statistical Journal of the IAOS* (31):317–26.

Land and Water Forum (2012). *Third report of the Land and Water Forum: managing water quality and allocating water*, Land and Water Forum, Wellington.

Māori Economic Development Panel (2012). *He kai kei aku ringa: the Crown–Māori economic growth partnership—strategy to 2040*, Māori Economic Development Panel, Wellington.

Ministry of Education (2014). *Profiles and trends: New Zealand's tertiary education sector 2013*, Tertiary sector performance analysis, Ministry of Education, Wellington.

Ministry of Science and Innovation [now Ministry of Business Innovation and Employment] (updated 2016). *Vision Mātauranga Capability Fund: questions and answers*, New Zealand Government, Wellington, msi.govt.nz/get-funded/research-organisations/vision-matauranga-capability-fund/.

Nana G, Stoke F, Hudson M, Haar J & Delaney P (2012). *Strategic step change: Māori entities and the science sector—case studies*, Report to Te Puni Kokiri, Wellington.

National Health and Medical Research Council (NHMRC) (2003). *Values and ethics: guidelines for ethical conduct in Aboriginal and Torres Strait Islander health research*, NHMRC, Canberra.

Nelson KD & Tipa G (2012). *Cultural indicators, monitoring frameworks and assessment tools*, Report for the Wheel of Water Project, Aqualinc Research Limited, Christchurch.

New Zealand Data Futures Forum (2015a). *Key recommendations and catalyst projects*, Statistics New Zealand, Wellington, nzdatafutures.org.nz/sites/default/files/NZDFF_Key_recommendations.pdf.

New Zealand Data Futures Forum (2015b). *Navigating the data future: four guiding principles*, Statistics New Zealand, Wellington, nzdatafutures.org.nz/sites/default/files/NZDFF_Discussion%20document%202.pdf.

New Zealand Institute of Economic Research (NZIER) (2014). *Research impact evaluation: NZIER report to Nga Pae o te Maramatanga*, NZIER, Wellington.

New Zealand Press Association (NZPA) (2008). Govt signs $400 million-plus 'Treelords' deal. *National Business Review*, 25 June 2008, nbr.co.nz/article/govt-signs-400-million-plus-treelords-deal-32500.

Radio NZ (2015). Deadline set for freshwater deal. *Radio NZ*, 5 February 2015, radionz.co.nz/news/te-manu-korihi/265413/deadline-set-for-freshwater-deal.

Royal C (2009). Te Kaimanga: towards a new vision for Mātauranga Māori, Lecture 1, Macmillan Brown Lecture Series, Macmillan Brown Centre for Pacific Studies, University of Canterbury, Christchurch, 16 September 2009.

Schnarch B (2004). Ownership, control, access and possession (OCAP) or self-determination applied to research: a critical analysis of contemporary First Nations research and some options for First Nations communities. *Journal of Aboriginal Health* (January):80–95, naho.ca/jah/english/jah01_01/journal_p80-95.pdf.

Smellie P (2014). Tainui assets top $1b as 20th anniversary of treaty settlement looms. *National Business Review*, 2 July 2014, nbr.co.nz/article/tainui-assets-top-1bln-20th-anniversary-treaty-settlement-looms-bd-158582.

Smith GH (1997). The development of Kau papa Māori: theory and praxis, PhD thesis, University of Auckland, Auckland.

Smith GH, Tinirau R, Gillies A & Warriner V (2015). *He Mangopare Amohia: strategies for Māori economic development*, Te Whare Wananga o Awanuiarangi, Whakatāne.

Smith LT (1999). *Decolonising methodologies: research and indigenous peoples*, Zed Books, London & New York.

Statistics New Zealand (no date). *Snapshots of New Zealand: integrated data infrastructure*, Statistics New Zealand, Wellington, stats.govt.nz/browse_for_stats/snapshots-of-nz/integrated-data-infrastructure.aspx.

Te Puni Kokiri (TPK) (2014). *Māori economy in the Waikato region*, TPK, Wellington.

Te Rūnanga o Ngāi Tahu (no date). *A pathway to prosperity for Ngāi Tahu Whānui*, Te Rūnanga o Ngāi Tahu, Christchurch, ngaitahu.iwi.nz/whanau/whai-rawa/.

Te Rūnanga o Ngāi Tahu (2014). *Annual report 2014*, Te Rūnanga o Ngāi Tahu, Christchurch, ngaitahu.iwi.nz/annual-report-2014/.

United Nations (UN) (2007). *United Nations declaration on the rights of indigenous peoples*, United Nations, New York, un.org/esa/socdev/unpfii/documents/DRIPS_en.pdf.

Waikato-Tainui (2014). *Waikato-Tainui, SODA Inc. partnership a boost to Maaori business*, 3 September 2014, Waikato-Tainui Te Kauhanganui Inc., Hamilton, NZ, waikatotainui.com/waikato-tainui-soda-inc-partnership-a-boost-to-maaori-business/.

Waitangi Tribunal (2011). *Ko Aotearoa Tenei: a report into claims concerning New Zealand law and policy affecting Māori culture and identity*, Te taumata tuarua [Waitangi Tribunal report], Legislation Direct, Wellington.

Walker R (2007). *Opotiki Mai Tawhiti*, Penguin Books, Auckland.

Whakatōhea Māori Trust Board (2011). *Whakatōhea Māori Trust Board: strategic plan 2010–2015*, Whakatōhea Māori Trust Board, Opotiki, NZ.

10

The world's most liveable city—for Māori: data advocacy and Māori wellbeing in Tāmaki Makaurau (Auckland)

James Hudson

What would the world's most liveable city look like? This is a question that is being considered by *iwi* (Māori tribes) and Māori communities within Tāmaki Makaurau (Auckland) in Aotearoa (New Zealand). This is a question that is also being considered by the Auckland Council, the local government authority for the Tāmaki Makaurau region. However, while Māori and the Auckland Council may be asking the same question, the responses are not necessarily, if at all, similar. This can be attributed (at the risk of oversimplifying) to dissimilar, and at times competing, values and world views underpinning the array of responses from Māori of Tāmaki Makaurau and Auckland Council.

Tāmaki Makaurau, as with the rest of Aotearoa, experienced colonisation by British settlers during the early 1800s, resulting in drastic loss of land, crippling depopulation and cultural erosion for Māori (Walker 2004). Today, however, due to a range of Māori-initiated developments, the Māori population has grown and arrived at a point where it is now larger and living longer than at any point in history (Durie 2005). And, during the past three decades, catalyst events such as the Hui Taumata (Māori Economic Summit) in 1984 have provided the contemporary thrust by which Māori have acted strategically at national and local government levels to establish laws and policies that empower their *iwi* and communities and which utilise more traditional Māori concepts and structures (Māori Economic Development Taskforce 2010). This is notwithstanding the custodial approaches of successive governments to apply assimilative policies to Māori development, which drove broader government agendas and quickly dismissed notions of Māori self-determination (Durie 2009).

This chapter explores the Māori and Auckland Council relationship within the context of negotiating a shared vision for Tāmaki Makaurau. The focal point is 'The Māori Plan for Tāmaki Makaurau', a plan constructed, with Māori of Tāmaki Makaurau, by the Independent Māori Statutory Board (IMSB), a statutory advisory board to the Auckland Council. The Māori Plan clearly articulates a Māori vision for Tāmaki Makaurau and is a touchstone for ongoing dialogue about Māori-specific data to support that vision. The chapter discusses the work of the IMSB in utilising and advocating for Māori-specific data to promote and advocate positive outcomes for Māori in Tāmaki Makaurau. And it shares some experiences and reflections to promote constructive discussion and reflective analysis that may be relevant for other local government contexts within Aotearoa or for wider international and indigenous contexts.

Background

Māori in Tāmaki Makaurau

The Māori population of Tāmaki Makaurau is approximately 142,767 people—one-quarter of the entire Māori population of Aotearoa (Statistics New Zealand 2013). It is overwhelmingly young, with over half the population aged 24 years or younger and less than 4 per cent aged 65 years or older (Statistics New Zealand 2013). And while there are more male Māori in age groups up to 19 years, females predominate in all remaining age groups (Statistics New Zealand 2013).

Mana whenua are 'the people of the land', the *iwi*, and have an enduring relationship with Tāmaki Makaurau. Tāmaki Makaurau is their *tūrangawaewae*—their place in the world. Mataawaka represent the wider Māori population and include Māori residents and ratepayers who are service users and stakeholders.

The Treaty of Waitangi and local government

Auckland Council's obligation to provide for Māori is ultimately grounded in and guided by the Crown's obligations under Aotearoa's founding constitutional document, the Treaty of Waitangi of 1840. In part due to the differences in interpretation in the English and Māori versions of the treaty, most contemporary legislation refers to *the principles of the treaty*, rather than the specific treaty provisions themselves (Belgrave 2012). The dominant principles articulated by the judiciary (though understood to be evolving) are: *partnership* (which includes the duty on both parties to act reasonably, honourably and in good faith), *active protection* (which requires the government to protect Māori interests) and *redress* (which requires the government to take active and positive steps to redress breaches of the treaty) (Wheen & Hayward 2012).

The *duty to consult* with Māori has been described as a principle inherent in the treaty and in the overarching principles of partnership and active protection.[1] At a local government level, the duty to consult with Māori is also required under two primary pieces of legislation. The first, the *Local Government Act 2002*, requires councils to establish and maintain processes to provide opportunities for Māori to contribute to the decision-making processes of the local authority. The second, the *Resource Management Act 1991*, requires that councils consult with Māori authorities at various stages under the Act, including during the development of resource management plans.

It is within this context of a treaty partnership, and the various legislative and policy requirements to adequately consult, that current discussions are occurring among Māori and the Auckland Council concerning a vision for Tāmaki Makaurau.

---

1   *New Zealand Māori Council v Attorney-General* [1897] 1 NZLR 683.

In 2009, the national government implemented bold changes to the governance system of Tāmaki Makaurau whereby the seven city and district councils existing at that time, along with the Auckland Regional Council, were disestablished and amalgamated into a new, unitary council, the Auckland Council.[2]

The amalgamation of these governing bodies, however, did not diminish Auckland Council's legal obligations and responsibilities towards Māori. And debate soon ensued concerning the best way in which treaty and legal obligations towards Māori in Tāmaki Makaurau could be met. A significant outcome of this debate was the establishment of the IMSB.

The Independent Māori Statutory Board

In its report to the government, the Royal Commission on Auckland Governance (2009) recognised that Māori constitute a unique community of interest with special status as a partner under the Treaty of Waitangi and recommended that Māori be guaranteed seats on the Auckland Council. However, the government chose *not* to adopt the Royal Commission's recommendation, opting instead to establish a Māori Advisory Board with a nonbinding consultative role before the Auckland Council. It was at this point that the IMSB was established under the *Local Government (Auckland Council) Act 2009*.

The IMSB's broad purpose is twofold: to assist the Auckland Council to make decisions, perform functions and exercise powers by promoting cultural, economic, environmental and social issues of significance for Māori in Tāmaki Makaurau; and to ensure that the Auckland Council acts in accordance with statutory provisions referring to the treaty. To achieve this purpose, the IMSB's primary functions include advising the Auckland Council on matters affecting Māori and working with the Auckland Council on the design and execution of documents and processes to implement the council's statutory responsibilities towards Māori.

---

2   *Local Government (Tamaki Makaurau Reorganisation) Act 2009, Local Government (Auckland Council) Act 2009* and *Local Government (Auckland Transitional Provisions) Act 2010.*

The IMSB is made up of nine representatives of Mana Whenua and Mataawaka, who are appointed by a process designed by Māori. They meet at least quarterly with the Auckland Council Governing Body. The IMSB members also sit on various targeted Auckland Council committees to advocate on behalf of Tāmaki Makaurau Māori. The IMSB is supported by a secretariat that includes policy advisors, technical staff and data analysts, each of whom engages with Auckland Council at an officer level. At these two levels of engagement—governance and operational—the IMSB is able to influence and advocate on behalf of Tāmaki Makaurau Māori.

The Māori Plan

Early in its inception, the IMSB identified that existing regional development frameworks and measures had failed to adequately provide for Māori identity and wellbeing. It also recognised the dearth of Māori-specific data at a regional level that were useful or relevant for informing their own and Auckland Council's regional strategies, policies and planning for Māori in Tāmaki Makaurau. While some data were available *about* Māori, few, if any, were available that could be viewed as data useful *for* Māori.

Therefore, in mid 2011, the IMSB initiated a process to explore an approach to monitor and measure Māori outcomes in Tāmaki Makaurau. The IMSB sought views from Mana Whenua and Mataawaka within Tāmaki Makaurau and reviewed relevant policy and planning documents from both Māori and Auckland Council. The process confirmed that, at that time, there was no existing framework that enabled the IMSB to measure Māori wellbeing in Tāmaki Makaurau in accordance with Māori world views and Māori values. Work therefore began on constructing such a framework.

An initial step was completing a critical review of the major approaches that are relevant to conceptualising and measuring Māori wellbeing. High-level approaches to wellbeing were analysed and the main strengths and shortcomings of each were identified. The review concluded that there were several kinds of approaches to measuring Māori wellbeing, all of which had the potential to provide a different snapshot of Māori wellbeing (Cunningham 1996; Durie et al. 2002; Kingi 2005; Baker 2010). Several of the approaches had a degree of overlap with respect to the concepts, indicators and data used, but varied in terms of how the information was framed and the underlying objectives or goals.

A mixed-method approach to constructing the Māori Plan was therefore proposed, which aligned with the priorities and interests of the Auckland Council, its business units and central government agencies, but still reflected the needs and aspirations of Māori in Tāmaki Makaurau. The review also found that the Māori Plan would need a robust translational process that ensured a good fit between the project's goals, the definition of wellbeing, the measurement dimensions and the available data sources.

Following this review, Mana Whenua and Mataawaka were engaged again to elicit an independent Māori voice to articulate their vision for their collective wellbeing in Tāmaki Makaurau. Significant engagement included 23 *hui* (gatherings) with Mana Whenua and Mataawaka and 10 *hui* with *rangatahi Māori* (Māori youth). The engagement exercise revealed a wide range of opinions about Māori wellbeing in Tāmaki Makaurau and contributors to improving it. Significantly, the engagement found that:

1. Mana Whenua and Mataawaka aspirations were holistic and crossed several domains
2. Māori values were integral to Mana Whenua and Mataawaka aspirations for the future
3. economic aspirations for Tāmaki Makaurau required further investigation and development
4. there were opportunities to connect and participate globally
5. greater value needed to be placed on Māori culture
6. there should be greater opportunities for Māori communities to connect with each other, and externally, to provide social cohesion.

Further, the engagement with Mana Whenua and Mataawaka also identified that the Māori Plan *belonged to* Māori; the role of the IMSB was as a *kaitiaki* (guardian) of, and advocate for, the Māori Plan rather than its owner.

The data and research gathered through the literature review and engagement processes were then analysed using Māori-centred approaches. An important output of this process was the Māori Plan, the indicators matrix of which is shown in Figure 10.1.

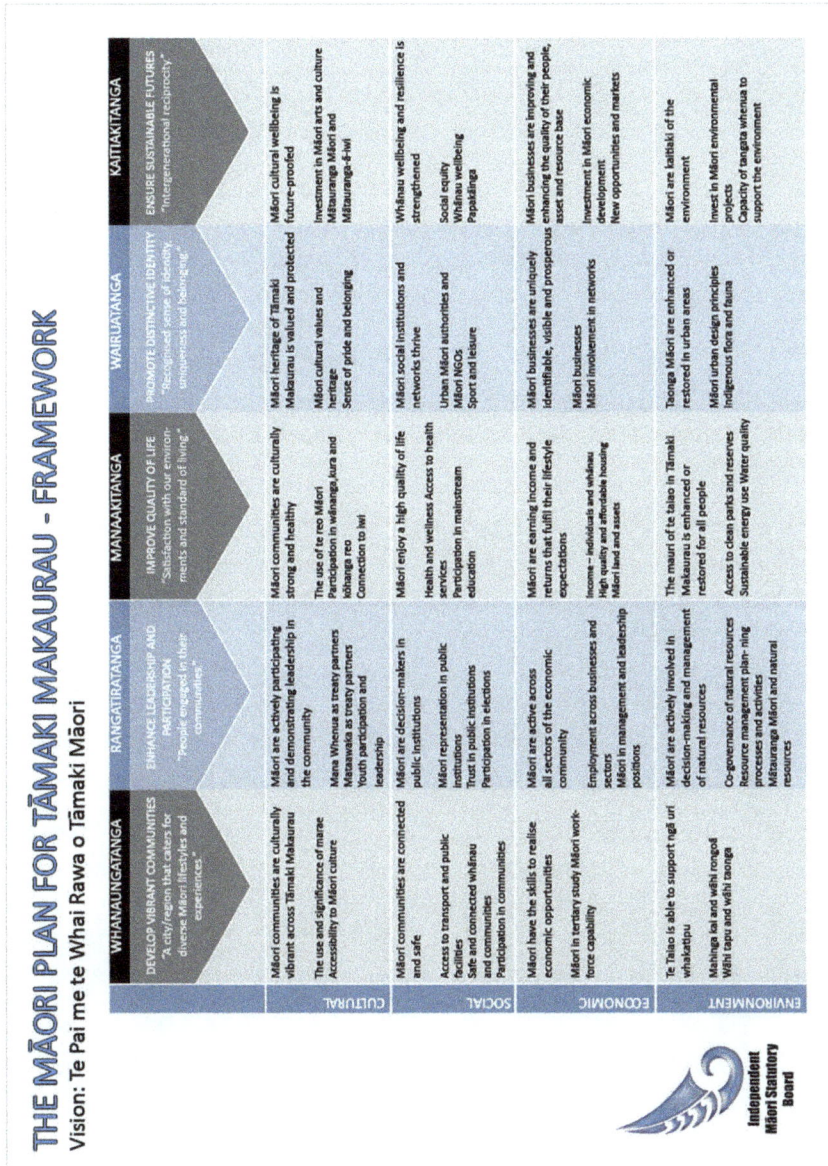

THE MĀORI PLAN FOR TĀMAKI MAKAURAU - FRAMEWORK
Vision: Te Pai me te Whai Rawa o Tāmaki Māori

	WHANAUNGATANGA — DEVELOP VIBRANT COMMUNITIES "A city/region that caters for diverse Māori lifestyles and experiences"	RANGATIRATANGA — ENHANCE LEADERSHIP AND PARTICIPATION "People engaged in their communities"	MANAAKITANGA — IMPROVE QUALITY OF LIFE "Satisfaction with our environments and standard of living"	WAIRUATANGA — PROMOTE DISTINCTIVE IDENTITY "Recognised sense of identity, uniqueness and belonging"	KAITIAKITANGA — ENSURE SUSTAINABLE FUTURES "Intergenerational reciprocity"
CULTURAL	Māori communities are culturally vibrant across Tāmaki Makaurau. The use and significance of marae. Accessibility to Māori culture	Māori are actively participating and demonstrating leadership in the community. Mana Whenua as treaty partners. Mataawaka as treaty partners. Youth participation and leadership	Māori communities are culturally strong and healthy. The use of te reo Māori. Participation in wānanga, kura and kōhanga reo. Connection to iwi	Māori heritage of Tāmaki Makaurau is valued and protected. Māori cultural values and heritage. Sense of pride and belonging	Māori cultural wellbeing is future-proofed. Investment in Māori arts and culture. Mātauranga Māori and Mātauranga-ā-iwi
SOCIAL	Māori communities are connected and safe. Access to transport and public facilities. Safe and connected whānau and communities. Participation in communities	Māori are decision-makers in public institutions. Māori representation in public institutions. Trust in public institutions. Participation in elections	Māori enjoy a high quality of life. Health and wellness Access to health services. Participation in mainstream education	Māori social institutions and networks thrive. Urban Māori authorities and Māori NGOs. Sport and leisure	Whānau wellbeing and resilience is strengthened. Social equity. Whānau wellbeing. Papakāinga
ECONOMIC	Māori have the skills to realise economic opportunities. Māori in tertiary study Māori workforce capability	Māori are active across all sectors of the economic community. Employment across businesses and sectors. Māori in management and leadership positions	Māori are earning income and returns that fulfil their lifestyle expectations. Income – individuals and whānau. High quality and affordable housing. Māori land and assets	Māori businesses are uniquely identifiable, visible and prosperous. Māori businesses. Māori involvement in networks	Māori businesses are improving and enhancing the quality of their people, asset and resource base. Investment in Māori economic development. New opportunities and markets
ENVIRONMENT	Te Taiao is able to support ngā uri whakatipu. Mahinga kai and wāhi rongoā Wāhi tapu and wāhi taonga	Māori are actively involved in decision-making and management of natural resources. Co-governance of natural resources. Resource management plan-ning processes and activities. Mātauranga Māori and natural resources	The mauri of te taiao in Tāmaki Makaurau is enhanced or restored for all people. Access to clean parks and reserves. Sustainable energy use Water quality	Taonga Māori are enhanced or restored in urban areas. Māori urban design principles. Indigenous flora and fauna	Māori are kaitiaki of the environment. Invest in Māori environmental projects. Capacity of tangata whenua to support the environment

Independent Māori Statutory Board

Figure 10.1 The Māori Plan for Tāmaki Makaurau
Source: IMSB (no date).

The Māori Plan is an aspirational 30-year plan for Māori in Tāmaki Makaurau. It provides the IMSB with a basis for prioritising issues, advocating for opportunities and forming partnerships with Auckland Council and other partners to deliver improved wellbeing for Māori communities. It is intended to be a touchpoint whereby the IMSB is able to provide direction to Auckland Council in developing policies, practices and plans relevant to Tāmaki Makaurau Māori. The Māori Plan was developed so it could be revised and refreshed over time to remain relevant to Mana Whenua and Mataawaka while providing the IMSB and Auckland Council with a basis from which to focus on key activities relating to Māori development within Tāmaki Makaurau.

The Māori Plan is underpinned by *Māori values*, emphasising the idea that Māori can contribute their own world views and practices to policies and plans in a way that is meaningful and constructive to them. The values are *whanaungatanga* (relationships), *rangatiratanga* (autonomy and leadership), *manaakitanga* (to protect and look after), *wairuatanga* (spirituality and identity) and *kaitiakitanga* (guardianship).

The Māori Plan includes *key directions*, which emerged from the analysis of the engagement meetings and key documents, and which reflect the overarching goals or aspirations that Māori have for their own tribes, organisations and communities. The key directions (which are located vertically in the plan) are: 1) developing vibrant communities; 2) enhancing leadership and participation; 3) improving quality of life; 4) promoting a distinctive Māori identity; and 5) ensuring sustainable futures.

The Māori Plan has four *domains*, or wellbeing areas: social, cultural, economic and environmental. And within each domain are *focus areas*, specific issues that Māori highlighted as being important to them—for example, accessibility to Māori culture, Māori in tertiary study, sustainable energy use and investment in Māori economic development.

Finally, and of particular relevance to this chapter, is the Māori Plan's set of *state of wellness* indicators—state indicators that provide the basis for the long-term measurement and monitoring of Māori wellbeing in Tāmaki Makaurau. They are relatively high level to identify trends and provide an evidential basis for the formulation of policies and actions. The indicators also act as accountability mechanisms to ensure that the Auckland Council and other agencies are responsive to Māori issues. The process of selecting indicators to populate the Māori Plan's framework was undertaken iteratively with the development of the focus areas and evaluated collaboratively with Māori and other stakeholders. The indicators rely on a range of data sources, including the New Zealand Census of Population and Dwellings, the Auckland Quality of Life Survey and central government and Auckland Council administrative data.

The Māori Plan: challenges and implications

There are a number of specific challenges to implementing and monitoring the Māori Plan, the first of which relates to considerations of *tikanga Māori* (Māori customs). Basically, the Māori Plan represents the aspirations and vision of Māori and the key directions and actions contained therein are guided by *tikanga Māori*. Proposed research and evaluation activities therefore need to be designed and carried out in a manner that is consistent with traditional Māori values, concepts and practices. These values imply the adoption of Māori-centred research practices where possible, the involvement of Māori in oversight of the implementation of the plan and the development of Māori research capability.

A second issue is the Māori Plan's long time horizon: 30 years. It is expected the Māori Plan will be refreshed and revised over this interval, which means the evaluation and monitoring of the plan will need to be flexible and able to accommodate change to ensure the plan remains relevant as priorities change. It also means that the reporting will need to blend short-term activities that enable early progress to be assessed with measurement of enduring indicators to enable long-term changes in wellbeing to be monitored.

Then, there is the broad range of issues of significance to Māori to consider. The Māori Plan spans a wide range of issues of significance and a diverse set of priorities. This mirrors, to a large extent, the broad range of factors that affect Māori wellbeing. It also reflects the wide span of influence of Auckland Council strategies, plans and activities. This presents challenges in terms of identifying monitoring and evaluation priorities, as it is simply not possible within available resources to monitor and evaluate every aspect of the Māori Plan's implementation. The IMSB is therefore required to engage in prioritisation exercises to best focus resources to progress towards positive Māori outcomes.

The review of data sources during the construction of the Māori Plan highlighted that considerable data gaps existed for Māori at the regional level, particularly in the environmental and cultural domains. In some cases, this was because ethnicity data were not collected or data were available only at the national level. The lack of existing indicators that reflect a Māori values-based approach to wellbeing was striking—both then and now—and highlights a tension that has long existed between the interests and statistical reporting requirements of government and Māori perceptions of what constitute useful and meaningful data. However, while there are a number of indicators for which no current data exist, this presents an opportunity to propose new primary research through new initiatives or ongoing collaboration between Māori, the Auckland Council and external partners.

Finally, evaluation and monitoring frameworks are typically developed for strategies, policies and programs for which there are dedicated resources and a clear intervention logic. In contrast, the Māori Plan is an aspirational document that sets out an intended vision and direction for Māori wellbeing and that has no dedicated resources committed to its implementation. The appropriate methodology for monitoring and evaluating implementation of the Māori Plan needs to reflect its aspirational status and the dependency on other parties' actions to give effect to it.

The IMSB data strategy

To some extent, the challenges above are mitigated by, first, the knowledge and experience of the IMSB members, who collectively are experts in *tikanga Māori*, Māori development and Māori cultural indicators. However, with respect to its work concerning Māori-specific data and research, these challenges are also being mitigated by the IMSB's recently launched 'Data strategy 2016–2020', which includes the establishment of a Data Strategy Expert Panel.

The data strategy is premised on the same five core Māori values and, in this way, is directly linked to the Māori Plan. The data strategy was designed to enable the IMSB to advocate for data that are Tāmaki Makaurau-focused, cost-effective, accessible in a timely manner, high quality and sustainable in the sense that they are collected regularly and systematically.

The strategy also identifies key partners with whom the IMSB has developed strategic relationships to both access and advocate for the future collection of Māori-specific data. Significant relationships include those with organisations such as Statistics New Zealand, Auckland Council's Research, Investigation and Monitoring Unit and Nga Pae o te Maramatanga, which is Aotearoa's Centre of Research Excellence in Māori and indigenous knowledge. These relationships have been prioritised primarily because of their aligned interests in progressing work with Māori data and also the contribution that each can make towards accessing or collecting data that are relevant for both the IMSB and Tāmaki Makaurau Māori.

Finally, the Data Strategy Expert Panel consists of members who, collectively, bring a significant breadth and depth of knowledge and experience in data and research, Māori development and policy and planning. The panel's primary purpose is to provide the IMSB with advice on the data strategy's implementation. The independent advice of the expert panel—who are, again, experts in data and research concerning Māori development—also ensures a degree of 'safety' around *tikanga Māori* and technical robustness.

Conclusion

While the Māori Plan presents challenges and implications, these are being addressed and they are nothing more than 'growing pains' in a relatively new and pioneering process. The Māori Plan ultimately still provides a Māori vision for Tāmaki Makaurau, which has never been articulated at any previous point in the history of local government.

The development of the plan and work relating to its implementation, monitoring and evaluation are an approach the IMSB is facilitating to contribute to positive outcomes for Māori in Tāmaki Makaurau. The hope is that the sharing of the IMSB's knowledge and experience gained to date with other Māori and indigenous collectives will usefully contribute to ongoing positive conceptualisations of Māori and indigenous wellbeing. Further, collective and collaborative efforts around the collation and analysis of related data will create and grow 'space' within which such Māori and indigenous conceptualisations may flourish.

References

Baker K (2010). *Whānau Taketake Māori: recession and Māori resilience—a report for the Families Commission*, Families Commission, Wellington.

Belgrave M (2012). Negotiations and settlements. In Wheen N & Hayward J (eds), *Treaty of Waitangi settlements*, Bridget Williams Books, Wellington.

Cunningham C (1996). *He Taura Tieke: measuring effective health services for Māori*, Ministry of Health, Wellington.

Durie M (2005). *Nga Tai Matatu tides of Māori endurance*, Oxford University Press, Auckland.

Durie M (2009). Pae Mana: Waitangi and the evolving state. In *The Paerangi Lectures: Māori horizons 2020 and beyond*, Massey University, Wellington.

Durie M, Fitzgerald E, Kingi TKR, McKinley S & Stevenson B (2002). *Māori specific outcomes and indicators: a report prepared for Te Puni Kokiri, the Ministry of Māori Development*, Massey University, Palmerston North, NZ.

Independent Māori Statutory Board (IMSB) (no date). *The Māori plan for Tāmaki Makaurau*, IMSB, Auckland, aucklandcouncil.govt.nz/ EN/planspoliciesprojects/plansstrategies/unitaryplan/Documents/ Section32report/Appendices/Appendix%203.16.4.pdf.

Kingi TK (2005). Evaluation and measurement of cultural outcomes, Paper presented at the 2005 Aotearoa New Zealand Evaluation Conference, Taupo, NZ, 18–20 July 2005.

Māori Economic Development Taskforce (2010). *Iwi infrastructure and investment*, Te Puni Kokiri, Wellington.

Royal Commission on Auckland Governance (2009). *Volume one: report*, Royal Commission on Auckland Governance, Auckland.

Statistics New Zealand (2013). *2013 census quickstats about Māori*, Statistics New Zealand, Wellington, stats.govt.nz.

Walker R (2004). *Ka whawhai tonui matou: struggle without end*, Penguin Books, Auckland.

Wheen R & Hayward J (eds) (2012). *Treaty of Waitangi settlements*, Bridget Williams Books, Wellington.

11

Indigenous data sovereignty: a Māori health perspective

Rawiri Jansen

Nā te kune te pupuke	From the conception the increase
Nā te pupuke te hihiri	From the increase the thought
Nā te hihiri te mahara	From the thought the remembrance
Nā te mahara te hinengaro	From the remembrance the consciousness
Nā te hinengaro te manako	From the consciousness the desire
Ka hua te wānanga[1]	Knowledge becomes productive.

Introduction

I work as a health practitioner with the National Hauora Coalition (NHC), a Māori primary health care organisation (PHO) and health provider. I come to the discussion of indigenous data sovereignty as a user of data, rather than as a data practitioner. Specifically, I am interested in how we can collect, analyse and use data—mainly health data—collected over time about individual Māori and collected from groups of Māori largely with a purpose of supporting improved health outcomes for individuals, *whānau* (extended family) and

---

1   This is part of a cosmological chant recited by Te Kohuora of Rongoroa (Salmond 1991: 171–2). It situates this discussion about data, information and knowledge in a broader cosmological and cultural context.

Māori communities. Māori engage with health providers, on average, many times a year and diagnosis, classifications, tests, investigations, treatments, prescriptions and so on will each have a data footprint. These data permit an appreciation of the experiences of the care generated—for example, which medicines are overprescribed or underprescribed to Māori, geographic variation or any unwarranted variation of prescriptions, investigations or referrals.

These sophisticated datasets and analyses are already driving evidence-led interventions for Māori primary health care. There is a need for enhanced Māori capability in the use and application of data and for more clearly specified client datasets. Māori are asserting that equity of outcomes is a fundamental element of quality in health care and an expression of our health rights. Our health data, both personally and collectively, are dispersed, distributed and disseminated. Exercising control over our data is challenging, as we need to navigate confidentiality, health privacy and commercial proprietary interests. And when we get data and convert it into intelligence and knowledge, we must use it wisely and tactically to influence the health system to deliver better outcomes.

The aim of this chapter is to explore indigenous data sovereignty from a Māori health perspective. I start, rather predictably, with a few words about rights to our data, beginning with treaty rights derived from the Treaty of Waitangi, and health and data rights derived from the United Nations Declaration on the Rights of Indigenous Peoples (UNDRIP). Then I examine a case study—or, more accurately, a set of connected case studies—that demonstrates how data can be used to inform interventions that address health and social inequalities. Specifically, I refer to a series of activities and interventions that the NHC leads to deliver improved health outcomes for Māori. These include the successful reduction of rheumatic fever in the Māori and Pacific populations of South Auckland and improved primary health care interventions across the NHC provider network. Additionally, I identify an opportunity to expand data views and data governance across the whole system rather than just data governance in one PHO. Finally, I address an issue, or an opportunity, depending on your perspective, adjacent to health data, and that is how our data can inform interventions that address inequities in the education system and may also contribute to developing a Māori health workforce that contributes to reducing health inequities.

Treaty of Waitangi

The Treaty of Waitangi was signed on 6 February 1840 and is a useful starting point because, as Nōpera Pana-kareao asserted: *'Ko te atarau o te whenua i riro i a te kuini, ko te tinana o te whenua i waiho ki ngā Māori'* ('The shadow of the land will go to the Queen [of England], but the substance of the land will remain with us'). He reversed his opinion within the year, declaring that the substance of the land had gone to the Queen and Māori retained only the shadow. Data governance, it seems, also requires thought about both the substance and the shadow of the data.

The assertion of sovereignty requires us as indigenous peoples to consider both substantive issues of data, its collection and storage and the shadow of data, its interrogation, analysis and application. Breaches of the treaty and the failure to observe the commitments therein—Māori control over lands and villages and *taonga* (resources) and Māori entitlement to the rights and privileges of British subjects— have led to persistent disparity across many domains of civil life, including access to and provision of services in education, health and justice and corrections.

Health rights

The right to health is contained in a broad range of international declarations, covenants and human rights instruments, from the Universal Declaration of Human Rights, the World Health Organization's constitution and the International Covenant on Economic, Social and Cultural Rights to, more recently, the UNDRIP. These human rights instruments establish the principles of equality and freedom from discrimination and also direct attention to ensuring that empowerment, participation in decision-making and accountability mechanisms contribute to the solutions and responses. Herein lies the import of data: to empower and inform the affected population, to enable our informed participation and, ultimately, to hold governments accountable.

Reid and Robson (2007: 3) assert that 'Māori have the right to monitor the Crown, and to evaluate Crown action and inaction'. They give primacy to the right of indigenous people to exercise self-determination, and provide a compelling critique of the health inequalities in New Zealand and the racism that underlies our current situation. They conclude with a challenge to use the data to debate fundamental questions:

> [W]hat are the current and evolving health challenges facing Māori; what are the likely underlying causes; where (and how) should we intervene; what resources (human, financial and knowledge) are needed to improve Māori health outcomes and eliminate inequalities; and how should progress be monitored? (Reid & Robson 2007: 8)

'Data is king' is a colloquialism (and, contestably, an ungrammatical one at that) that recalls a truism from financial planning[2] and which I appropriate to my own purposes—that is, our ability to declaim that Māori are more likely than non-Māori to be arrested, more likely to be charged, more likely to be charged with serious offences, more likely to be found guilty, more likely to be sentenced to imprisonment (or equivalently disadvantaged at every step of the cancer journey or any number of other journeys through the health, housing, education, justice or corrections systems). Access to data—and especially access to our data—and our ability to analyse those data give us the resources to deconstruct such institutionalised racism. Indeed, our critical understanding is predicated on access to real, reliable, accurate data and robust analysis. Thus informed and resourced, we can resist and defy or reclaim and occupy—exercising a full range of responses in our struggle for equity.

The role of data in reducing inequities: examples and possibilities

Rheumatic fever

High rates of rheumatic fever, cellulitis and other preventable conditions affect Māori, Pacific and low socioeconomic populations in South Auckland (Wilson 2010; Vogel et al. 2013). This has significant costs to the individual, to families and communities and to the district

---

2   Of uncertain provenance and sometimes asserted as 'cash flow is king', it is a strident reminder to the business owner to pay close attention to managing income and expenditure (Lant 1991:48–56; Bremner 1995:37; The Economist 1995:80).

health board (DHB) and wider society. Research by Carapetis et al. (2005) shows that the median incidence of acute rheumatic fever (ARF) is more than three times higher among Pacific and indigenous populations in Australia and New Zealand than in any other region in the world (Figure 11.1).

The influential work of Jackson and Lennon (2011) on rheumatic fever in New Zealand from 1998 to 2010 showed that rheumatic fever rates vary by age, by ethnicity, by geography (in a north–south gradient) and by deprivation. Māori children have rates that are 47 times higher and Pacific children 69 times higher than non-Māori and non-Pacific children. Children living in the most socioeconomically deprived areas in the Auckland region (decile 9–10) have a 36 times higher rate of contracting rheumatic fever than children living in the least deprived areas (decile 1–2). The highest rates of ARF also occur in school years one to eight (ages 5–14), where the school has a low decile (1–2)[3] and high Māori or Pacific enrolment (Jackson & Lennon 2011).

There is also a strong link between household crowding and rheumatic fever (Jaine et al. 2011). Living in crowded housing conditions increases the transmission rates of a range of infectious conditions including Group A Streptococcal (GAS) throat infections. Structural crowding and functional overcrowding both contribute to rheumatic fever risk. Information from the 2006 census demonstrates the prevalence of structural household crowding (1+ bedroom deficit) is higher among the Māori (23 per cent) and Pacific (43 per cent) populations (Baker et al. 2012). In the Auckland metro area, the levels of crowding are higher than national levels, particularly for Pacific children and youth (Craig et al. 2012: 93).

Rheumatic fever prevention strategies were needed at three levels:

- Addressing social determinants of health, including interventions that address household crowding and raising community awareness.
- Improving access to primary care to treat GAS-positive sore throats, including school-based clinics to treat sore throats and health promotion messages and activities.

---

3   The areas of greatest socioeconomic disadvantage are those at the high end of the spatial deprivation scale (9–10). In contrast, the most deprived schools are those at the low end of the school decile ranking (1–2).

- Secondary prevention activities through the active provision of prophylactic antibiotics to reduce recurrent cases and rheumatic heart disease.

To address these prevention strategies, the NHC led the development of a comprehensive program that included 'Mana Kidz', a nurse-led school-based health service that has now been established in 61 primary and intermediate schools in South Auckland; 'Rapid Response' sore throat clinics in 16 secondary schools and 30 primary care clinics; and the Auckland Wide Healthy Homes Initiative (AWHI) to improve housing conditions (see AWHI 2014).

Rheumatic fever prevention: Mana Kidz

The NHC was awarded a Ministry of Health contract in 2012 to provide a nurse-led school-based rheumatic fever prevention program, Mana Kidz, which aimed to improve access to primary care, treat GAS-positive sore throats and skin infections and provide a comprehensive school health service. The design stages of the program were evidence informed by the work of the public health physicians at the Auckland Regional Public Health Service and the district health boards alongside clinical leadership from paediatricians.

Spatial analysis of cases by school location was critical for the design of the program that was funded by the Ministry of Health and the Counties Manukau District Health Board (see Counties Manukau District Health Board 2013). This analysis informed the deployment of a school-based comprehensive health service in 61 schools across the South Auckland region where Māori children are concentrated. Similar analysis either is not available in other districts or, where it is, does not indicate sufficient rate density distributed by school to warrant the deployment and investment required to support the school-based service model.

Critical contributions to the design and deployment of a program such as Mana Kidz have been the data collection, analysis and measures reporting. Through Mana Kidz, more than 25,000 children and *whānau* now have daily access to health services addressing skin infections and sore throat assessment and management. As of March 2015, 98 per cent of eligible children were given consent to join the program, over 21,000 GAS-positive sore throats were treated and a further 19,510 skin infections were treated (the majority through cleaning and covering and a smaller number with antibiotics).

Participation and progress are monitored via a regularly updated Mana Kidz scorecard (Figure 11.1), which ensures that children and *whānau* who test positive for GAS receive speedy treatment and that eligible families are referred to the AWHI for housing solutions to reduce the likelihood of developing rheumatic fever.

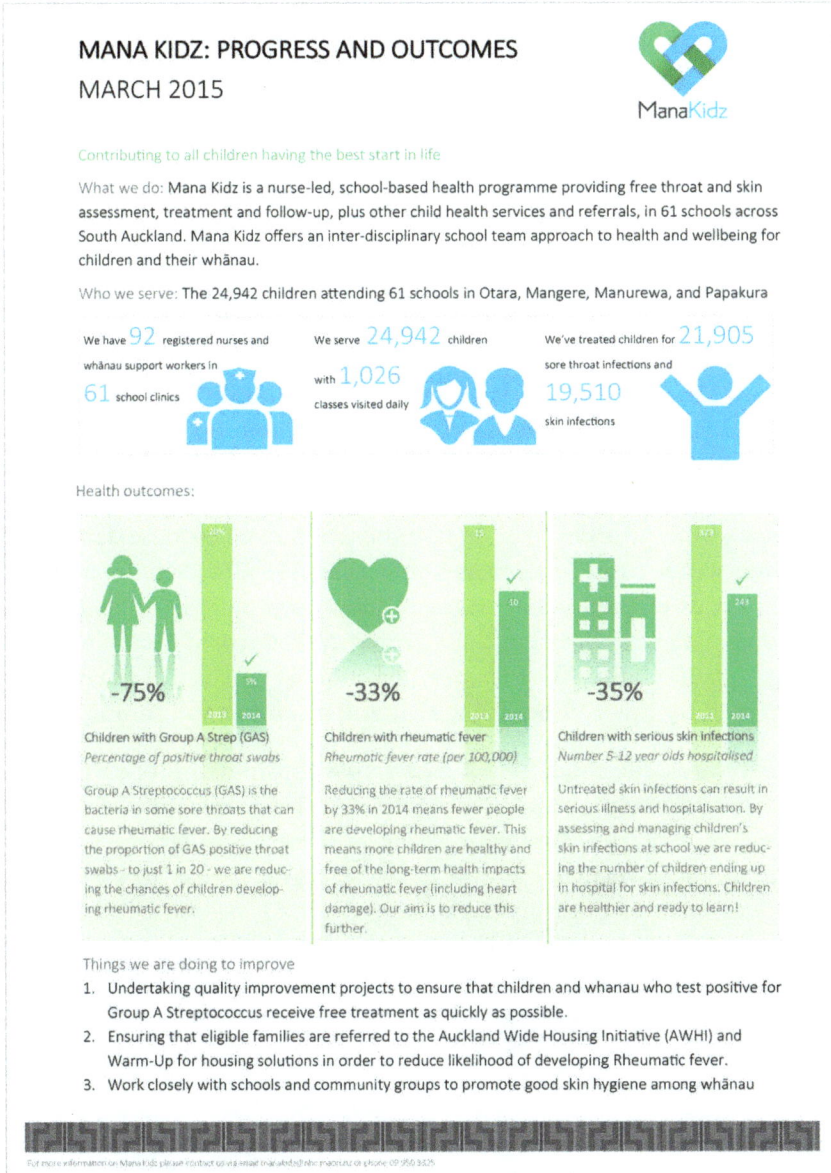

Figure 11.1 Mana Kidz data scorecard
Source: National Hauora Coalition, Auckland.

Rheumatic fever prevention: rapid response clinics

'Rapid Response (Sore Throat Management in Secondary Schools and Primary Care Clinics)' services more than 65,000 4–19-year-olds at high risk of rheumatic fever and provides free access to assessment and treatment of sore throats.

Similar to Mana Kidz, here data collection and analysis have informed the deployment and distribution of free primary care clinics delivering rapid response, nurse-led sore throat assessment and treatment clinics. The NHC developed and deployed the electronic forms to capture the activity in the rapid response clinics. This includes demographic data (age, gender, ethnicity, geocoded domicile, school attended) and clinical data (sore throat as the presenting complaint, weight, clinical signs including temperature and clinical assessment of the patient's throat, symptomatology including cough, prescription and medication supply). Related activity data are also collected including date and time of visits and laboratory data including lab request forms and lab results. Analysis of these linked data provides the project team with a rich picture and allows it to assess whether patient cohorts receiving the service align with the program's intention (by age, ethnicity and quintile).[4] The NHC regularly transmits these data to our provider clinics and funders as a scorecard. We also conduct analyses to inform us of the quality of the clinical services (tested against the National Heart Foundation Sore Throat Management Guideline) and the program quality (for instance, the number of clinical attendances completed by practitioner type or attendances versus funding).

In these ways, the collection of data across this network of 61 primary and secondary schools and 30 primary care clinics informs the ongoing management of the rheumatic fever prevention program. It allows the program governance group to drive performance, to strengthen the investment or to disinvest decisively.

---

4   The NZDep2006 index of socioeconomic deprivation uses a reduced five-point scale (quintiles), each of which collapses two deciles. That is, NZDep2006 values 9 and 10 are combined as quintile 5, which indicates the most deprived 20 per cent of the population for small areas (meshblocks or census area units) (White et al. 2008).

Rheumatic fever prevention: the AWHI

The NHC, with our partner, the OLA Coalition Limited,[5] has designed and established a regional housing hub that works with families who have a high risk of rheumatic fever. Our role is to connect people to local services and organisations that can help them to create healthy homes. We help families to develop their own housing plans and to increase housing literacy. At the heart of our approach is the recognition that supporting our families also means ensuring they have the skills to make better choices in the future in ways that are meaningful to them.

The eligibility criteria are very specific: children must have had a specific diagnosis from an admission to one of three Auckland hospitals[6] or three confirmed GAS throat infections in a three-month period, and the families must have income below set thresholds and have household crowding and more than one child in the household. The complexities should be obvious: the intention to provide a coordinated, customised and targeted service intervention for an eligible population through a complex intersection of clinical events and investigations, with income, housing and household membership characteristics. Construction of these datasets has been challenging— in terms of access to the data and in terms of concordance across datasets. This has led to a significant reduction in the numbers of families identified to receive the service interventions, from 3,000 per year to 1,600 per year.

The service interventions need to align with housing outcomes for families: measurable and reliable changes in circumstances for families to have warm, dry, safe homes. Overcrowding will have predictable drivers, including the obvious financial benefit from families sharing the costs of rent, power or food, and other cultural benefits of being connected with a wider family network, supportive interrelationships and alignment with traditional family customs. A housing literacy approach asserts that families are entitled to know and understand the risks and benefits of their living arrangements and make reasonable and rational decisions to manage those risks and maximise the benefits. The service interventions include insulation, heating, beds and

---

5   The OLA Coalition Limited is a joint-venture limited liability company 50 per cent owned by the NHC and 50 per cent owned by AllianceHealth Plus, an Auckland-based Pacific PHO.
6   www.starship.org.nz/media/259329/starship_30_july_nc_.pdf.

bedding and minor repairs (all of which address functional rather than structural overcrowding), housing entitlements and income assessments and Housing NZ fast-tracking (which addresses structural overcrowding).[7]

Noting the complex development issues in building the service delivery model, the program is now demonstrating outcomes for families. The data challenges in this include coordination across a network of eight nongovernmental organisation (NGO) providers and five major suppliers while neither suppliers nor providers share a single information technology (IT) platform. Nonetheless, a successful monitoring and reporting scorecard platform has been established, showing eligible referrals received by referral source, housing assessments undertaken and housing plans implemented according to housing outcomes (income, insulation, minor repairs, and so on)—all classifiable by Māori, Pacific and other ethnic status (Figure 11.2).

It is clear that data privacy complexities must be managed. Should the referring hospital service be entitled to know the result of the income benefit assessment or just that such an assessment was undertaken? A family living in an overcrowded house may decline to have the insulation provider involved because that may alert the landlord to, for example, overcrowding, which would represent a breach of the tenancy agreement and potentially lead to termination of tenancy. Again, control and use of the data have predictable risks and benefits, at an individual as well as a collective level.

The scorecards for the AWHI can quickly and effectively demonstrate data that show the number of families and their progress in the journey from referral through to interventions, and to follow-up months later. We use the scorecard to provide visibility of reliable, accurate data. For our provider network, this supports them to deliver high performance in terms of timeliness and quality. For referrers and funders, this supports them in knowing that the referred families are receiving interventions that are appropriate. Finally, and most importantly, *whānau* and communities need to see that the AWHI is delivering the appropriate interventions in a timely way and that

7   See the Housing New Zealand website: hnzc.co.nz/news/older-news-items/september-2013/rheumatic-fever-sas.

the interventions deliver durable changes in circumstances to the vulnerable families that we serve. Data—specifically our data (that is, data about us)—accessed and controlled by us, help us drive performance and deliver outcomes.

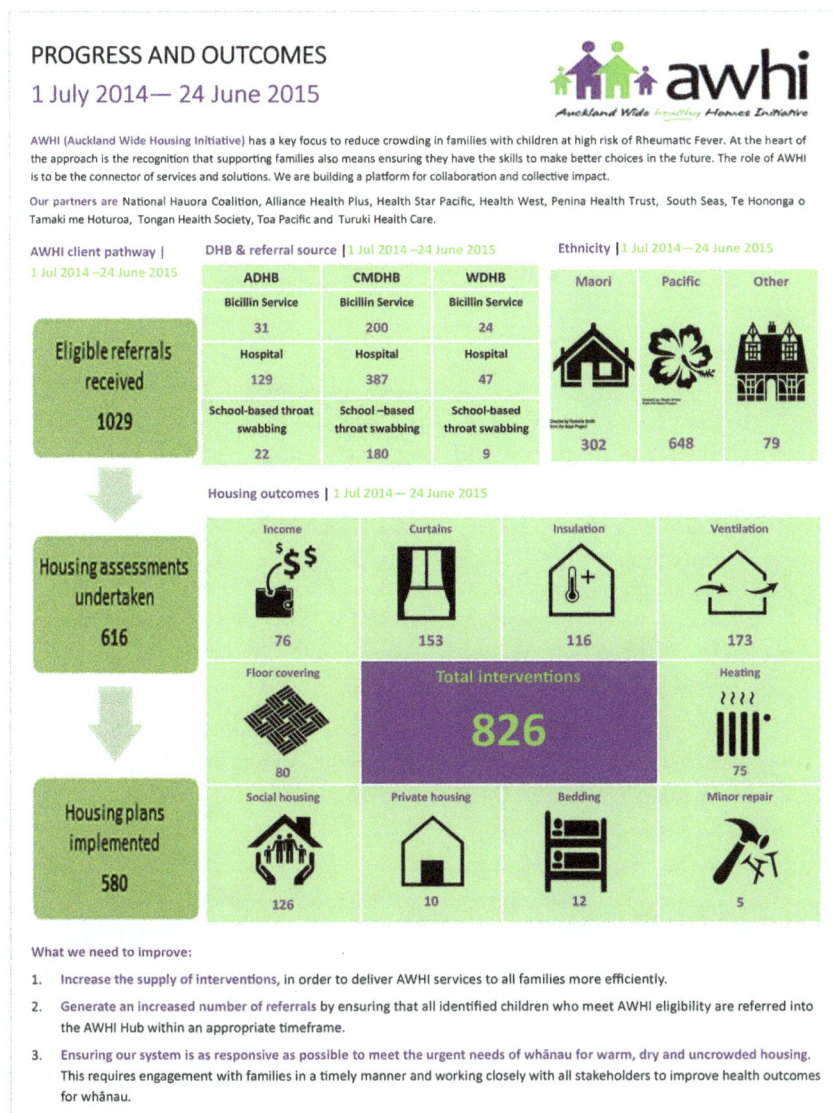

Figure 11.2 The AWHI data scorecard
Source: National Hauora Coalition, Auckland.

Cardiovascular disease

The NHC, as a PHO, has some 35 primary care clinics with 135,000 enrolled patients. Managing our data has been useful in focusing our provider network to deliver to our Māori enrolled population. Specifically, the NHC accesses and controls these data directly from our provider network; they are not mediated through a Crown agent or other intermediary.

Māori have a disproportionately higher rate of cardiovascular disease (CVD) than the rest of the population and a significant inequity of appropriate screening and management. CVD risk assessment is a national health target (NHT), and performance against this generates an incentive payment to the NHC (which is passed through to the provider network). Through the application of our own discretionary funding pool, the NHC provides incentives for the management of Māori with a CVD risk of 15 per cent or greater. This arrangement supports providers to undertake the CVD risk screening (contributing to their NHT performance and incentive payment) and then access CVD management funding. The rationale is that management (and not screening) is the driver of improved CVD outcomes. Real-time decision support is provided and real-time data are collected.

To facilitate this, Mōhio Forms (the NHC IT platform used nationally across the NHC provider network) delivers electronic claim forms with budget control, a dashboard with program and contact information, real-time data collection and reporting. Mōhio is available via the internet or within the patient management system where electronic forms are auto-populated. Data are validated as they are entered and claims are invoiced and budgets allocated in real time. When users submit the form, a receipt is provided and relevant health, process or claims data are written back to the patient management system. Mōhio Forms provides a rich data picture of the activity of our provider network in real time that allows us to drive performance and tailor direct and responsive feedback to the NHC provider network.

As with the Mana Kidz and AIHW platforms, the Mōhio dashboard visually presents data on the performance of individual health targets and can be disaggregated by ethnicity and detailed geography. It also displays the results of individual providers or by district or in aggregate across the NHC network. This output will be further developed to show performance by relative rate ratios (comparing the rates at which a health target is achieved by the provider for the Māori and non-Māori populations) as a measure of equity performance.

Once again, access, control and, in this case, ownership of our data are informing and resourcing us to identify rational responses to health inequities and to drive performance. Based on analysis of our health data, the NHC is able to deploy a tactical funding response to improving the service delivery of our provider network and is lifting performance in strategic interventions (such as CVD risk management, immunisations and cervical screening).[8]

Expanding access to primary care data: data-sharing protocols

In the previous section, I discussed some opportunities for using data over which we currently exercise control or access to inform our activities and interventions. The immediately adjacent space is to consider similar data that are held and controlled by other organisations active in primary care. This includes other PHOs and also Crown entities such as DHBs.

PHOs and DHBs have overlapping service delivery and accountability for health service planning. In Auckland, there are three DHBs and seven PHOs serving a population of over 1.3 million. Sharing data to inform health service planning, delivery and performance underpins a rational collaboration.[9] The Metro Auckland Data Stewardship Group (MADSG) has been formed to navigate the issues of health information use, management and privacy across the health system. A purpose–use matrix has been developed to provide the guidelines to support the need to share information to support the whole-of-system approach while maintaining patient privacy and professional confidentiality requirements.[10] PHOs and DHBs have jointly agreed to the following purposes as the basis of the purpose–use matrix:

---

8   For a detailed discussion on which interventions are likely to contribute to improved health outcomes or life expectancy (and why), please see Robson and Harris (2007).
9   Shared Health Information Privacy Framework Version 10, 20 June 2013. For a recent discussion of electronic shared care records, see: www.privacy.org.nz/assets/Files/Reports-to-ParlGovt/Electronic-Shared-Care-Records-Elements-of-Trust-report-1.pdf.
10   See Auckland District Health Board (2015).

- direct patient care
- clinical audit
- service management, monitoring and resource allocation
- planning and service development
- research.

The NHC is committed to improving health outcomes for Māori and other underserved populations, whether or not they are our enrolled patients. The data-sharing agreement suggests that a basis for examining data across the whole system is now possible and it is consistent with the overarching principles of quality and equity. For example, examining general practitioner (GP) utilisation data for patients seen in hospital emergency departments might uncover enrolment practices that disadvantage Māori. Examination of GP utilisation data and pharmaceutical prescribing and dispensing data may identify specific cohorts of patients who are underserved in CVD risk management or diabetes management or overprescribed reno-toxic medications for gout, and so on. The data are likely available and amenable to an equity analysis right now, but access to the data is currently proprietary—they are owned and held by autonomous and sometimes commercial health provider organisations. The governance organisations have agreed that the data-sharing protocols will enable the establishment of a Māori data-sharing governance framework. An indigenous data sovereignty framework such as this can provide opportunities for an equity analysis and, informed by such an analysis, we can resource appropriate interventions to deliver improved health equity.

Intersectoral data to deliver health equity: the education system and Māori doctors

Associated with the push for greater access to and control of our health data for use in addressing health inequities are the intersections that exist between health equity and the education system. I have been a member of Te Ohu Rata o Aotearoa (Māori Medical Practitioners Association) since I was a medical student and currently (and recurrently) serve on the board. To generate more Māori doctors, we need to examine the education journey for Māori, including the upstream delivery: the secondary school system. Unfortunately, many Māori students attend secondary schools that do not teach science to the National Certificate of Educational Achievement Level 3. And for those who do achieve that standard, we recruit many of them—and, questionably, too many of them—into medical undergraduate courses. Tactically, we should perhaps be trying to grow both Māori secondary science teachers and Māori doctors.

Further downstream, however, Aotearoa/New Zealand has achieved a remarkable feat:[11] to my knowledge, it is the only jurisdiction in the world to have achieved equitable per capita representation of indigenous students in medical undergraduate entry. Currently, some 15 per cent of the medical school intake into both Auckland and Otago schools of medicine are Māori, and it is reasonably expected that this proportion will continue.

Similarly, the Royal New Zealand College of General Practitioners (RNZCGP) is, to my knowledge, the first medical vocational college in any jurisdiction to establish an indigenous faculty (RNZCGP 2016). The Māori faculty of the RNZCGP is named after the first Māori doctor, the late Sir Maui Pomare, who graduated in 1899 from the Adventist Medical College in Chicago. Te Akoranga a Maui (the Māori faculty) has more than 100 Māori GPs networking throughout Aotearoa/New Zealand—predictably, involved in all aspects of recruiting, supporting and mentoring Māori doctors through their vocational training and in community health care settings.

Additionally, Māori GPs exert their influence across all aspects of the college's business, seeking to give a Māori voice and a Māori perspective to the curriculum and to the college's structures and leadership. One area of interest is accessing and using the data that the college collects about Māori patients through its activities. For instance, applicants for college fellowships are required to collect experience-of-care data from a sample of patients.[12] The patient questionnaire data collected from Māori patients might be analysed across all applicants or over time to illuminate some aspects of care provision for Māori. Similarly, the patient questionnaires that form part of the cornerstone accreditation

---

11   All credit to the two medical schools and their impressive Māori women leaders, Professor Papaarangi Reid and Associate Professor Joanne Baxter, who have resourced this achievement.
12   Better Practice Patient Questionnaire, see RNZCGP (2011: 19). The RNZCGP Better Practice Patient Questionnaire is available from the college in Māori, Samoan, Chinese and Korean.

process (by clinic provider, rather than by practitioner) should also yield some interesting information when disaggregated by ethnicity. Te Akoranga a Maui is currently asserting a Māori data governance role in those datasets. Access and control of Māori data held by the RNZCGP could inform training programs for GPs and GP registrars. Improving GP training programs can contribute to better primary care service delivery and to primary health care services that focus on delivering interventions to reduce inequities.

Conclusion

In this chapter, I have used examples from the health sector to discuss how indigenous data sovereignty in Aotearoa/New Zealand can contribute to Māori health outcomes and to health equity. The assertion that data sovereignty comes from our right to our data can be sourced from the Treaty of Waitangi and from the UNDRIP, to which Aotearoa/New Zealand is a signatory. For myself, working as a Māori health practitioner, in a Māori-led, *kaupapa*-driven organisation,[13] I assert that Māori sovereignty is informed by knowing about ourselves. Knowing who we are, where we are, what we do, when we do it, how we do it or how much we do what we do—all of the data that describe who we are are our data, and are likely to be useful and informative and amenable to our analysis.

Robson and Reid (2001) promoted the idea 15 years ago that data produced by the Crown should be at least as effective for Māori as for non-Māori. With other Māori health colleagues, they also argued persuasively that health surveys should be constructed consistent with the principle of 'equal explanatory power' (Te Rōpū Rangahau Hauora a Eru Pomare 2002). Those seminal papers have been hugely influential in the design of official surveys and have contributed to ensuring Māori data visibility. Data visibility has been a useful tool in monitoring the Crown (again, Robson & Reid 2001) and is especially relevant when considering official data. The next development—one that I think becomes explicit in the examples from this chapter— is data accessibility. The datasets that inform Mana Kidz sometimes sit in official sources (government ministries, DHBs and schools), but they

---

13   Kaupapa Māori health provision is based on a set of distinctively Māori principles and values. See, for example: rangahau.co.nz/research-idea/27/.

also sit in adjacent entities (private companies, commercial entities, PHOs and NGOs) that are funded by the Crown through the Ministry of Health or DHBs. It seems that we move up a hierarchy from data visibility and data accessibility to data sharing and data control. These are forms of data governance that, consistent with indigenous data sovereignty, can inform and resource Māori to influence, monitor and hold the health system to account for Māori health outcomes and for equity. Data sovereignty is more than holding the health system or the Crown to account. Māori sovereignty is informed by Māori data sovereignty.

References

Auckland District Health Board (2015). *Metro Auckland data sharing guideline, application of the information purpose–use matrix*, Auckland District Health Board, Auckland.

Auckland District Health Board (2014). *AWHI (Auckland Wide Healthy Homes Initiative) documentation*, Auckland District Health Board, Auckland.

Baker MG, Goodyear R, Telfar-Barnard L & Howden-Chapman P (2012). *The distribution of household crowding in New Zealand: an analysis based on 1991 to 2006 census data*, He Kainga Oranga/Housing and Health Research Programme, University of Otago, Wellington.

Bremner B (1995). Cash is king for corporate Japan. *Business Week*, 1 May 1995, bloomberg.com/news/articles/1995-04-30/cash-is-king-for-corporate-japan.

Carapetis JR, Steer AC, Mulholland EK & Weber M (2005). The global burden of group A streptococcal diseases. *Lancet Infectious Diseases* 5(11)(November):685–94.

Counties Manukau District Health Board (2013). *Shared health information privacy framework*, Ministry of Health, Auckland.

Craig E, Dell M, Reddington A, Adams J, Oben G, Wicken A & Simpson J (2012). *The determinants of health for children and young people in New Zealand*, Ministry of Health, Wellington.

Jackson C & Lennon D (2011). *Rheumatic fever in the Auckland regions 1998–2010: data from the rheumatic fever register*, Paediatric Infectious Diseases, Starship Children's Health & Auckland Regional Public Health Service, Auckland District Health Board, Auckland.

Jaine R, Baker M & Venugopal K (2011). Acute rheumatic fever associated with household crowding in a developed country. *Paediatric Infectious Diseases* 30(4)(April):315–19.

Lant J (1991). Cash is king. *Small Business Reports.*

Reid P & Robson B (2007). Understanding health inequities. In Robson R & Harris R (eds), *Hauora: Māori standards of health. IV: a study of the years 2000–2005*, Te Rōpū Rangahau Hauora a Eru Pōmare, Wellington.

Robson B & Reid, P (2001). *Ethnicity matters*, Statistics New Zealand, Wellington.

Robson R & Harris R (eds) (2007). *Hauora: Māori standards of health. IV: a study of the years 2000–2005*, Te Rōpū Rangahau Hauora a Eru Pōmare, Wellington.

Royal New Zealand College of General Practitioners (RNZCGP) (2011). *Aiming for excellence, RNZCGP standard for NZ general practice*, RNZCGP, Wellington.

Royal New Zealand College of General Practitioners (RNZCGP) (2016). Faculties & chapters, RNZCGP, Wellington, oldgp16.rnzcgp.org.nz/assets/documents/News--Events/WEBRGP-8115-Maori-strategy.pdf.

Salmond A (1991). *Two worlds: first meetings between Māori and Europeans, 1642–1772*, Viking, Auckland.

Te Rōpū Rangahau Hauora a Eru Pomare (2002). *Mana whamamārama: equal explanatory power—Māori and non-Māori sample size in national health surveys*, Ministry of Health, Wellington.

The Economist (1995). Where cash flow is king. *The Economist*, 18 February 1995.

Vogel AM, Lennon DR, Gray S, Farrell E & Anderson P (2013). Registered nurse assessment and treatment of skin sepsis in New Zealand schools: the development of protocols. *New Zealand Medical Journal* 126(1380):27–38.

White P, Gunston J, Salmond C, Atkinson J & Crampton P (2008). *Atlas of socioeconomic deprivation in New Zealand*, NZDep2006, Ministry of Health, Wellington.

Wilson N (2010). Rheumatic heart disease in indigenous populations: New Zealand experience. *Heart, Lung and Circulation* 19(5–6):282–8.

12

Aboriginal and Torres Strait Islander community wellbeing: identified needs for statistical capacity

Ray Lovett

Introduction

The ability of Aboriginal and Torres Strait Islander nations to inform and influence policy, program decisions and outcomes is heavily reliant on there being appropriate data to inform results and therefore direction. The cost to our nations, and to Australia broadly, of unreliable or inappropriate data in the area of Aboriginal and Torres Strait Islander health and wellbeing means that, at best, we progress little because of uncertainty about the direction in which to proceed. At worst, unreliable or inappropriate data lead to the perpetuation of ineffective policies and programs because our ability to assess their outcomes and effectiveness is limited.

In addition to concerns about the reliability and appropriateness of data, the manner of its collection, manipulation and reporting also causes great consternation among those of us who lament the inability of the questions on which statistical collections are based to reflect our individual and community realities. This need for data to reflect reality is what Walter and Andersen (2013) refer to as 'the cultural framework of Indigenous statistics'. At the national statistics office (NSO) level, there is seemingly a difficulty converting concepts into questions that capture meaningful data about important constructs that give Aboriginal and Torres Strait Islander lives meaning and value, despite having Indigenous advisory structures. The result is a large 'evidence gap' (see Walter, this volume).

Aboriginal and Torres Strait Islander people have observed the inability of NSOs (despite the advice) to progress in this area and have become disengaged or distrustful (Yu 2012). This concern is the likely result of previous experience in research broadly, such as concerns over who controls the process of question (data) development, sampling, data collection, data analysis, data interpretation (context) and reporting of those data. Calls for 'indigenous data sovereignty' stem from these historical legacies and point to a future where indigenous polities maintain, control and protect their data and resulting intellectual property (FNIGC 2007; UN 2007).

Some groups—both domestically and internationally—have turned to their own approaches in progressing what NSOs have been unable to do (Taylor et al. 2012; Nguyen & Cairney 2013). With this movement has come the assertion of data sovereignty (FNIGC 2007).

The primary way data sovereignty will be achieved in Australian Aboriginal and Torres Strait Islander health and wellbeing policy, program development and review processes is to have the statistical capacity within our population to build these data and to then better inform direction. In addition, we need to connect with non-Indigenous people with statistical capacity who are aware of the current concerns about the statistical construct of our lives and how some analyses are currently being conducted and reported to our detriment.

Unfortunately, there are no readily available data on how many Aboriginal and Torres Strait Islander people have the capacity to undertake statistical analysis and reporting, but proxy estimates suggest the situation is poor. While the focus of this chapter is on health and wellbeing statistics, it is important to recognise that statistical capacity and literacy within the Aboriginal and Torres Strait Islander population are required across all areas of social policy and analysis. Having said that, the building of statistical capacity is also a priority area of need for Australia more broadly (Goldacre 2011; BCA 2015).

This chapter is presented in two parts. The first part provides a brief historical overview of statistical collections of the Aboriginal and Torres Strait Islander peoples in Australia and then discusses why statistical capacity is important from an Indigenous perspective—specifically for the realisation of data sovereignty. It concludes by outlining what we currently know about this capacity. Part two provides an overview of current initiatives and approaches that are aimed at improving Indigenous statistical capacity. The chapter concludes with a proposed model for building statistical capacity via research processes using the first national longitudinal study of Aboriginal and Torres Strait Islander wellbeing: Mayi Kuwayu.

Statistical subject or the subject of statistics

The *Commonwealth of Australia Constitution Act 1901* mentions Aboriginal people in section 127: 'In reckoning the numbers of the people of the Commonwealth, or of a State or other part of the Commonwealth, aboriginal natives shall not be counted.' Despite the exclusion of 'full-blood' Aboriginal and Torres Strait Islander people from the Commonwealth census-based count of the Australian population, the states had been collecting or planning to collect data about the Aboriginal populations resident within them from the 1830s onwards (Cannon & MacFarlane 1982; Briscoe & Smith 2011).

The inclusion of Aboriginal and Torres Strait Islander people in census counting was one of the primary reasons for the *Constitution Alteration (Aboriginals) Act 1967* (the 1967 referendum). Due to the resulting changes to the constitution, Aboriginal and Torres Strait Islander people have been included in the Australian census as a self-identified population from 1971 (CBCS 1972). The counting of Indigenous people in Australia has since flowed through to many other government administrative data collections including hospitals (AIHW 2011a), death and cancer registers (AIHW 2015) and immunisation registers (Centre for Indigenous Health 2004), among others, with a guideline produced to assist (AIHW 2010). More recent developments have included pathology and infectious disease notifications.

These collections are important for the same reasons they are important for the entire population—for example, in planning services and in developing policy. But there have been and continue to be complex issues with administrative data that are influenced by a wide range of factors such as systematic racism and a lack of indices reflecting factors that are important to Aboriginal and Torres Strait Islander people (Paradies et al. 2008; Walter & Andersen 2013). The Australian Bureau of Statistics (ABS) has examined factors affecting reporting of Indigenous status in statistical collections using focus groups. It found that the reliability of Aboriginal and Torres Strait Islander data was negatively affected by the purpose of the data collection, who is conducting it (researchers, government or community organisation) and the mode of collection (ABS 2012). These focus groups also identified that Aboriginal and Torres Strait Islander peoples are less likely to participate in studies and data collections if the data are utilised to create a homogenous Indigenous population and where the analysis portrays Indigeneity as problematic in the manner described by Fforde et al. (2013).

The political, media and social climates can be significant factors in the reliability of Indigenous administrative data. A recent workshop on factors influencing Aboriginal and Torres Strait Islander identification in administrative data discussed how key national events might shape changes in identification:

> Positive events that may have influenced the number of people identifying as Indigenous were the Mabo High Court decision in 1992 and the National Apology to the Stolen Generations in 2008. Negative events that seemed to have some influence include the Northern Territory Emergency Response that was rolled out in 2007. Concerns were raised about the next census and the negative symbolism of the current events in Western Australia with the proposed forced closure of many Aboriginal communities. The effects of these events are amplified through media coverage. Participants noted that media can be a barrier to identification by reinforcing internalised racism but also as strength when positive stories are told well. (Nous Group 2015: 2)

Indigenous national engagement with statistical agencies

Both the ABS and the Australian Institute of Health and Welfare (AIHW) have Indigenous engagement processes for their statistical collections. The ABS has an Aboriginal and Torres Strait Islander Demographic Statistics Expert Advisory Group, which has been tasked with providing technical advice and guidance on methodological issues relating to the ABS program of Aboriginal and Torres Strait Islander demographic statistics and advising on communication and engagement strategies (ABS 2011). The most recent meeting notes available online from this group are for December 2011. On examination of the appointment requirements for the advisory group, participants must have 'knowledge of demographic statistics, in particular their technical expertise'. This appears to be limiting given what we know about this expertise among the Aboriginal and Torres Strait Islander population, particularly where it also states that appointees are to have 'knowledge and understanding of the culture and needs of Aboriginal and Torres Strait Islander Peoples' (ABS 2011). It is hard to assess whether the advisory group is meeting its aims, as there is no reference to whom it is advising or whether this advice is being taken up.

The AIHW, in conjunction with the ABS, also administers the National Advisory Group on Aboriginal and Torres Strait Islander Health Information and Data (NAGATSIHID). The main role of NAGATSIHID is to provide strategic advice to the Australian Health Ministers Advisory Council (AHMAC) on Indigenous health data issues. NAGATSIHID has specific responsibility to 'advise and advocate on improving the quality of Indigenous health information and advise on the use of Indigenous health information' (AIHW 2011b). One of the highlighted features of NAGATSIHID is that it has majority Aboriginal and Torres Strait Islander membership drawn from across the different fields of research and teaching, service provision and policy. While an AHMAC member chairs the group, for any decisions, an Indigenous quorum needs to be present (AIHW 2011b).

Common to both structures is the somewhat limiting ability to 'advise', not direct. In addition, the accountability mechanisms for advice provided by membership of both structures are not detailed. While noting the inherent problem of limited statistical capacity, neither structure allows Aboriginal or Torres Strait Islander chairmanship of the advisory structure despite there being greater capacity now than at any time before. Therein lies the problem: with greater Indigenous engagement in these advisory structures comes the advice regarding what Walter and Andersen (2013) call 'the guiding quantitative methodology', and this often conflicts with existing statistical frameworks. Having Aboriginal and Torres Strait Islander voices in the discourse surrounding statistical methodologies now, more than at any time before, has the potential to cause conflict or improve the path forward, depending on your view.

The cultural context of health and wellbeing statistics

There are two main reasons for communicating to Aboriginal and Torres Strait Islander people why statistical capacity is important in our population. The first concerns the current data from the *Overcoming Indigenous Disadvantage* (*OID*) report, which tell us that only one indicator is improving and, overall, 'the gap' is not closing (SCRGSP 2014). The health and wellbeing of Aboriginal and Torres Strait Islander peoples continue to be the poorest in Australia (AIHW 2014). Despite this, and despite the consequences of two centuries of colonisation, Aboriginal culture and values remain strong; yet this fact would not be known from reading the *OID* report. These strengths are considered to be just as important and significant to Aboriginal and Torres Strait Islander people, and they are what should be influencing the statistical agenda (see Bishop, this volume).

Thus, a major barrier to the effective measurement of Aboriginal and Torres Strait Islander health and wellbeing is the lack of a relevant evidence base for factors that Aboriginal and Torres Strait Islander peoples themselves consider important, resulting in the application to data collection of underlying assumptions that other Australians apply to Aboriginal and Torres Strait Islander people. Moreover, there is a lack of integration into data analysis of culture, cultural practices and experiences. Features of the cultural landscape and Aboriginal experience that are highlighted as negatively impacting on wellbeing include exposure to racism, exclusion, marginalisation and negative identity formation (Daniel et al. 2011). The limited available data indicate that there may be relationships between 'on country' practices and risk factors, and that people with a 'strong' sense of identity and higher levels of attachment to culture are happier and display better mental health (Dockery 2011). Hence, interventions devised on the basis of standard evidence lack integration with evidence regarding key dimensions that are central to Aboriginal and Torres Strait Islander health and wellbeing—dimensions that are critical to the effectiveness and acceptability of data.

The problem, then, is not so much with gap analysis in and of itself, but rather how we measure and collect data on gaps. We accept that we need to understand what is sustaining the lack of change in key outcomes such as education and employment (upstream indicators) and headline indicators such as life expectancy, but there remain a number of key systemic limitations to the existing framework. In particular, there appears to be an unwillingness to move to more distal levels of measurement and analysis. We seem content to know that we are not reaching equality in educational outcomes, for example, but are unwilling to find out what distal factors may be contributing. These factors are acknowledged in policy reports (Australian Government 2013: 9; SCRGSP 2014: 85), but there appears to be no movement on how these 'data gaps' might be resolved. The fear might be that policies need to focus on the very things current approaches are avoiding: social and cultural differences. What of the distal indicator of a strong connection to mob and country showing a positive correlation with reductions in cardiovascular disease outcomes (Rowley et al. 2008)? Based on this finding and from this perspective, the policy shift would surely need to be cultural strengthening not closure of communities. Local and international literature on the subject of Aboriginal and Torres Strait Islander, Māori and other First Nations groups propose measures that are consistent with indigenous conceptions of wellbeing. These conceptions include:

- relationships with country, spirituality and rituals (Assembly of First Nations 2002; Burgess et al. 2008; Ganesharajah 2009; Prout 2011; Knibb-Lamouche 2012)
- identity and identity representation and racism (Chandler et al. 2003; Henry et al. 2004; Hallett et al. 2007; Paradies et al. 2008; Reading & Wien 2009; Cunningham & Paradies 2012; Fforde et al. 2013; Zubrick et al. 2014)
- heritage and language (Chandler et al. 2003; Hallett et al. 2007; Reading & Wien 2009)
- agency, self-determination, empowerment, fate and control (Hallett et al. 2007; Reading & Wien 2009; Larsen et al. 2010; Knibb-Lamouche 2012; Taylor et al. 2012)

- cultural continuity (Assembly of First Nations 2002; Chandler et al. 2003; Reading & Wien 2009; Knibb-Lamouche 2012).

These themes address many of the current concerns that indigenous peoples have with contemporary epidemiological approaches to illness measurement in that they are mostly positively focused and are applicable at the local community level as well as at individual and national levels.

The 2008 National Aboriginal and Torres Strait Islander Social Survey (NATSISS) included Aboriginal and Torres Strait Islander community and expert workshops to inform indicators of community wellbeing included in the final survey. To date, only one analysis has examined the 2008 NATSISS data on the relationship between these 'holistic' measures and wellbeing (Dockery 2011), with the results showing that greater participation in cultural events and activities was associated with better mental wellbeing.

There were differences between the results when analysed by rurality in that the positive affects of cultural identity, language use and traditional economic activities accrued mostly within remote areas. Associations between these attributes and greater psychological distress appeared to apply only in nonremote areas. It is hypothesised that this is related to the notion of 'living between cultures' (Dockery 2011: 14) and further evidence of this phenomenon is evident through experiences of racism. Both nonremote and remote groups reported similar rates of exposure to racism overall, but the stronger a non-remote Aboriginal person's identity became, the more likely they were to experience racism in the preceding 12 months (up to 41 per cent) (Dockery 2011).

This work is the first in Australia to empirically demonstrate that Indigenous culture 'should be maintained and leveraged as a solution to Aboriginal and Torres Strait Islander disadvantage, rather than being seen as the problem' (Dockery 2011: 3). It therefore supports the view that Aboriginal and Torres Strait Islander people must be afforded influence over the statistical agenda and, if this is to be revised, improved and managed in a way that is consistent with Aboriginal and Torres Strait Islander values, Aboriginal and Torres Strait Islander people need to be front and centre in any related decision-making process. A related need is to enhance Indigenous statistical capacity.

What do we mean by Indigenous statistical capacity?

Statistics is a form of mathematical analysis involving the use of quantified representations, models and summaries for a given set of empirical data or real-world observations. Statistical analysis involves the process of collecting and analysing data and then summarising the data into numerical format. There are two elements to statistical capacity. The first is having the relevant training in methods and approaches to appropriately inform the compilation of statistics. The second concerns the 'frame of view' used in preparing the questions we seek to answer; this also invariably informs the *way* we analyse and report data—the way we give it meaning (Walter & Andersen 2013; Walter, this volume). This second aspect is critical to understanding how we engage in the measurement of Aboriginal and Torres Strait Islander health and wellbeing in Australia.

Capacity describes an ability to do something. In this sense, then, Aboriginal and Torres Strait Islander statistical capacity is the ability of Aboriginal and Torres Strait Islander people to perform mathematical analysis involving the use of quantified representations, models and summaries for a given set of empirical data or real-world observations within a frame of view that gives the data meaning to our nations and peoples. This frame of view constitutes how the world around us is connected. For Aboriginal people, this includes the centrality of family connections (mob), our connection to country or countries and the stories that maintain those links with family and country. Family and country are crucial as, without these, connection is limited or lost. Importantly, these elements endure across the country and across the statistical classifications of remote, regional and urban. Operationalising these concepts requires those with this frame of view to be at the forefront of question design and analysis.

School-based statistical capacity

The foundation of statistics is mathematics. Every three years Australian students participate in the Programme for International Student Assessment (PISA), which measures three educational outcomes—literacy in: mathematics, science and reading. In 2012, about 14,500 Australian 15-year-olds participated in PISA, including

1,991 Indigenous students from across urban, regional and remote settings. The 2012 PISA results for mathematical literacy indicated that Indigenous students were more than 2.5 years behind their non-Indigenous peers and that these results were particularly stark compared with those for reading and science (Dreise & Thomson 2014). Consistently, we see education outcome reports identify a growing inequality of educational outcomes between Indigenous and other students as they move through the school years; and this gap has been growing for some time (Mellor & Corrigan 2004).

Previous research has identified that methods of teaching primary mathematics can be ineffective for Aboriginal students because they are not related to their world and everyday experiences (Matthews et al. 2007). This results in alienation from maths in the later years of primary school (Matthews et al. 2003). It is encouraging, then, to see an increasing use of more novel approaches to primary and secondary school teaching of maths (AAMT 2015). This includes projects such as 'Maths as Story Telling' (MAST), a teaching approach designed to assist Indigenous students in their understanding of algebra through the creation and manipulation of their own symbols for equations (Matthews et al. 2007; Ewing et al. 2010). Coincidentally, issues with data integrity have meant results have not been released, although some sites have reported positive outcomes at the student and school levels (AAMT 2013).

There is also a range of other high school statistical and mathematics programs that are designed to engage students in statistics. These include the Statistical Society of Australia National Secondary Schools Poster Competition and the Commonwealth Scientific and Industrial Research Organisation Mathematics in Schools project (CSIRO 2014; SSA 2014). While these programs are available, there are no data on their uptake by Aboriginal and Torres Strait Islander students or by specific schools.

Tertiary and further education–based statistical capacity

In the vocational education and training (VET) sector, statistical training is usually embedded within broader mathematics programs (TAFE NSW 2015). These are generalist programs and provide the basic requirements of mathematics for statistical concepts and are relatively common across Australia. Data about the number of Aboriginal and Torres Strait Islander students enrolled in and completing these courses (and units) are limited due to reliability issues. As for the university sector, some courses at the undergraduate level teach research methods including quantitative analysis (sociology, economics and psychology, for example), however, access to data concerning Aboriginal and Torres Strait Islander enrolment and completions requires a specific request to the Department of Education (only aggregated broadly themed data are available on their website). Advanced statistics training is undertaken in specialist postgraduate teaching and research programs in the disciplines of epidemiology, public health, biostatistics, demography, econometrics and psychology. These courses are less common throughout the country and access to enrolment data for Aboriginal and Torres Strait Islander students is limited and the data are unreliable due to the variable recording of Indigenous status at enrolment. The Statistical Society of Australia lists seven accredited statistics courses across 10 universities, keeping in mind there are other courses that provide education in statistics (SSA 2015).

A successful higher education model?

The National Centre of Epidemiology and Population Health (NCEPH) at The Australian National University (ANU) has been running a Field Epidemiology Training Program (FETP) for the past 20 years. The MPhil (Applied Epidemiology), previously the Master of Applied Epidemiology (MAE), is a two-year research degree that emphasises learning-by-doing. The program teaches epidemiology through coursework and learning in a field placement, such as with a health department. The MPhil (Applied Epidemiology) is Australia's only FETP and is part of the international network of Field Training Programs in Epidemiology & Public Health Interventions Network. The program has been extremely successful both as a field-based training program and for the high proportion of Aboriginal and Torres Strait Islander graduates (about 30 of the total of more than 150 graduates) as a result of introducing a specific Indigenous training commitment in 1998 (Guthrie et al. 2011). In 2010 funding from the Australian Government Department of Health and Ageing, which had been responsible for the growth in Master of Public Health degrees across the country, was withdrawn (Lin et al. 2009). This had a severe impact on the MAE as the funds were no longer available to support the students' living expenses (a stipend) and, although the field-based training element remained, the host organisations are now required to find upwards of $50,000 each year to host a student. These changes came despite compelling arguments for the program's continuation, including the potential detrimental impact on statistical and epidemiological capacity (Guthrie et al. 2011).

Inclusion of statistical capacity in research programs: Mayi Kuwayu

As with international examples (Assembly of First Nations 2002; Larsen et al. 2010), the idea for the first national longitudinal study of Aboriginal and Torres Strait Islander wellbeing, Mayi Kuwayu, was born out of concern about the absence of constructs that are important to Aboriginal and Torres Strait Islander peoples' wellbeing in existing administrative data (Lovett et al. 2015). While the study is still in the early development phase, built into the proposal is the establishment of a community-based statistical capacity-building program, which will be developed between three Aboriginal and Torres Strait Islander peak research and community groups and The Australian National University. The program aims to run a residential-based short course in quantitative methods among staff working within Aboriginal and Torres Strait Islander health services. Given the number of these services across the country, the pool of participants is potentially large. The aim is to provide the administrative and Aboriginal and Torres Strait Islander health staff with statistical skills that will enable them to collect, prepare, analyse and report their own service data in ways that are meaningful to their service and the community. This capacity-building program was written into the research proposal as a result of the research team seeing community-based organisations, including Aboriginal and Torres Strait Islander health services, struggle with their electronic databases. The opportunity to assist in the building of statistical capacity so that data can be used for advocacy and resourcing enables the research team to meet a need that will have tangible and sustained benefits for individuals and organisations, as required by National Health and Medical Research Council ethical guidelines (NHMRC 2003).

Conclusion

There has been slow progress in developing statistics that are conceptualised from an Aboriginal and Torres Strait Islander 'frame of view'. This is likely a result of the poor level of statistical capacity and the restrictive processes of defining wellbeing indicators to date. Statistical capacity has the potential to enhance the development of indices relevant to Aboriginal and Torres Strait Islander people's lives from our frame of view, and to position us at the table to assert data sovereignty. These new data will give Aboriginal and Torres Strait Islander peoples and nations the power to demonstrate to individuals, institutions, communities and governments evidence for the development of policy and programs.

Greater direct engagement in the conceptualisation, design and data collection, analysis and reporting will enable more meaningful information to be provided to policymakers and also enable communities to engage in a circular process whereby they are able to welcome the benefits of data collection and analysis, leading to more open discourse about the information needed to inform the evidence base. To ensure there is enhanced statistical capacity within our nations, mathematics education and statistical training that encompass direct relevance to our world views and ways of being are required. Programs such as the MPhil Epidemiology program and other community-based statistical capacity-building programs have the potential to facilitate statistical capacity and need to be supported. As well as these programs assisting with statistical capacity, they will also help to develop quantitative indicators of wellbeing from an Aboriginal and Torres Strait Islander frame of view. The combination of capacity and frame of view will then influence Indigenous data sovereignty.

References

Assembly of First Nations (2002). *Community health indicators: second year of the project*, Institute of the Environment, Ottawa.

Australian Association of Mathematics Teachers (AAMT) (2013). *Make it count: numeracy, mathematics and Indigenous learners project summary*, AAMT, Adelaide, mic.aamt.edu.au/Resources/Make-It-Count-2009-2012/Publications-and-statements.

Australian Association of Mathematics Teachers (AAMT) (2015). *Make it count: maths and indigenous learners*, AAMT, Adelaide, mic.aamt. edu.au/.

Australian Bureau of Statistics (ABS) (2011). *Aboriginal and Torres Strait Islander Demographic Statistics Expert Advisory Group terms of reference*, ABS, Canberra, abs.gov.au/websitedbs/ c311215.nsf/88e17471717cdbc5ca25778a001d9500/0a906fcb6f13c 76dca257a93001f7bcc/$FILE/Terms%20of%20Reference.pdf.

Australian Bureau of Statistics (ABS) (2012). *Perspectives on Aboriginal and Torres Strait Islander identification in selected data collection contexts*, Cat. no. 4726.0, ABS, Canberra.

Australian Government (2013). *National Aboriginal and Torres Strait Islander health plan (NATSIHP) 2013–2023*, Department of Health and Ageing, Canberra.

Australian Institute of Health and Welfare (AIHW) (2010). *National best practice guidelines for collecting Indigenous status in health data sets*, AIHW, Canberra, aihw.gov.au/WorkArea/DownloadAsset. aspx?id=6442458760.

Australian Institute of Health and Welfare (AIHW) (2011a). *The health and welfare of Australia's Aboriginal and Torres Strait Islander people: an overview, 2011*, AIHW, Canberra.

Australian Institute of Health and Welfare (AIHW) (2011b). *National advisory group on Aboriginal and Torres Strait Islander health information and data: strategic plan 2010–2015*, AIHW, Canberra.

Australian Institute of Health and Welfare (AIHW) (2014). *Australia's health 2014*, AIHW, Canberra.

Australian Institute of Health and Welfare (AIHW) (2015). *Australian burden of disease study: fatal burden of disease in Aboriginal and Torres Strait Islander people 2010*, Australian Burden of Disease Study, Series 2. Cat. no. BOD 2, AIHW, Canberra.

Biostatisticians Collaboration of Australia (BCA) (2015). *About the BCA*, BCA, Sydney, bca.edu.au/aboutbca.html.

Briscoe G & Smith L (2011). *Australian Aboriginal census, 1921–1944*, Australian Social Science Data Archive, The Australian National University, Canberra, Dataset ID:au.edu.anu.ada.ddi.20002-nsw.

Burgess C, Berry H, Gunthorpe W & Bailie R (2008). Development and preliminary validation of the 'Caring for Country' questionnaire: measurement of an Indigenous Australian health determinant. *International Journal for Equity in Health* 7(26).

Cannon M & MacFarlane I (eds) (1982). *The Aborigines of Port Phillip, 1835–1839*, Victorian Government Printing Office, Melbourne.

Centre for Indigenous Health (2004). *Needs analysis of immunisation for Aboriginal and Torres Strait Islander people in Queensland: general practitioner survey of Indigenous immunisation issues*, Centre for Indigenous Health, University of Queensland, Brisbane.

Chandler MJ, Lalonde CE, Sokol B & Hallett D (2003). *Personal persistence, identity development, and suicide: a study of native and non-native North American adolescents*, Monographs of the Society for Research in Child Development Vol. 68, Wiley-Blackwell, Boston & Oxford.

Commonwealth Bureau of Census and Statistics (CBCS) (1972). *Official year book of the Commonwealth of Australia*, No. 58, CBCS, Canberra.

Commonwealth Scientific and Industrial Research Organisation (CSIRO) (2014). *Mathematicians in schools*, CSIRO, Canberra, mathematiciansinschools.edu.au/.

Cunningham J & Paradies YC (2012). Socio-demographic factors and psychological distress in Indigenous and non-Indigenous Australian adults aged 18–64 years: analysis of national survey data. *BMC Public Health* 12(95), doi:10.1186/1471-2458-12-95.

Daniel M, Lekkas P & Cargo M (2011). Environments and cardiometabolic diseases in Aboriginal populations. *Heart, Lung and Circulation* 19(5):306–15, doi:10.1016/j.hlc.2010.01.005.

Dockery AM (2011). *Traditional culture and the wellbeing of Indigenous Australians: an analysis of the 2008 NATSISS*, CLMR Discussion Paper 2011/01, Centre for Labour Market Research, Curtin Business School, Curtin University, Perth.

Dreise T & Thomson S (2014). *Unfinished business: PISA shows Indigenous youth are being left behind*, ACER Occasional Essay, February 2014, Australian Council for Educational Research, Melbourne.

Ewing B, Cooper T, Baturo A, Matthews C & Sun H (2010). Contextualising the teaching and learning of measurement within Torres Strait Islander schools. *Australian Journal of Indigenous Education* 39:11–23.

Fforde C, Bamblett L, Lovett R, Gorringe S & Fogarty B (2013). Discourse, deficit and identity: Aboriginality, the race paradigm and the language of representation in contemporary Australia. *Media International Australia Incorporating Culture and Policy* 149:162–73.

First Nations Information Governance Centre (FNIGC) (2007). *OCAP: ownership, control, access and possession, sanctioned by the First Nations Information Governance Committee*, Assembly of First Nations, National Aboriginal Health Organization, Ottawa.

Ganesharajah C (2009). *Indigenous health and wellbeing: the importance of country*, Native Title Research Report No. 1/2009, Australian Institute of Aboriginal and Torres Strait Islander Studies, Canberra.

Goldacre B (2011). The statistical error that just keeps on coming. *The Guardian*, 10 September 2011, theguardian.com/commentisfree/2011/sep/09/bad-science-research-error.

Guthrie J, Dance P, Kelly P, Lokuge K, McPherson M & Faulkner S (2011). Public health capacity development through Indigenous involvement in the Master of Applied Epidemiology program: celebrations and commiserations. *Australian Aboriginal Studies* 2011(2):102–10.

Hallett D, Chandler MJ & Lalonde CE (2007). Aboriginal language knowledge and youth suicide. *Cognitive Development* 22:392–9.

Henry BR, Houston S & Mooney GH (2004). Institutional racism in Australian healthcare: a plea for decency. *Medical Journal of Australia* 180(10):517–20.

Knibb-Lamouche J (2012). Culture as a social determinant of health: examples from native communities, Paper prepared for the Roundtable on the Promotion of Health Equity and the Elimination of Health Disparities, Institute on Medicine, Seattle, 14 November 2012.

Larsen JN, Schweitzer P & Fondahl G (eds) (2010). *Arctic social indicators: a follow-up to the Arctic Human Development Report*, Nordic Council of Ministers, Copenhagen.

Lin V, Watson R & Oldenburg B (2009). The future of public health: the importance of workforce. *Australia and New Zealand Health Policy* 9(6):4, doi:10.1186/1743-8462-6-4.

Lovett R, Banks E, Chapman J & Strelein L (2015). *Development of the first national Aboriginal and Torres Strait Islander longitudinal study of wellbeing: research proposal*, Unpublished report, The Australian National University and the Australian Institute of Aboriginal and Torres Strait Islander Studies, Canberra, aiatsis.gov.au/mayi-kuwayu.

Matthews C, Cooper TJ & Baturo AR (2007). Creating your own symbols: beginning algebraic thinking with indigenous students, Paper presented at the 31st Annual Conference of the International Group for the Psychology of Mathematics Education, Seoul, 8–13 July 2007, eprints.qut.edu.au/14627/.

Matthews S, Howard P & Perry JR (2003). Working together to enhance Australian Aboriginal students' mathematics learning. In Bragg L, Campbell C, Herbert G & Mousley J (eds), *Mathematics education research: innovation, networking, opportunity. Proceedings of the 26th Annual Conference of the Mathematics Education Research Group of Australasia, Deakin University, Geelong, 6–10 July 2003*, MERGA, Geelong, Vic.

Mellor S & Corrigan M (2004). *The case for change: a review of contemporary research on Indigenous education outcomes*, Australian Council for Educational Research, Melbourne, research.acer.edu.au/cgi/viewcontent.cgi?article=1006&context=aer.

National Health and Medical Research Council (NHMRC) (2003). *Values and ethics: guidelines for ethical conduct in Aboriginal and Torres Strait Islander health research (values and ethics)*, NHMRC, Canberra.

Nguyen O & Cairney S (2013). *Literature review of the interplay between education, employment, health and wellbeing for Aboriginal and Torres Strait Islander people in remote areas: working towards an Aboriginal and Torres Strait Islander wellbeing framework*, CRC-REP Working Paper CW013, Ninti One Limited, Alice Springs, NT.

Nous Group (2015). *Understanding Aboriginal and Torres Strait Islander identification: draft workshop report*, Nous Group, Canberra.

Paradies Y, Harris R & Anderson I (2008). *The impact of racism on Indigenous health in Australia and Aotearoa: towards a research agenda*, CRCAH Discussion Paper Series No. 4, Cooperative Research Centre for Aboriginal Health and Flinders University, Adelaide.

Prout S (2011). Indigenous wellbeing frameworks in Australia and the quest for quaification. *Social Indicators Research* 109(2):317–36.

Reading CL & Wien F (2009). *Health inequalities and social determinants of Aboriginal peoples' health*, National Collaborating Centre for Aboriginal Health, Prince George, British Columbia.

Rowley KG, O'Dea K, Anderson I, McDermott R, Saraswati K, Tilmouth R & Brown A (2008). Lower than expected morbidity and mortality for an Australian Aboriginal population: 10-year follow-up in a decentralised community. *Medical Journal of Australia* 188(5):283–7.

Statistical Society of Australia (SSA) (2014). *SSA national secondary schools poster competition*, SSA, Canberra, www.ssaipostercomp.info/:SSAI.

Statistical Society of Australia (SSA) (2015). *Accredited university courses in statistics 2015*, SSA, Canberra, statsoc.org.au/careers-accreditation/professional-accreditation/accredited-courses/.

Steering Committee for the Review of Government Service Provision (SCRGSP) (2014). *Overcoming Indigenous disadvantage: key indicators 2014*, Productivity Commission, Canberra.

TAFE NSW (2015). *Mathematics and science for further study*, TAFE NSW, Sydney, tafensw.edu.au/course/10222NAT-01V01-15WCN-002/mathematics-and-science-for-further-study.

Taylor J, Doran B, Parriman M & Yu E (2012). *Statistics for community governance: the Yawuru Indigenous population survey of Broome*, CAEPR Working Paper No. 82/2012, Centre for Aboriginal Economic Policy Research, The Australian National University, Canberra.

United Nations (UN) (2007). *United Nations declaration on the rights of indigenous peoples*, General Assembly Resolution 61/295, 13 September 2007, United Nations, New York.

Walter M & Andersen C (2013). *Indigenous statistics: a quantitative research methodology*, Left Coast Press, Walnut Creek, CA.

Yu P (2012). *The power of data in Aboriginal hands*, CAEPR Topical Issue 2012/4, Centre for Aboriginal Economic Policy Research, The Australian National University, Canberra, caepr.anu.edu.au/Publications/topical/2012TI4.php.

Zubrick S, Dudgeon P, Gee G, Glaskin B, Kelly K, Paradies Y & Walker R (2014). Social determinants of Aboriginal and Torres Strait Islander social and emotional wellbeing. In Dudgeon P, Milroy H & Walker R (eds), *Working together: Aboriginal and Torres Strait Islander mental health and wellbeing principles and practice*, 2nd edn, Telethon Kids Institute, Perth, aboriginal.telethonkids.org.au/media/699863/Working-Together-Book.pdf.

13

Data sovereignty for the Yawuru in Western Australia

Mandy Yap and Eunice Yu[1]

Introduction

A report by the United Nations (UN) Secretary-General's Independent Expert Advisory Group on the data revolution for sustainable development suggests:

> Data are the lifeblood of decision making and the raw material for accountability. Without high-quality data providing the right information on the right trend, at the right time, designing, monitoring and evaluating effective policies becomes almost impossible. (Secretary-General's IEAG 2014: 2)

This report captures the growing preoccupation with and reliance on data and indicators to guide decision-making and to design policies and programs at the international and national levels.

1   The authors would like to acknowledge that this work was undertaken on Yawuru country and extend their gratitude to the following organisations: Nyamba Buru Yawuru, Nagula Jarndu and the Yawuru Prescribed Body Corporate. We would also like to express thanks to the Centre for Aboriginal Economic Policy Research (The Australian National University) and the Kimberley Institute Limited (Broome) for in-kind and financial support given to the research. Last but not least, this chapter would not have been possible without the generous time and knowledge afforded by the Yawuru community who made the Yawuru Knowledge and Wellbeing Project come to fruition.

Indigenous peoples around the world are not immune from this growing trend of quantification-based accountability (Espeland & Vannebo 2007). There is a plethora of information pertaining to Australia's First Peoples compiled by the state and other organisations for the purposes of knowing and counting the population base for service delivery and resource allocation. Despite this, Indigenous scholars and leaders have argued that these datasets are not necessarily collected to inform the agenda and priorities of Aboriginal and Torres Strait Islander communities and organisations (Yu 2011; Walter 2013; Kukutai & Walter 2015). Furthermore, a substantial amount of data collected within the overarching government policy framework of 'closing the gap' are narrowly defined against mainstream criteria with the objective of monitoring the extent to which Indigenous people conform to a set of predetermined characteristics of the general population. As Peter Yu, a prominent Aboriginal leader and Yawuru man, noted in his address to the Australian Bureau of Statistics (ABS) national conference in 2011:

> I contend that there is a much more fundamental flaw to the Closing the Gap Strategy. And that is that the underlying assumption is wrong. COAG [the Council of Australian Governments] is pursuing this agenda unquestioningly on the basis that Indigenous wellbeing will be improved through Indigenous people adopting values and practices of mainstream western society … The intended use of data by governments does not measure the fundamental imperatives of Aboriginal life. (Yu 2011)

This narrow view renders other, uniquely positive, aspects of being Aboriginal or Torres Strait Islander less relevant because of their minimal contribution to the evidence base (Pholi et al. 2009). In particular, what is 'recognised' as evidence is increasingly synonymous with the creation of indicators, which are primarily quantitative in nature. These statistical indicators are commonly sourced from existing data sources collected for the purpose of informing government frameworks. The tension that exists between the world views of Indigenous peoples and government reporting frameworks is what Taylor (2008) has conceived of as existing within 'the recognition space'. The recognition space is a framework for examining the different positioning, world views and aspirations on the one side and national and international targets set by governments and international bodies on the other (Watene & Yap 2015).

Taylor (2008) further notes that it is in this intersectional space that meaningful engagement can begin to develop measures that reflect indigenous world views and aspirations.

Charles Taylor (1992: 25) argued for the importance of 'recognition' as a vital human need, saying that misrecognition can be seen as another form of oppression. Furthermore, the recognition of oneself and the importance of one's values and identities occurs through the interaction with others and as a product of history and institutional structures. The renegotiation and reclaiming of what is 'recognised' therefore have to occur through those same channels. One of the ways in which this space has been created is through the transformation of Western research paradigms that prioritise Indigenous ways of knowing, being and doing (Smith 1999, 2005; Martin 2003; Moreton-Robinson & Walter 2009).

In the practice of demography, Kukutai and Taylor (2013: 14) offer some insights as to how data might be 'indigenised' to better meet the needs of indigenous communities. The Yawuru people of the north-west of Western Australia (WA) have risen to this challenge: the Yawuru Knowing our Community (YKC) survey in 2011 is the first Yawuru endeavour to exercise self-determination from the ground up in their data collection efforts (Kukutai & Taylor 2013). This chapter offers two other examples of Yawuru furthering that self-determination exercise.

Data, indicators and the recognition space

The report on the measurement of economic performance and social progress by Stiglitz et al. (2010) brought into the spotlight the inadequacies of extant measures of quality of life in terms of the need for environmental sustainability and the financial challenges that are faced globally. The statement by the authors that 'what we measure affects what we do and if our measures are flawed policies will be misguided' (Stiglitz et al. 2010: 7) astutely sums up the importance of being cognisant of what the measures represent and the unintended consequences that arise from utilising measures and indicators uncritically (Merry 2011; Fukuda-Parr 2014; see also Morphy, this volume). The report has rekindled an interest among scholars, governments and peoples around the world in interrogating how quality of life has been measured to date and how it can be better measured internationally as well as within different population groups and, following that, in the canvassing of indicators and associated data repositories that best reflect and capture these redefined notions of wellbeing.

At the global level, indigenous groups and organisations such as the United Nations Permanent Forum on Indigenous Issues (UNPFII) are driving a self-determination agenda to mobilise the international community to consider how to develop indicators that are culturally appropriate and reflect indigenous world views. Of particular interest is how the sustainability goals of the UN and the UN Secretary-General's Independent Expert Advisory Group (IEAG) and their various targets can incorporate and be informed by indigenous world views and aspirations for wellbeing. The themes that have been tabled include traditional knowledge and practices, health, rights, leadership, access to and control of land, self-determination and participation in matters pertaining to indigenous peoples (UNPFII 2006; PUMC-UNAM 2008).

Perhaps not surprisingly, given the breadth and depth of core themes covered, there has been a concerted effort to produce statistics and measures for indigenous populations around the world. At the very least, there is a need for better information capture and representation through disaggregation of pre-existing information by countries, by ethnicity and by gender internationally. However, a more fundamental need is to capture data that reflect indigenous aspirations and world views. This is not just information relating to indigenous peoples' social, economic and demographic circumstances, but is also information on cultural dimensions, indigenous ecological values and indigenous peoples' unique relationship to nature and the living landscape. Various scholars, many of whom are contributors to this monograph, have alluded to the fact that despite the wealth of data that national statistical agencies worldwide collect and manage, the functionality of the data in informing indigenous aspirations and world views remains questionable (Taylor 2008, 2010; Jordan et al. 2010; Prout 2011; Yu 2011; Walter & Andersen 2013; Kukutai & Walter 2015).

In Australia, a survey of the literature, information databases and national statistics collection agencies reveals a commonality: the production of a population binary contrasting Indigenous and non-Indigenous through the inclusion of questions on self-identification as an Indigenous person (Walter & Andersen 2013; Taylor 2010). For some time now, in an effort to address the weakness of postcolonial data collection frameworks, there has been a concentrated effort to produce surveys specifically designed to capture Indigenous cultural connections and social lives, such as the National Aboriginal and Torres Strait Islander Social Survey (NATSISS), the Australian Aboriginal and Torres Strait Islander Health Survey (AATSIHS) and the Longitudinal Survey of Indigenous Children (LSIC). However, these surveys do not go far enough to address the geographical and cultural diversity of the hundreds of language groups and nations that make up Australia's First Peoples, and this limits the usability of the data for informing on the wellbeing and aspirations of groups such as the Yawuru.

Clearly, there is a pressing need to improve the functionality of the current data environment for the Aboriginal and Torres Strait Islander population, but how does one begin to operationalise the recognition space so that the information reflects Indigenous aspirations and world views while simultaneously informing government planning and reporting needs? Two fundamental issues arise here: first, for what purpose are these measures or indicators being collected and represented; and second, by whom and by what process are these measures decided?

Building on Taylor's idea of the recognition space, Kukutai and Walter (2015) identify five recognition principles to address statistical functionality for indigenous peoples: geographical diversity, cultural diversity, other ways of knowing, mutual capability building and indigenous decision-making. The authors argue that these five recognition principles are the beginnings of a meaningful meeting in the recognition space, in particular for genuine participation and decision-making by indigenous peoples to shape the functionality of indigenous statistics. These principles form the building blocks of implementing the United Nations Declaration on the Rights of Indigenous Peoples (UNDRIP) in the data context.

UNDRIP, ratified in 2007, provided an international standard-setting mechanism to support indigenous peoples' right for a development paradigm that is balanced between development and sustainability; that is collective while inclusive; and, most importantly, that is reflective of and built on strength of culture and identity and is in balance and harmony with the environment. The principles of self-determination, participation, cultural rights, land rights, ownership, control and free prior and informed consent all form the basis for supporting indigenous groups worldwide in their efforts to set an agenda for the maintenance of their wellbeing (UN 2007).

At more localised levels, indigenous communities have begun the process of setting their own wellbeing agenda and priorities. Events set in train by the Yawuru people of Broome in WA provide a prime example of how the principles of UNDRIP can be implemented on the ground. Articles 3, 18, 19, 25, 26, 29, 31, 32 and 43 of UNDRIP were all pivotal in guiding Yawuru to develop the Knowledge and Wellbeing Project in which participation by members of the community, respect, control of information and cultural rights were central. Two case studies from this project are presented later, but first we must examine some of the background to its establishment.

Native title: process and challenges

In the seminal case of *Mabo vs Queensland (No. 2)* (1992), the High Court of Australia handed down its decision recognising the connection of Aboriginal and Torres Strait Islander groups to their land as passed down through their traditional laws and customs. Following that decision, the *Native Title Act 1993* created the legal framework through which connection to Indigenous laws, customs and traditions is recognised to enable native title holders to deal with multiple interests on their land.

Native title brings with it significant challenges and opportunities for the native title holders. While there are potential economic benefits resulting from landholdings through native title agreements, there are significant barriers relating to property rights that need to be addressed before economic development and its benefits can be fully enjoyed. In May 2015, these challenges and issues were discussed at the high-level Indigenous Leadership Roundtable convened by the Aboriginal and Torres Strait Islander Social Justice Commissioner and the Human Rights Commissioner.

There are significant non-economic benefits arising from the recognition of native title holders, such as the pride of being recognised as traditional owners. Perhaps most important of all, however, native title brings with it a self-determination agenda, an opportunity to negotiate and have a say on outcomes that will affect the native title holders and, with that, an opportunity to maintain and improve their sense of wellbeing. Native title brings with it the rights and responsibilities of a seat at the table, to negotiate and manage the different competing interests on country and waters and to make decisions about what happens on their traditional land and waters (Neate 2010; Webb 2015).

Notwithstanding the difficulties of living and managing native title across two cultures and two worlds, native title determination processes act as a catalyst for thinking about data collection, data sovereignty and data usability in the context of fulfilling the rights and responsibilities that come with securing native title.

Yawuru and the native title process

Since the Bugarrigarra[2] gave shape and life to the living landscape and country we now know as Broome, the Yawuru people have practised their traditions, law and customs. As custodians of the land, Yawuru have long fished and hunted in and managed their traditional ecological knowledge systems and habitats, and have held and passed their stories on to future generations despite the harsh colonisation practices instituted by the state (Dodson 2013). These stories, rituals and law handed down from the Bugarrigarra are what Yawuru women and men continued to maintain through their responsibilities and obligations as Yawuru people, which gave rise to recognition through the native title process.

---

2   Bugarrigarra is the core of Yawuru cosmology. Bugarrigarra is the time before time, when the creative forces shaped and gave meaning and form to the landscape, putting the languages to the people within those landscapes and creating the protocol and laws for living within this environment (Yawuru RNTBC 2011: 13).

In 2010, the Yawuru were granted native title.[3] This determination signalled a shift in the relationship between Yawuru and other groups living in Broome as well in their relationship with the state of Western Australia. The native title determination has provided Yawuru with the opportunity to have a say over the land and its use and also to have input into issues affecting Yawuru in local and regional settings (Yawuru RNTBC 2011). The native title process provided a platform for the process of knowledge building and capacity building among Yawuru. Now key players within the community, Yawuru have a significant say about and input to the growth trajectories of Broome and neighbouring areas. With that responsibility and those rights now in place, Yawuru identified the immediate need for information that will enable them to make sound decisions that will secure their economic, social, cultural and environmental base as First Peoples of Australia. There was a recognised need to, first and foremost, invest in data and knowledge development for Yawuru, driven by Yawuru, to inform Yawuru development and wellbeing aspirations. The Yawuru Knowledge and Wellbeing Project was a response to this need. It centres on four key themes: knowing Yawuru country, knowing Yawuru stories, knowing Yawuru community and building economic prosperity.

Yawuru response to data needs: an exercise in self-determination

In addressing the need to negotiate with multiple stakeholders under multiple pressures, Yawuru embarked on a project to build knowledge around their country, community and stories in an effort to 'be at the table' with information for negotiation rather than at the margins receiving information. The beginning of that knowledge project was identifying the availability and scope of data to contribute to Yawuru's knowledge base and decision-making processes (Taylor et al. 2014). Despite the wealth of data available on the Indigenous population of Australia, the usefulness of those datasets for Yawuru's purposes

---

3   Native title comprises the rights and interests of Indigenous Australian peoples to their traditional lands and waters, which for each group derive from their own laws and customs and are recognised by the Federal Court, in accordance with Australian statutory and common law, although subject to a judicial process of application by prospective native title holders. If determined to exist, this title is held in trust by a prescribed body corporate as per the requirements of the *Native Title Act 1993*.

is limited. The Yawuru Knowing our Community (YKC) survey was Yawuru's first response to the Yawuru Knowledge and Wellbeing Project (Table 13.1).

Table 13.1 Timeline of the Yawuru native title determination and subsequent actions to implement the Knowledge and Wellbeing Project

Year	Event
1994	First native title claim lodged with the National Native Title Tribunal
2006	Federal Court decides that Yawuru have maintained their law and customs from the time of the Bugarrigarra
2008	Appeal by the state of Western Australia against the determination and finalisation of determination
2010	Yawuru agreements signed
2011	Yawuru Knowing our Community survey (Broome)
2013	Yawuru Knowledge and Wellbeing Project commences

Source: The authors.

Yawuru Knowledge and Wellbeing Project

Dodson (2013) has called for a new narrative of how Indigenous people intend to assert their place in the modern world, defined by their local perspectives and reflecting values that Indigenous people (in this case, Yawuru) value and aspire to. The Yawuru Knowledge and Wellbeing Project Framework is based on Yawuru knowledge systems, ways of being and doing and the Yawuru philosophy of *mabu liyan*. *Mabu liyan* reflects the Yawuru sense of belonging and being, living well in connection with country, culture, others and oneself. In other words, *liyan* is relational wellbeing and concerns relationships with country, family, community and oneself (McKenna & Anderson 2011; Dodson 2013).

Mabu buru, mabu liyan and *mabu ngarrungunil* are the aspirations and guiding principles of the journey that Yawuru have taken since time immemorial and they are critical for the rebuilding of the Yawuru nation in the aftermath of native title. They form the pillars of the Yawuru Knowledge and Wellbeing Project. *Mabu buru* refers to strong country and *mabu ngarrungunil* refers to strong community. Together, the interconnectedness between the country, its people and its culture brings about *mabu liyan* (Yawuru RNTBC 2011).

The Yawuru demographic survey of the Broome community taken in partnership with the Kimberley Institute and The Australian National University (Table 13.1) filled the gap in 'knowing' the Broome community from the ground up (Kukutai & Taylor 2013; Taylor et al. 2014). In the next two projects, discussed below, Indigenous ecological knowledge and Indigenous ways of knowing are critical to the foundation of a meaningful engagement in the recognition space, as a means to implement UNDRIP at the community level.

While the end product of these studies is important in itself, the methodology employed is equally significant. The innovative use of participatory methods and tools that reflect Yawuru ways of knowing, being and doing serves to challenge the existing paradigms of what matters in defining wellbeing. It takes a strength-based rather than a deficit approach and, in the case of ecological knowledge systems, paints the landscape as a living, breathing life force for transmission of knowledge, culture and the reinforcement of identity.

Case study 1: Knowing our Country—mabu buru

As traditional custodians of the land and waters in Broome, Yawuru women and men hold responsibilities arising from the Bugarrigarra to manage and protect their traditional country and waters. Traditional ecological knowledge recognises a cycle of six seasons and nine habitats, and this knowledge is part of Yawuru's spiritual relationship with the land. As with other Aboriginal groups in Australia, for Yawuru the six seasons and nine habitats are identified through weather patterns, tidal movements and the availability of traditional food sources for harvesting and hunting. Native title gave rise to the right to protect, access and live on Yawuru traditional land. It is therefore imperative for Yawuru to be informed about and consulted by any parties with interests in their land—in particular, interests and activities that have uncertain and long-lasting impacts on the land and waters in Broome. Indigenous peoples have long engaged in conceptual mapping of country, both land and sea. The biodiversity, stories, songs and history are held in their minds (Tobias 2000; Crawhall 2008). Cultural mapping has been used for some time to promote intercultural dialogue and to provide an interface where Indigenous people's knowledge and interactions with their land and sea are made visible (Crawhall 2008: 4). Working with First Nations communities in British Columbia, Terry Tobias (2000) proposed mapping as a way of documenting land use and occupancy by aboriginal groups. Some examples of land use and occupancy information that have been mapped include sacred sites, travel routes, aboriginal placenames, ecological knowledge, ceremonial sites and harvesting places (Tobias 2000).

Yu (2013: 26–7) states that Aboriginal groups, governments and industry need to explore ways to build workable relationships in post–native title Australia. He further notes that cultural mapping methodologies are emerging as a vital tool to assist in negotiations over and implementation of UNDRIP principles of 'free prior and informed consent'. These geospatial tools provide an interface between governments, land users and local authorities to map country so that greater transparency and accountability can be delivered to create greater social cohesion and equity between traditional societies and other citizens in their local environments and communities. Utilising Geographical Information System (GIS) mapping to digitally map places of cultural and social significance for Yawuru, alongside the Cultural Management Plan, provides Yawuru with vital information to make informed decisions about access to and use of their country to ensure its sustainability.

This mapping of Yawuru use and occupancy of country, and of important cultural and ceremony sites, is part of the compilation of vital information for Yawuru in the negotiation of land use management—in particular, around resource extraction. The information provides Yawuru with the leverage to identify potential interference with country that is not just environmental but also cultural. An example of this was highlighted in the Yawuru submission to the WA Standing Committee on Environment and Public Affairs, which stated:

> Yawuru considers water sites on country to be 'living waters' which are permanent springs and manifestations of the Bugarrigarra. Many water sites are inhabited by powerful snake-like spiritual beings. Contaminated waters as a result of fracking would impact upon the sustainability and cultural integrity of water sites and therefore impinge on Yawuru's fundamental native title rights and responsibility to look after country. (Yawuru RNTBC 2013: 6)

The maps generated through Yawuru's Knowing our Country efforts have been critical in casting a spotlight on their significant cultural and hunting sites and use of country to inform negotiation and management processes with various government departments and stakeholders in the region (Rangelands NRM 2016).

Case study 2: Knowing our Community—mabu liyan

Following on from the native title determination, there has been a need to pause to reflect on whether the programs and policies in place are improving the lives of Yawuru men and women. Conceptions of wellbeing cannot be meaningfully disentangled from place, time and history. To investigate whether the wellbeing of Yawuru women and men is being maintained and improving, there is a need to first understand how Yawuru conceptualise wellbeing and to understand what social, cultural and economic aspects they most value.

The Yawuru Knowledge and Wellbeing Project is a sequential mixed-methods project aimed at understanding Yawuru conceptions of and priorities for wellbeing. For the most part, measures of wellbeing are often sourced from existing surveys with limited functionality in representing community-level wellbeing (Taylor 2008; Yu 2011). Furthermore, where composite measures of wellbeing are created, the weights attached to the various dimensions of wellbeing tend to be determined by the researchers, either as equally important or through using statistical weights (Biddle 2009; Yap & Biddle 2010).

In this project, Yawuru ways of being, knowing and doing are prioritised in several ways: first, through the framing of Yawuru wellbeing through the philosophy of *mabu liyan*, and second, in the participatory way in which measures of wellbeing were derived, validated, collected and weighted.

Mabu liyan is a central notion of wellbeing for Yawuru. Pursuits of various aspects of wellbeing identified by Yawuru women and men were often associated with achieving and maintaining *mabu liyan* or 'good' *liyan*. Starting with *mabu liyan* as the central focus of Yawuru wellbeing is recognising that there are other ways of 'knowing'. This means that the wellbeing measures are grounded in Yawuru values through a process that results in data that are fit for purpose.

This is done with the aim of evaluating how Yawuru women and men are faring over time against their own determined benchmarks (see Morphy, this volume).

The participation and guidance of Yawuru women and men through all stages of the research process, from content and design to collection, are the second way in which Yawuru voices are prioritised. This bottom-up approach for conceptualising wellbeing, selecting wellbeing dimensions and the weighting of wellbeing ensures that if Yawuru set out on the road to constructing a Yawuru wellbeing index, as suggested by Yu (2011) in his address at the ABS conference, the index in its entirety will be grounded in Yawuru world views, reflecting Yawuru priorities, with Yawuru voices and inputs interwoven throughout the process. A further way in which the Yawuru's critical voice has been prioritised in the conceptualisations of wellbeing and *liyan* is through the formation of a steering committee consisting of Yawuru women and men to ensure that the information generated through the research reflects local aspirations and values but, more importantly, is functional for community purposes.

There were two broad stages to the research, with the qualitative component informing the quantitative instrument of the Yawuru Wellbeing Survey 2015. The first stage comprised two interconnected phases involving face-to-face semistructured interviews and focus group workshops with Yawuru women and men to conceptualise ideas of a good life. Together, the interviews and focus groups formed the Yawuru Wellbeing Framework (for women and men separately) and the Yawuru Wellbeing Survey, which was conducted in the quantitative stage (Yap & Yu, in press). The construction of a gender-specific Yawuru Wellbeing Framework, reflecting the different but overlapping priorities and concerns of Yawuru women and men, is an innovative contribution to this process. The grounding of the process in Yawuru world views not only facilitated the derivation of culturally relevant measures, but also created a sense of 'ownership' in the operation of the recognition space (Table 13.2).

Table 13.2 Examples of grounded community-driven approaches for deriving measures of wellbeing

Themes	Examples of interview	Indicators	Selected/not selected by focus groups	Survey question
Connection to country	'I try and get back into country in the afternoons. I go back and I sit down on the rocks, get out on country and go fishing and that makes my liyan *feel good'*	Fishing and hunting	Picked by Yawuru women Picked by Yawuru men	In the past 12 months, how often did you fish or hunt?
	'Yawuru use[d] to get blood cockle … we are saltwater people and we hunt from the sea. The cockles have disappeared now. People feel very low from a wellbeing perspective that this cockle has gone … our liyan *no good when we see that'*	Quality and quantity of catch and kill	Picked by Yawuru women Picked by Yawuru men	In the past 12 months, did you eat traditional food (catch, kill or bushfood)?

Source: Adapted from Yap and Yu (in press).

Summary and discussion

It is clear from the case studies provided that the guiding principles around the Yawuru Knowledge and Wellbeing Project are not dissimilar to the spirit and values underpinning UNDRIP. Both emphasise the importance of geographical and cultural context, and of empowering communities to fashion their own development agendas and solutions.

The projects are also strength based, stemming from Yawuru aspirations and the values that underpin *knowing our country*, *knowing our stories* and *knowing our community*. Together, these key pillars can bring about healthy country, strong community and *mabu liyan* in parallel with the pursuit of economic development. The importance of building and recognising Yawuru ways of knowing and being is a key foundation of the meaningful operation of Taylor's recognition space through the key recognition principles outlined by Kukutai and Walter (2015).

The exercise of self-determination through active and meaningful participation by members of the community in both of the projects discussed above is crucial to building an evidence base that is relevant but reflective of the diversity and lived experiences of different members of the community: women and men, young and old, those living on country and those living away from country. This is important in the endeavour of being inclusive and transparent while moving ahead as a collective.

Last but not least, the capacity-building component of both research projects through research partnerships with universities, community organisations such as Kimberley Institute and the prescribed bodies corporate, and the training of a local research team, ensures that there is co-production of knowledge. This brings together different ways of knowing, both traditional and Western, in a manner that is more consistent with the recognition space.

There are, however, challenges associated with operationalising the recognition space. The investment required in both time and resources is extensive and there is a need to ensure enduring consistency and comparability over time. Evaluation of wellbeing and priorities needs to be undertaken periodically—especially in a time when there are environmental and economic pressures that need to be balanced against social and cultural considerations, with sometimes very short time frames for decision-making.

As the reality of native title sets in, the information gathered to inform Yawuru priorities acts as a compass showing where Yawuru are and where they are heading. A key to the implementation of self-determination is ensuring that the utility of Yawuru data is communicated so that such projects are always accountable to the native title holders, the community, and the elders and senior lawmen whose efforts and stories gave rise to the recognition of Yawuru as traditional custodians of Broome, long before European contact. Their stories, their investment of time and their knowledge serve to populate the data collection instruments that Yawuru have initiated and, ultimately, they are the ones who will benefit from the fruits of these processes and the data and information that they produce.

References

Biddle N (2009). *Ranking regions: revisiting an index of relative indigenous socioeconomic outcomes*, CAEPR Working Paper 50, Centre for Aboriginal Economic Policy Research, The Australian National University, Canberra, anu.edu.au/caepr/working.php.

Crawhall N (2008). *The role of participatory cultural mapping in promoting intercultural dialogue: 'we are not hyenas'*, Concept Paper prepared for Division of Cultural Policies and Intercultural Dialogue, February 2007, United Nations Educational, Scientific and Cultural Organization, Paris.

Dodson P (2013). Doctrine I: an Indigenous doctrine of discovery post terra nullius, Presentation to Thinking for yourself: a conference in honour of Robert Manne, La Trobe University, Melbourne, 28 February 2013.

Espeland W & Vannebo B (2007). Accountability, quantification and law. *Annual Review of Law and Social Science* 3:21–43.

Fukuda-Parr S (2014). Global goals as a policy tool: intended and unintended consequences. *Journal of Human Development and Capabilities* 15(2–3):118–31, doi:10.1080/19452829.2014.91018.

Jordan K, Bullock H & Buchanan G (2010). Exploring the tensions between statistical equality and cultural difference in Indigenous wellbeing frameworks: a new expression of an enduring debate. *Australian Journal of Social Issues* 45(3):333–62.

Kukutai T & Taylor J (2013). Postcolonial profiling of indigenous populations: limitations and responses in Australia and New Zealand. *Espace Populations Sociétés* 1:13–27.

Kukutai T & Walter M (2015). Recognition and indigenizing official statistics: reflections from Aotearoa New Zealand and Australia. *Statistical Journal of the IAOS* 31:317–26.

McKenna V & Anderson K (2011). Kimberley Dreaming: old law, new ways—finding new meaning, Presentation to World Congress for Psychotherapy, Sydney, 24–28 August 2011.

Martin K (2003). Ways of knowing, ways of being and ways of doing: a theoretical framework and methods for Indigenous research and Indigenist research. *Journal of Australian Studies* 76:203–14.

Merry S (2011). Measuring the world indicators, human rights, and global governance. *Current Anthropology* 52(S3):s83–95.

Moreton-Robinson AM & Walter M (2009). Indigenous methodologies in social research. In Walter M (ed.), *Social research methods: an Australian perspective*, 2nd edn, Oxford University Press, Melbourne.

Neate G (2010). Using native title to increase Indigenous economic opportunities, Presentation to fifth Indigenous Recruitment and Training Summit, Brisbane, 6 December 2010.

Pholi K, Black D & Richards C (2009). Is 'Close the Gap' a useful approach to improving the health and wellbeing of Indigenous Australians? *Australian Review of Public Affairs* 9(2):1–13.

Prout S (2011). Indigenous wellbeing frameworks in Australia and the quest for quantification. *Social Indicators Research* 109(2):317–36.

Rangelands NRM (2016). *GIS plan highlights diverse values of Roebuck Plains*, Rangelands NRM WA, Perth, rangelandswa.com.au/856/gis-plan-highlights-diverse-values-of-roebuck-plains-.

Secretary-General's Independent Expert Advisory Group (IEAG) (2014). *A world that counts: mobilising the data revolution for sustainable development*, United Nations, New York.

Smith LT (1999). *Decolonising methodologies: research and indigenous peoples*, Zed Books, London & New York.

Smith LT (2005). On tricky ground: researching the native in the age of uncertainty. In Denzin NK & Lincoln YS (eds), *The SAGE handbook of qualitative research*, 3rd edn, SAGE Publications, Thousand Oaks, CA.

Stiglitz J, Sen A & Fitoussi J (2010). *Report by the Commission on the Measurement of Economic Performance and Social Progress*, Paris.

Taylor C (1992). The politics of recognition. In Guttmann A & Taylor C (eds), *Multiculturalism and the 'politics of recognition'*, Princeton University Press, Princeton, NJ.

Taylor J (2008). Indigenous peoples and indicators of well-being: Australian perspectives on United Nations global frameworks. *Social Indicators Research* 87(1):111–26.

Taylor J (2010). Postcolonial transformation of the Australian Indigenous population. *Geographical Research* 49(3):286–300.

Taylor J, Doran B, Parriman M & Yu E (2014). Statistics for community governance: the Yawuru Indigenous population survey, Western Australia. *International Indigenous Policy Journal* 5(2):1–31.

Tobias T (2000). *Chief Kerry's moose: a guidebook to land use and occupancy mapping, research design and data collection*, Union of British Columbia Indian Chiefs and Ecotrust Canada, Vancouver.

United Nations (UN) (2007). *United Nations declaration on the rights of indigenous peoples*, General Assembly Resolution 61/295, 13 September 2007, United Nations, New York, www.un.org/esa/socdev/unpfii/documents/DRIPS_en.pdf.

United Nations Permanent Forum on Indigenous Issues (UNPFII) (2006). *Report on the meeting on indigenous peoples and indicators of wellbeing*, United Nations Permanent Forum on Indigenous Issues, Fifth Session, New York.

Walter M (2013). The 2014 National Aboriginal and Torres Strait Islander Social Survey is an anachronism, *Online Opinion*, 6 August 2013, onlineopinion.com.au/view.asp?article=15317.

Walter M & Andersen C (2013). *Indigenous statistics: a quantitative research methodology*, Left Coast Press, Walnut Creek, CA.

Watene K & Yap M (2015). Culture and sustainable development: indigenous contributions. *Journal of Global Ethics* 11:51–5.

Webb R (2015). Historic Tenure Certainty Project: a tool for sharing the knowledge, sharing the future, Paper presented at the 2015 World Bank Conference on Land and Poverty, Washington, DC, 23–27 March 2015.

Working Group Mexico Multicultural Nation University Programme and the National Autonomous University of Mexico (PUMC-UNAM) (2008). *Indigenous peoples and the indicators of well-being and development*, Preliminary Report, Seventh Session of the United Nations Permanent Forum on Indigenous Issues, New York.

Yap M & Biddle N (2010). Gender gaps in Indigenous socioeconomic outcomes: Australian regional comparisons and international possibilities. *International Indigenous Policy Journal* 1(2).

Yap M & Yu E (in press). Operationalising the capability approach: developing culturally relevant indicators of Indigenous wellbeing—an Australian example. *Oxford Development Studies*.

Yawuru Native Title Holders Aboriginal Corporation Native Title Prescribed Body Corporate (Yawuru RNTBC) (2011). *Walyjala-jala buru jayida jarringgun Nyamba Yawuru ngan-ga mirlimirli: planning for the future—Yawuru cultural management plan*, Pindan Printing, Broome, WA.

Yawuru Native Title Holders Aboriginal Corporation Native Title Prescribed Body Corporate (Yawuru RNTBC) (2013). *Submission to the Standing Committee on Environment and Public Affairs: inquiry into the implications for Western Australia of hydraulic fracturing for unconventional gas*, September 2013, Perth.

Yu P (2011). Aboriginal development: making data work, Paper presented at the ABS Conference Census: beyond the count, Melbourne, 3 March 2011.

Yu P (2013). Process from the other side: *liyan* in the cultural and natural estate. *Landscape Architecture Australia* 139(August).

14

Building a data revolution in Indian country

Desi Rodriguez-Lonebear

Introduction

From Twitter to the World Bank, the data revolution is transforming business as usual. Everything from our spending habits to our health status is now captured as data for use by governments, industry, nongovernmental organisations (NGOs) and whoever can get access. Information about us is becoming a valuable global currency. With 90 per cent of data in the world created in the past two years alone (IBM, no date), we are undoubtedly in the data age. Yet, this unparalleled profusion of data does not serve everyone. Marginalised populations across the globe continue to face glaring data inequities. Indigenous peoples, for example, suffer from a dearth of relevant information about their populations, and this is so despite generations of contentious external data collection efforts in their communities. In the data mecca of the United States, American Indian tribes[1] face a paucity of data about their own populations.

---

1   For the sake of brevity, I use American Indian tribe and tribe interchangeably throughout. I also utilise American Indian, Indian, Native American and indigenous peoples synonymously.

American Indian nations, like other nations, are decision-making entities that need reliable information about their citizens. However, existing data on tribal populations are often limited to those developed by others—usually federal, state and local governments. Tribes must grapple with the task of building strong nations while utilising data that have been collected to advance the aims of other governments. I do five things in this chapter. First, I argue that data are not a new concept to American Indians; they have long been data gatherers and data experts. Second, I trace the movement of American Indian nations from data sovereignty to data dependence. Third, I review some of the data challenges now facing American Indian nations, including the current state of American Indian population data. Fourth, I explore the nascent data revolution now getting under way in Indian country as some tribes reclaim data sovereignty. Finally, I close by considering how tribal data sovereignty can be a powerful tool in decolonisation and in pursuit of tribal development goals.

Our peoples have always been data gatherers

Science and technology are often considered markers of civilisation, with progress measured in units of data (Misa et al. 2003). Despite centuries of indigenous knowledge production steeped in histories of data collection and analysis (Cajete 1999; Smith 1999), progress is defined largely in Western terms and measured by Western-identified and controlled indices. In the United States, the hegemony of the Western approach means that information that does not originate in or is not validated by Western constructs is rejected or coopted at best, and destroyed at worst. Yet, contrary to colonial narratives of savagery and unsophistication, indigenous peoples were relentlessly empirical with advanced systems of knowledge. For indigenous peoples, data were everywhere, and survival was often tied to one's ability to gather, analyse and share this knowledge. The winter counts by the Plains Indians are an example of the meticulous and methodological nature of indigenous data. The Lakota, Blackfeet and other Plains tribes recorded winter counts on animal hides to enumerate important aspects of their world. These detailed counts included numbers of tribal citizens, allies, enemies, wild game, lodges and so on: histories and assemblages of data that were instruments of survival. They are among the earliest population and wildlife records in all of North America (Raczka 1979). Another instance of indigenous peoples' detailed data-keeping are the totem poles carved in the Pacific North-West. Totem poles document everything from family histories and tribal origin stories to achievements, marriages and land rights (Stewart 1993). While the purpose and significance of totem poles vary greatly across the peoples of the Pacific North-West, they all hold deep meaning to their creators and remain relevant and valuable data sources today.

An additional example comes from the oral history of my tribe, the Northern Cheyenne. We are often labelled 'anti-progress' due to our intergenerational stance—despite pervasive poverty—against developing lucrative coal and natural gas deposits on our lands. Reasons for and against resource development vary and factions within the tribe abound. However, one salient argument against development comes from the oral history of the Cheyenne people. The Cheyenne prophet Sweet Medicine, one of our most powerful figures, foretold that the Cheyenne would one day encounter a black stone beneath our lands. Sweet Medicine warned that this stone was to be left alone if the Cheyenne were to remain Cheyenne. This prophecy, along with many others by Sweet Medicine, has been passed down from generation to generation. They have been shared by Cheyenne and non-Cheyenne alike (Powell 1979), and continue to influence contemporary decisions within the tribe. As with many tribes, Cheyenne oral history remains a critical source of data as we grapple with contemporary issues. It directly challenges the idea of data as products of modernity with little relevance to indigenous lived experiences or traditions. These and other examples indicate that the indigenous peoples of the United States identified, gathered and used essential data in pursuit of their own goals.

From data sovereignty to data dependence

The word 'data' comes from the Latin *datum*, meaning 'something given' (OED Online, no date). However, indigenous experiences under colonial control suggest that data more often means 'something taken'. An extreme, yet common, version of the taking of indigenous data stems from the perverse fascination of Europeans with the faculties and nature of indigenous peoples turned into objects of research (Smith 1999; see also the FNIGC, this volume). This has been apparent in the United States in the desecration of countless Indian graves, looting of funerary objects and theft of human remains. The remains of thousands of American Indians held in museums and private collections across the globe illustrate the ultimate theft of indigenous peoples' data: their bodies (Fine-Dare 2002). The life of Ishi, a native man who was sensationalised as the last member of the Yahi tribe in the early-twentieth century, exemplifies how the 'taking' of indigenous knowledge and the theft of Indian remains played a significant role in advancing academic disciplines—markedly, American anthropology.[2] Ishi's story also demonstrates how the exertion of tribal sovereignty over data can achieve some measure of justice.

Ishi is said to have wandered out of the wild in 1911 and was 'taken in' by University of California anthropologist Alfred Kroeber (Kroeber 1961). He spent the last years of his life as a living exhibit at the university's Museum of Anthropology, drawing huge crowds (Starn 2004). Kroeber and others talked at length with Ishi, trying to learn all they could about his language and the ways of his people. In effect, Ishi was a source of data and provided an opportunity to secure the data that he and his people had gathered over the generations. Ultimately, even Ishi's brain became data to be secured. After his death, his brain was removed and sent to the National Museum of Natural History as a 'gift from the University of California' (Starn 2004). In 1997, four federally recognised tribes of the Maidu people[3] of northern California passed a resolution to locate Ishi's brain. The tribes leveraged their relationships with state and local governments, gaining support for the investigation from the US Forest Service, the City of Oroville and the Butte County Board of Supervisors (Rockafellar, no date). The tribes' efforts resulted in an official inquiry into the location of Ishi's brain, which was ultimately discovered in the Smithsonian Institution's collections. The *National Museum of the Native American Act* of 1989

---

2   For an example, see Mead (1961); for a critique, see Deloria (1969).
3   These four tribes banded together to form the Butte County Native American Cultural Committee, which served as the collective advocating for Ishi's repatriation.

mandates the return of Native American human remains and associated funerary objects if requested by federally recognised tribes.[4] Ishi's brain was eventually repatriated to the Redding Rancheria and Pit River tribes, restoring their control over a small portion of tribal data and gaining some semblance of overdue justice.

The concept of data is imbued with a host of meanings within and across contexts. To some, it is simply information, while, for others, it is the very pulse of a revolution. In the indigenous world, data have a contentious history tied to the survival of native peoples on one hand, and to the instruments of the coloniser on the other. Indigenous data engagement in the United States is inextricably tied to the subjugation of American Indians and federal policies of Indian extermination and assimilation. Historically, this relationship is apparent in the concurrent exclusion of American Indians from official statistics and the peak of the colonial engine. Article I, section 2 of the US Constitution mandates a census be taken every 10 years to determine congressional representation by apportionment. The only people explicitly excluded from this count are 'Indians not taxed'—defined as 'those Indians living on reservations or those roaming in unsettled areas of the country' (Collins 2006). Under this definition, the majority of American Indians were deliberately omitted from the US Census for over 100 years (1790–1924) until the passage of the *1924 Indian Citizenship Act*.[5] While censuses are intended to serve as the pre-eminent source of data on all individuals of a population, the act of counting people is political (Walter & Andersen 2013). The exclusion of American Indians from official enumeration throughout the nineteenth century justified the colonial narrative of a vast and unpopulated land in the west ripe for settling. However, the Indian Wars told a very different story (Utley & Washburn 1985).

---

4   See 103 STAT.1336, Public Law 101-185, *National Museum of the American Indian Act*, 28 November 1989.
5   From 1885 to 1940, special Indian census rolls were collected by federal Indian agents in charge of Indian reservations. These counts were collected at the discretion of Indian agents and were maintained separately from the general decennial census. Often, these rolls became the basis of tribal enrolment policy and federal tribal recognition. See File 595276, Indian Census Rolls, 1885–1941, Record Group 75: Records of the Bureau of Indian Affairs, 1793–1999, National Archives Building, Washington, DC.

As the Indian Wars concluded and American Indians were relegated to reservations, much of the data gathering on which they depended for generations also forcibly ceased. Removal from their ancestral homelands, coupled with the decimation of wild game, population decline and the boarding school system, stripped Indians of their traditional sources of knowledge and survival. It also marked the inception of federal assimilation policies, starting with the *General Allotment Act* of 1887, which sought to 'civilise' the Indians by privatising tribal lands (Otis & Prucha 1973). This new chapter in federal–Indian relations precipitated a shift to data dependency for American Indian tribes. Indigenous data transitioned from a means of survival to mechanisms of federal administration. In 1824, the Bureau of Indian Affairs (BIA) was established under the War Department to oversee American Indians. It was charged with 'the administration of the fund for the civilization of the Indians'.[6] The BIA was later relocated to the Department of the Interior, where American Indian populations are now managed alongside national parks, natural resources and fish and wildlife.

Though no longer designated enemies of war, American Indians are still treated as a population in need of federal oversight. Often in competition with each other, tribes vie for federal grants disbursed through a host of agencies, including the BIA, the Department of Housing and Urban Development (HUD) and the Administration for Native Americans, among others. Given the destruction of traditional tribal economies in the aftermath of colonisation, these federal monies sustain vital tribal services on reservation lands, such as health care, education and housing. The reality is that contemporary tribal governments endure varying stages of federal dependency, including data dependency. The data collection activities of tribes now largely revolve around mandatory federal grant reporting, and many tribes employ grant officers or administrators to oversee these efforts.

---

6   See House Document No. 146, 19th Congress, 1st session, serial 138: 6.

The key issue: data by whom for whom?

Data sovereignty deals with the right and ability of tribes to develop their own systems for gathering and using data and to influence the collection of data by external actors. With respect to the latter, the United States has not kept pace with some other countries, such as New Zealand, where national statistics offices are becoming more responsive to the data priorities of Māori tribes (Walling et al. 2009; Kukutai & Rarere 2013). The focus of American Indian demography remains on the national and regional levels, utilising census counts of American Indians. Too often missing from this data picture is analysis at the tribal population or subpopulation level. American Indian tribes are policymaking bodies currently operating without accurate and reliable data that are or can be disaggregated at levels that facilitate sound tribal policy. Both the tribal pursuit of nation rebuilding and the federal investment pursuant to the fiduciary relationship between tribes and the US Government point to the need for more comprehensive tribal data systems.

Many of the issues tribes face in using existing data about their citizens stem from the use of inconsistent criteria to delimit tribal populations in tribal, county, state and federal datasets. Unlike in other countries, in the United States no statistical data standard exists to govern the collection and reporting of American Indian tribal population data across agencies.[7] Todd (2012) compiled a list of 295 sources of Indian country data, which provides a window into the daunting maze that tribes must work through to ascertain information about their populations. Less than 2 per cent of the data reported in this exhaustive list are from a tribal source. Five sources about tribal governance structures are reported from tribal constitutions, and one account of historical tribal data was identified. The remaining 98 per cent of sources span the US Census, administrative agencies such as the BIA and HUD, national surveys and numerous scholarly references.

Table 14.1 provides one illustration of the resulting problems. It lists 10 data sources of significance to Indian country and how each source identifies tribal citizens. This provides a small glimpse into

---

7   See Statistics New Zealand's Statistical Standard for *iwi* (tribes) as an example: stats.govt.nz/ methods/classifications-and-standards/classification-related-stats-standards/iwi.aspx.

the competing data landscape that tribal leaders, communities and researchers face. Confronted with hundreds of such data sources and no consistent standards or measures, it is small wonder tribes often find effective policymaking difficult.

Table 14.1 Tribal data sources and identifiers

Data source	Tribal identifier
US Census	Self-identification
American Community Survey	Self-identification
Tribal Enrolment Data	Minimum blood quantum, lineal descent and residency are the most common measures enforced by tribes
Department of Housing and Urban Development	Census counts
Department of Education Scholarships	Tribal enrolment verification; Certificate Degree of Indian Blood from the Bureau of Indian Affairs
Bureau of Indian Affairs	A tribal service population is defined as all American Indians and Alaska Natives, citizens and non-citizens, living 'on or near' a tribe's reservation during the calendar year and who were eligible for Bureau of Indian Affairs-funded services (see Evans & Topoleski 2002)
Indian Health Service	Federally recognised tribal member living within the service area
State and county agencies	Census counts
Official vital statistics	Lack of data at the tribal level inhibits the ability to calculate vital statistics for enrolled tribal populations
US Armed Forces	Certificate Degree of Indian Blood from the Bureau of Indian Affairs

Source: The author's research.

Furthermore, little systematic evidence has been gathered to date to identify what types of tribal data exist, what processes govern access to those data, what analyses have been conducted using those data and what use these analyses have been to tribes. The tribal data that do exist are often framed as inferior to data collected by other governments. For example, in 2015 the state of Montana issued a press release explaining that the state's Department of Labor and Industry will now calculate monthly unemployment rates for Montana's seven Indian reservations. Previously, the state calculated only annual reservation statistics. The department's chief economist issued the following reason: 'Reservations were struggling to find accurate numbers, and some were creating their own methods' (Associated

Press 2015). This statement ignores the fact that tribes often are in the best position to capture the realities of their tribal citizens' situations. Given the shortage of skilled data analysts throughout Indian country, analysing data in statistically sound ways that yield robust figures may be a challenge. But both tribal and state governments would benefit from an initiative that focused on assisting tribes to improve their data capabilities to take advantage of their insider knowledge. Instead, Montana's chief economist further entrenches the idea that state statistics are valid and tribal statistics are the ones in need of correction.

Also missing from this story are those data that can transform native communities. Walter & Andersen (2013: 14) note the power of statistics to perpetuate 'very narrow, but largely accepted lenses' through which governments and researchers alike understand indigenous peoples. Mainstream understandings of indigenous peoples are constrained by data that inform the prevailing narratives. We witness this time and again in native communities. High rates of suicide, diabetes, unemployment and substance abuse are but a few of the pervasive deficit statistics used to characterise native populations, so it is time to develop our own data that speak to our strengths. For example, what do we know about tribal youth, who make up the majority of tribal populations? Do they desire to return home after getting their education to help their nations? These are the 'data warriors' we need to steer the data revolution.

It is evident that dominant demographic approaches and methods remain limited in facilitating tribal development. The 'collision of systems' that characterises the collection of indigenous data by the state is pervasive across Indian country (Morphy 2004). In light of this, census and administrative agencies are criticised for failing to fully appreciate the complexity of native identities and communities. Scholars in indigenous demography contend that this is largely because official data drive mainstream agendas and do not reflect indigenous social structures, realities or aspirations (Taylor 2009; Axelsson & Sköld 2011). This issue needs to be addressed from both sides. Tribal data sovereignty has two prongs. On one side, it involves tribes exercising their sovereignty by developing tribal data sources; on the other, it involves improved collection of official statistics on tribal citizens and finding ways to make those statistics maximally useful to tribes. Despite the limitations of official statistics, they remain critical sources of evidence that tribes can use in pursuit of their goals. This will require meaningful and deliberate partnership, not just consultation, between American Indian tribes and the US Census Bureau and other federal, state and county agencies.

The case of tribal population data

Tribal population data provide an excellent example of both the data problem and the start of a possible solution. Tribal citizenship and American Indian identity are not mutually inclusive. A key aspect of tribal sovereignty is the sole right of tribes to determine tribal citizenship. This is one of the few areas of Indian affairs that the federal government explicitly leaves to the prerogative of tribes. Tribes determine citizenship through various means including ancestry, residency, maternal/paternal lineage and minimum blood quantum.[8] Without delving into the tribal blood quantum debate, suffice to say that every tribe has clearly defined tribal population boundaries. Though tribes maintain records on their citizens, these data are rarely used by any other entity. The federal government does not rely on tribal records for official tribal population numbers; instead, most agencies utilise tribal self-identification counts from the US Census. This has serious implications for tribes because tribal census counts are used to calculate federal funding formulas, which in turn allocate money for vital services to American Indian tribes. For example, HUD distributes US$650 million annually to tribes through the Indian Housing Block Grant, based largely on population figures from the census (Sackett 2015).

Federal funding formulas directly test tribal data sovereignty as they prioritise tribal data collected by the federal government over those collected by tribes for national decision-making. For HUD grants, tribes can challenge the census counts; however, doing so is particularly burdensome as tribes must show that their data were collected in the same manner as for the US Census and, ultimately,

---

8   The US Government first implemented blood quantum as the basis for racially identifying American Indians in the late-nineteenth century—most markedly, beginning with the *1877 Dawes Act* (also known as the *General Allotment Act*). The concept stems from the now debunked quasi-scientific belief that blood was the carrier of not only genetic material, but also cultural traits and social behaviour (Snipp 1989). This belief later influenced the eugenics movement (Berkhofer 1978).

HUD has the final authority to accept or dismiss a tribal challenge (HUD 2012). Over the course of interviews with 15 tribal leaders about tribal data, I consistently heard that the census numbers do not accurately enumerate tribal populations—specifically, that the census undercounts their tribal citizens.[9] While there are no comparative studies in the United States, international research supports this position, demonstrating an incongruence between tribal populations enumerated in tribal data sources and those in official statistics. A tribal demographic study in New Zealand found significant variation in the characteristics of a tribal population enumerated in the New Zealand Census and those of the tribe's own citizenship register, particularly with regard to gender and age (Walling et al. 2009).[10]

In the United States, scholarship is focused on the American Indian and Alaska Native (AIAN) aggregate population, with an emphasis on population size, composition, undercounting and processes of changing racial identification (Eschbach 1995; Nagel 1996; Sandefur et al. 1996; Snipp 1997; Liebler & Ortyl 2014). Little attention has been paid to tribal demography. This is a major oversight given the political, social and cultural importance of American Indian tribes as sovereign nations within the US political system. Furthermore, as governance entities, tribes are the pre-eminent units of measurement for the collective dispersal of federal funding. Regarding tribal data from the US Census, one must first ask whether capturing tribal populations in the census is even within the purview of the federal government given the reach of tribal sovereignty. What is the value of self-identified tribal counts in the US Census if tribes maintain their own citizenship records? Instead of collecting self-identified tribal counts, should the US Census Bureau invest in tribal capacity building and tribal data infrastructure to support tribal censuses?

Beyond these questions of principle, there is also the methodological question of whether the US Census can accurately enumerate the general AIAN population, much less tribal subpopulations. American Indians and Alaska Natives experienced the largest undercount

---

9   Based on 15 personal interviews with tribal leaders at the National Congress of American Indians Mid-Year Conference in Minneapolis, Minnesota, 20 June – 1 July 2015. This research was approved by the University of Waikato Faculty of Arts and Social Sciences Human Research Ethics Committee on 18 February 2015.
10   I seek to undertake similar research comparing American Indian tribal data with US Census data as part of an upcoming research project.

(4.9 per cent) of any racial or ethnic group in the 2010 census (US Census Bureau 2012). Currently, the Census Bureau is testing the possibility of a tribal enrolment question in the 2020 census. This question will enable more detailed analyses of self-identified tribal populations and could perhaps yield more accurate tribal counts. Conversely, nonresponse to the enrolment question could be high and thus contribute to more data inequities for American Indians and Alaska Natives. In 2015–16, the US Census Bureau hosted eight tribal consultations to discuss the tribal enrolment question with tribal leaders. While an official report is yet to be released, tribal leaders have made clear that this is a matter of tribal sovereignty and that such decisions require more than mere consultation, but rather genuine collaboration and careful joint deliberation (El Nasser 2015).

The pursuit of tribal data sovereignty

Today, there is a tribal data revolution under way in the United States. Some tribes are retaking control of data governance. In particular, the 25 per cent (n = 155) of federally recognised tribes that are now designated 'self-governance tribes'[11] are leaders in the data revolution. A self-governance designation enables tribes to hold the federal government accountable to its trust responsibility to Indian tribes with limited federal intervention. These tribes are able to restructure federal programs and utilise federal funding as they see fit to meet the needs of their citizens. As these tribes are already exercising tribal sovereignty to a greater extent than 'direct service tribes', they are ideally positioned to guide the tribal data revolution.

'Tribal sovereignty is only as strong as we exercise it.'[12] This statement by a mentor and former tribal president of the Northern Cheyenne Nation, John J. Robinson, describes the precarious position of Indian tribes as quasi-sovereign nations operating within a federal governance structure that was founded on the erosion of tribal sovereignty. It speaks further to the need for tribes to engage in governance endeavours on par with any other sovereign. The legal foundation

---

11 Tribes can apply for 'self-governance' designation per the *Tribal Self Governance Act of 1995* (PL 103-413).

12 Personal communication with John J. Robinson, former president of the Northern Cheyenne Nation (2012–13), 10 October 2015.

of tribal sovereignty vis-a-vis the US Government is critical to understanding the opportunities and challenges inherent in American Indian data governance. Each of the 567 federally recognised American Indian tribes has their own nation-to-nation relationship with the US Government, which is expressly addressed in Article 1, section 8 of the US Constitution—also referred to as the 'Commerce Clause'. In the 1830s, a series of Supreme Court decisions known as the Marshall Trilogy delineated the sovereignty of tribes as 'domestic dependent nations' (Fixico 2008). The sovereign status of Indian tribes enables legal and political authority over tribal citizens and activities occurring within the jurisdiction of tribal lands (Davies & Clow 2009). However, the state of domestic dependency on the federal government leads to a well-argued position in federal Indian law that tribal sovereignty exists 'only where the acts of Congress have not displaced it' (Gould 1996: 811). While American Indian tribes continuously fight legal battles to uphold sovereignty and tribal jurisdiction, less attention is paid to tribal sovereignty as a self-reinforcing exercise. Data governance, for example, is facilitated by tribal sovereignty; it also reinforces tribal sovereignty by providing the tribal evidence base required to advance self-determination.

Tribal sovereignty over tribal citizens and resources extends to control over data and research (NCAI Policy Research Center 2012). Data sovereignty explains the process by which American Indian tribes regulate all aspects of tribal data, including access, collection, management, analysis and reporting. Viewing data governance through the lens of tribal sovereignty strengthens the nation-to-nation relationship between tribes and other sovereigns because it commands policy development on tribal terms. For too long, tribes have relied on external data sources for tribal decision-making. This dependency is no less a threat to tribal sovereignty than any other legal constraint facing tribes. The necessity to ground data within a tribal sovereignty framework is critical given that the information tribes need to support their own conceptions of development is not being produced by colonial administrative systems. Tribal data are perhaps the most valuable tools of self-determination because they drive tribal nation building by tribes for tribes.

Ripples of change are starting to emanate from tribes. This was the sentiment I gathered from my interviews with tribal leaders at the National Congress of American Indians Mid-Year Conference in

July 2015. These semi-structured interviews with tribal leaders covered a range of data topics, including current tribal data use and infrastructure, data needs and the connection between tribal sovereignty and data. As I am still in the process of analysing these interviews, a complete analysis is not possible in this chapter.[13] However, I wish to address the unexpected response I received to one set of questions because it leads to an important conclusion about how the data revolution can take root in Indian country.

I asked the following questions pertaining to tribal enrolment:

> Please tell me about your tribe's enrolment policy and process for enrolment. How is this information captured and maintained? Does it differ for tribal citizens who live on the reservation or off?

My intent in asking these questions was to understand the mechanisms and structures of tribal enrolment systems. Much to my surprise, the conversations that ensued included extensive discussion of attitudes towards blood quantum[14] and citizenship. Our conversations turned very personal as tribal leaders shared examples from within their own families of how the exclusivity of blood quantum is harmful. As these were semi-structured interviews, our conversations were allowed to evolve organically. Several of my interviewees talked at length about the need to depart from blood quantum. One mentioned the sense of responsibility he felt as a tribal leader to change the system. This is evident in his statement: 'We have to do something. Just because these kids don't have enough blood, that doesn't make them any less [name of tribe].' Other tribal leaders expressed similar concerns about the future of their tribes if current and future generations cannot formally claim a tribal identity. Moreover, the role of tribal data in advancing citizenship changes became clear. One of the most impassioned interviewees said:

> We need data! I can't go to my fellow legislators and talk to them about dropping the blood quantum unless I have data to show them how in five years we're going to be here, in 10 years we're going to be here [referring to decreases in the size of the tribe]. They'll just think I'm doing this to get my cousin enrolled or something. That's why we need the data.

---

13   I anticipate publishing my findings from these data sovereignty interviews with tribal leaders towards the end of 2016.

14   See Note 9 for more details on blood quantum.

This conversation highlights a critical connection between tribal decision-making and tribal data. This tribal leader referred to data as objective—the opposite of a personal motivation. The importance of having unbiased evidence when developing strategies for tribal decisions, especially those steeped in controversy, cannot be overstated. Moreover, this statement identifies another connection between tribal data and tribal survival. All but one of the tribal leaders I interviewed were concerned about the future of their tribes if citizenship criteria remained in their current state. Further, there is a sense of urgency with which tribal leaders feel they must act to better align citizenship criteria and the demographic realities of their populations. To this end, they identified data as a critical tool. Intertribal partnerships—tribes helping tribes—must be a key component of the data sovereignty revolution in Indian country.

I asked the same tribal leader who shared the above quote to elaborate on the data to which he was referring. He explained that his tribe needs all kinds of data, but especially population projections. To that end, the importance of tribal population projections was also evident in a project undertaken by the Minnesota Chippewa Tribe (MCT) from 2012 to 2013. The MCT contracted with a research firm, Wilder Research, to conduct a series of tribal population projections based on hypothetical citizenship criteria to evaluate tribal citizenship changes (MartinRogers & Gillaspy 2014). The MCT project, in addition to being an excellent example of tribal demographic research, demonstrates how 'by tribes for tribes' does not mean that external expertise cannot be utilised. Data sovereignty is about tribal control: control over who, what, when, where and why for all data projects pertaining to tribal citizens and resources. While the ultimate goal might be 100 per cent 'by us for us', the reality is that many tribes are not in a position to undertake expansive research projects that require extensive technical infrastructure, time and skills. Securing the right research expertise and steering the course are also important exercises of data sovereignty.

Concluding thoughts: the foundation of a data revolution

Tribes in the United States are still catching up to the levels of indigenous data governance occurring in our sister countries: New Zealand, Australia and Canada. In talking to tribal leaders and scanning the data landscape of Indian country, it is promising to at least say we are moving in the right direction. Each of the tribal leaders with whom I spoke is a visionary; they all expressed the view that the futures of their tribes need to be built on data that are controlled by tribes. One of the biggest barriers expressed by all 15 tribal leaders in regards to tribal data development was the need for skilled staff to meet their data needs. All Indian tribes are currently facing the same data circumstances: they encounter gaps in their own tribal data infrastructure; they are subject to administrative data collections that do not meet their needs; they contend with problematic and inaccurate enumeration by other sovereigns; and they face barriers to creating a skilled data workforce, or 'data warriors'. Despite these resounding obstacles, we see that tribes are engaging in data sovereignty projects and developing best practices that other tribes can utilise to meet similar objectives. One of the obstacles, however, is that we still operate in silos in Indian country. It is time to move beyond these silos and embrace intertribal and international indigenous data partnerships to pave the way for data sovereignty. The data sovereignty revolution in Indian country is going to be built tribe by tribe and community by community. Reclaiming the right to understand the diverse realities of our peoples on our terms and to chart sustainable courses for future generations is a matter of contemporary survival for indigenous peoples.

A tribal leader whom I had the honour to interview powerfully summarised the transcendent connection between tribal data and tribal governance: 'Sovereignty as tribal nations was given to us by the Creator. It is sacred. Data to exercise our sovereignty is also sacred.'[15] This statement illustrates how the autonomy of Indian tribes extends far beyond the quasi-sovereign status afforded by the federal government. Indigenous peoples and tribal nations have survived despite every effort to ensure our demise. The key to our survival is

---

15   Personal interview with tribal leader at the National Congress of American Indians Mid-Year Conference in Minneapolis, Minnesota, 1 July 2015.

the fact that our peoples have always been data gatherers. Whereas our ancestors practised data gathering for survival and resistance, today, tribes are engaged in data gathering for sovereignty. Yet, I question whether there is in fact a difference. Tribal data building continues as a critical catalyst for tribal nation rebuilding. In the United States, we are witnessing the beginning of a paradigm shift in which American Indian tribes are becoming data gatherers again, reclaiming the data-rich practices of survival that our ancestors employed since time immemorial. Drawing from this tradition, tribes are disrupting the legacy of colonisation and systems of data administration to which they have been subject. The tribal data revolution demands new approaches, new warriors, new structures and new partnerships to meet the contemporary challenges of tribal data governance in the twenty-first century.

References

Associated Press (2015). For first time, Montana reports unemployment rate on reservations. *Billings Gazette*, 19 June 2015, billingsgazette.com/news/state-and-regional/montana/for-first-time-montana-reportsunemployment-rate-on-reservations/article_f8a0d505-effb-5d29-b870-beb1a26ebfc0.html.

Axelsson P & Sköld P (2011). *Indigenous peoples and demography: the complex relation between identity and statistics*, Berghahn Books, New York.

Berkhofer R (1978). *The white man's Indian: images of the American Indian from Columbus to the present*, Knopf, New York.

Cajete G (1999). *A people's ecology: explorations in sustainable living*, Clear Light, Santa Fe, NM.

Collins JP (2006). Native Americans in the census, 1860–1890. *Prologue* 38(2)(Summer), archives.gov/publications/prologue/2006/summer/indian-census.html.

Davies W & Clow R (2009). *American Indian sovereignty and law: an annotated bibliography*, Scarecrow Press, Lanham, Md.

Deloria V (1969). *Custer died for your sins: an Indian manifesto*, Macmillan, New York.

El Nasser H (2015). US Census challenge: counting every Native American and Alaska Native. *Al Jazeera America*, 3 November 2015, america.aljazeera.com/articles/2015/11/3/us-census-challenge-counting-every-american-indian-and-alaska-native.html.

Eschbach K (1995). The enduring and vanishing American Indian: American Indian population growth and intermarriage in 1990. *Ethnic and Racial Studies* 18(1):89–108.

Evans WN & Topoleski JH (2002). *The social and economic impact of Native American casinos*, NBER Working Paper 9198, National Bureau of Economic Research, Cambridge, Mass.

Fine-Dare K (2002). *Grave injustice: the American Indian repatriation movement and NAGPRA*, University of Nebraska Press, Lincoln, Nebr.

Fixico D (2008). *Treaties with American Indians: an encyclopedia of rights, conflicts, and sovereignty*, ABC-CLIO, Santa Barbara, CA.

Gould SL (1996). The consent paradigm: tribal sovereignty at the millennium. *Columbia Law Review* 96(4):809–902.

IBM (no date). Bringing big data to the enterprise. *IBM InfoSphere Platform*, IBM, New York, www-01.ibm.com/software/data/bigdata/what-is-big-data.html.

Kroeber T (1961). *Ishi in two worlds: a biography of the last wild Indian in North America*, University of California Press, Berkeley, CA.

Kukutai T & Rarere M (2013). Tracking patterns of tribal identification in the New Zealand Census, 1991–2006. *New Zealand Population Review* 39:1–24.

Liebler C & Ortyl T (2014). More than one million new America Indians in 2000: who are they? *Demography* 51(3):1101–30.

MartinRogers N & Gillaspy T (2014). *Minnesota Chippewa Tribe population projections methodology report*, Wilder Research, St Paul, mnchippewatribe.org/pdf/MCT%20Methodology%20Report.pdf.

Mead M (1961). *Coming of age in Samoa: a psychological study of primitive youth for Western civilization*, Morrow, New York.

Misa T, Brey P & Feenberg A (2003). *Modernity and technology*, MIT Press, Cambridge, Mass.

Morphy F (2004). *Indigenous household structures and ABS definitions of the family: what happens when systems collide, and does it matter?*, CAEPR Working Paper No. 26/2004, Centre for Aboriginal Economic Policy Research, The Australian National University, Canberra.

Nagel J (1996). *American Indian ethnic renewal: red power and the resurgence of identity and culture*, Oxford University Press, New York.

National Congress of American Indians (NCAI) Policy Research Center (2012). *Walk softly and listen carefully: building research relationships with tribal communities*, NCAI, Washington, DC.

Otis D and Prucha F (1973). *The Dawes Act and the allotment of Indian lands*, University of Oklahoma Press, Norman, OK.

Oxford English Dictionary (OED) Online (no date). *Oxford English dictionary*, Oxford University Press, Oxford, oxforddictionaries. com/us/definition/american_english/datum.

Powell P (1979). *Sweet Medicine*, University of Oklahoma Press, Norman, OK.

Raczka P (1979). *Winter count: a history of the Blackfoot people*, Oldman River Culture Center, Brocket, Alberta.

Rockafellar N (no date). *The story of Ishi: a chronology*, University of California, Berkeley, history.library.ucsf.edu/ishi.html.

Sackett C (2015). Who counts? Identifying Native American populations. *Evidence Matters* (Spring), US Department of Housing and Urban Development, Washington, DC, huduser.gov/portal/ periodicals/em/spring15/highlight2.html.

Sandefur G, Rindfuss R & Cohen B (1996). *Changing numbers, changing needs: American Indian demography and public health*, National Academy Press, Washington, DC.

Smith LT (1999). *Decolonizing methodologies: research and indigenous peoples*, Zed Books, London.

Snipp CM (1989). *American Indians: the first of this land*, Russell Sage Foundation, New York.

Snipp CM (1997). The size and distribution of the American Indian population: fertility, mortality, migration, and residence. *Population Research and Policy Review* 16:61–93.

Starn O (2004). *Ishi's brain: in search of America's last 'wild' Indian*, WW Norton & Company, New York.

Stewart H (1993). *Looking at totem poles*, Douglas & McIntyre & University of Washington Press, Vancouver & Seattle.

Taylor J (2009). Indigenous demography and public policy in Australia: population or peoples? *Journal of Population Research* 26:115–30.

Todd RM (2012). *Indian country economic development: data and data gaps.* Federal Reserve Bank of Minneapolis, Minneapolis, minneapolisfed.org/community/indian-country/events/~/media/Files/community/indiancountry/Todd_Data_and_Data_Gaps_Paper.pdf.

United States Census Bureau (2012). Census Bureau releases estimates of undercount and overcount in the 2010 census, Media release, Washington, DC, 22 May 2012.

United States Department of Housing and Urban Development (HUD) (2012). Challenging US decennial census data: guidelines for the Indian Housing Block Grant Formula, Media release, Washington, DC, 31 July 2012.

Utley RM & Washburn WE (1985). *The Indian wars*, American Heritage, New York.

Walling J, Small-Rodriguez D & Kukutai T (2009). Tallying tribes: Waikato-Tainui in the census and iwi register. *Social Policy Journal of New Zealand* 36:2–15.

Walter M & Andersen C (2013). *Indigenous statistics: a quantitative research methodology*, Left Coast Press, Walnut Creek, CA.

Part 4: State agency responses

15

The Australian Bureau of Statistics' Aboriginal and Torres Strait Islander enumeration and engagement strategies: challenges and future options

Paul Jelfs

The Australian Bureau of Statistics (ABS) has an Aboriginal and Torres Strait Islander Statistics Program, led by the National Centre for Aboriginal and Torres Strait Islander Statistics (NCATSIS). The role of NCATSIS is to support best practice in the enumeration of Aboriginal and Torres Strait Islander statistics, and maintaining wide-reaching consultation with the Aboriginal and Torres Strait Islander community remains a key strategy in the coordination and development of national statistics. The ABS has a dedicated team devoted to building and strengthening engagement with Aboriginal and Torres Strait Islander peoples, communities and organisations. The ABS supports and is endeavouring to maintain alignment with the United Nations Declaration on the Rights of Indigenous Peoples (UNDRIP) in producing statistics for Aboriginal and Torres Strait Islander peoples. This chapter presents examples of the ABS's acknowledgement of and compliance with UNDRIP in applying many of the organisation's strategies.

What do we know? Literature review

A literature review was conducted to explore viewpoints on existing statistical frameworks and research into alternative enumeration and engagement strategies for indigenous populations, using case studies from Australia, Canada, New Zealand and the United States.

Issues with existing data in Australia

The research reflects concern among analysts that current outputs are of little relevance to Aboriginal and Torres Strait Islander people, and are based on the assumption that their wellbeing is achieved through absorption into mainstream society (Yu 2011: 4). For instance, the Productivity Commission's 'Overcoming Indigenous Disadvantage' framework emphasises statistical socioeconomic equality at the expense of recognising Aboriginal and Torres Strait Islander perspectives and priorities, such as living on remote homelands (Taylor 2009: 118, 122–4; Jordan et al. 2010: 339, 352). Additionally, the literature indicates that outputs from data collections such as the Australian Census and the National Aboriginal and Torres Strait Islander Social Survey (NATSISS) do not meet community needs for localised data. Analysts attribute this to data being aggregated at national or state levels (Yu 2011: 2; Taylor et al. 2012) and to problems with the existing 'Aboriginal and Torres Strait Islander population' demographic (Biddle & Wilson 2013: 107). Analysts suggest addressing the demographic issues by applying consistent parameters across collections and by recognising groups within the broader Aboriginal and Torres Strait Islander population such as native title holders (Taylor 2009: 125; Taylor et al. 2012: 28).

Community initiatives

The literature suggests that a lack of relevant official data is forcing Indigenous groups to collect and manage their own demographic data. These initiatives illustrate not only the inadequacy of existing data but also an opportunity for statistics agencies to engage with Indigenous groups to improve official data collections, as well as to assist community-driven projects such as:

- collections of localised cultural and demographic data to inform community planning and longitudinal datasets such as the Knowing our Community survey undertaken by the Yawuru people of Broome in Western Australia (Yu 2011: 5; Taylor et al. 2012: 8, 28); the International Network of Demographic Evaluation of Populations and Their Health in Africa and Asia (Taylor 2009: 125)
- statistical frameworks measuring Indigenous capabilities and wellbeing such as those developed by the Cape York Institute for Policy and Leadership (Jordan et al. 2010: 347–8, 353).

National and international initiatives

The research reveals a growing interest among governments in developing partnerships with indigenous peoples to develop statistical products that reflect indigenous interests as well as those of government. For instance, Canada has several longstanding survey and research data relationships between government bodies and indigenous groups, as well as health data-sharing initiatives and data infrastructure projects (Bruhn 2014: 16–7). Australia and the United States have also established data governance projects, such as Australia's Aboriginal and Torres Strait Islander Data Archive (Bruhn 2014: 18–9, 23–4).

New Zealand and the United Nations Permanent Forum on Indigenous Issues (UNPFII) have developed indigenous statistical frameworks in close consultation with indigenous peoples. The United Nations (UN) framework reflects indigenous cultural concepts and perspectives in addition to common concerns such as income and education. One key point evident from the indicators is the interdependence of indigenous peoples with the wellbeing of their lands, identities and cultures (Jordan et al. 2010: 351). This point is also reflected in the Māori Statistics Framework, which aims to measure and promote Māori wellbeing (Wereta & Bishop 2006: 266–7, 270).

Common themes and challenges

Certain challenges faced in the development of data governance initiatives for indigenous peoples are discussed in the literature. These include:

- collection and stewardship of culturally sensitive data (Boulton et al. 2014)
- conceptual issues—in particular, unpacking the concept of 'wellbeing' (Wereta & Bishop 2006: 271).

Analysts note that measures of cultural specificity may have limited influence on public policy, as public policy is not easily able to incorporate diverse perspectives (Jordan et al. 2010: 333–5). The literature indicates that this challenge is best addressed through partnerships between indigenous peoples and official agencies, for mutual benefit (Wereta & Bishop 2006; Jordan et al. 2010; Yu 2011; Bruhn 2014: 16). A common priority should be to ensure that communities have access to and a voice in the governance of data concerning them (Bruhn 2014: 25–6).

ABS strategies and data management

Current practice

Key elements of the Aboriginal and Torres Strait Islander Statistics Program include a commitment to ongoing engagement with Aboriginal and Torres Strait Islander peoples in ABS planning, collection and dissemination activities. The ABS collects statistics about the wellbeing of Aboriginal and Torres Strait Islander peoples and is striving to meet the growing need for data about Aboriginal and Torres Strait Islander peoples that are available to and understood by all. The ABS has strived to form a sound history of working collaboratively with the Aboriginal and Torres Strait Islander community across Australia to address statistical collection and dissemination challenges to improve our understanding of their statistical needs. By better understanding the needs of Aboriginal and Torres Strait Islander stakeholders, the ABS is trying to produce data that are informative, relevant and meaningful to all users. To meet this objective, the ABS has implemented strategies and is learning to adapt them as needed, as well as forming important relationships and strengthening existing ones to more effectively report on matters of importance to Aboriginal and Torres Strait Islander peoples.

The strategies used by the ABS aim to:

- improve the survey/data collection experience for Aboriginal and Torres Strait Islander peoples
- collect data that are culturally appropriate, relevant and of high quality for items of importance to Aboriginal and Torres Strait Islander peoples
- promote the range of information available for Aboriginal and Torres Strait Islander peoples and provide support for them to use it effectively, recognising that use may extend from issues awareness to service planning and budgeting.

Key ongoing activities flowing from these strategies, which reflect examples of where the ABS recognises the values of UNDRIP and has been proactive in establishing good relations and understanding across the Aboriginal and Torres Strait Islander population and also the wider community, include the following.

Indigenous Community Engagement Strategy (ICES)

The ICES is a long-running ABS strategy that has helped the organisation build a good relationship with the Aboriginal and Torres Strait Islander community. It aims to enhance ABS engagement with the Aboriginal and Torres Strait Islander community in both data collection and data dissemination, as well as to deliver accessible, appropriate and relevant statistics to meet the needs of Aboriginal and Torres Strait Islander peoples. The objectives of the ICES are delivered by a team of Indigenous Engagement Managers (IEMs) located in each state and the Northern Territory. The IEMs play a crucial role in building relationships based on mutual trust to facilitate honest and open feedback and are actively involved in advising the Aboriginal and Torres Strait Islander community and organisations on the effective use of ABS statistics. The ICES also supports and facilitates the return of information collected from the census and surveys back to the Aboriginal and Torres Strait Islander community in a culturally appropriate way.

The ABS is committed to local-level facilitation and engagement, ensuring continued cooperation and high-quality data for Aboriginal and Torres Strait Islander peoples. Under the ICES program, the IEMs work closely with communities and organisations. For example, before the 2011 census, the Australian Statistician championed the need to expand the ICES, resulting in an increase in the number of IEMs employed by the ABS. This led to improved partnerships with Aboriginal and Torres Strait Islander communities and representative bodies, which the ABS values highly. The strategy resulted in good response rates to the census and an improved range of data for Aboriginal and Torres Strait Islander peoples.[1] Participation and sponsorship at key Aboriginal and Torres Strait Islander events were a key focus for the ABS in the period leading up to the 2011 census.

The ICES program is central to the success of ABS consultation with the Aboriginal and Torres Strait Islander community. The program is committed to targeted engagement for mutually beneficial outcomes and to achieving sustainable and effective partnerships with Aboriginal and Torres Strait Islander communities and organisations. The ICES network also plays a key role across ABS offices in the delivery of cross-cultural training and raising the cultural competency of staff working or engaging with Aboriginal and Torres Strait Islander peoples. Most recently, the network has reviewed and redrafted the ABS Cultural Protocols and Procedures for Working with or Engaging with Aboriginal and Torres Strait Islander Peoples and Communities. These protocols support the ABS's commitment to reconciliation and provide ethical principles to guide behaviours when engaging with Aboriginal and Torres Strait Islander peoples. The review has resulted in streamlining the ABS's approach to engagement and emphasises the need to continue managing engagement in a culturally appropriate way.

Roundtable on Aboriginal and Torres Strait Islander Statistics

In 2013, the ABS established the roundtable, with meetings held twice a year. Members are Aboriginal and Torres Strait Islander people with grassroots experience of working with their communities. The roundtable's operational grassroots focus allows it to provide important insights into improving data quality, engagement strategies and statistical literacy strategies for Aboriginal and Torres Strait Islander peoples. The roundtable's membership includes one IEM from the ABS, with the feedback adding to the information provided from the ICES network. The regular meetings provide a venue for discussion

---

1   Despite this, the net census undercount rate for the Indigenous population increased from 11.5 per cent in 2006 to 17.2 per cent in 2011 — *Editors*.

and exploration of new approaches to overcoming old challenges. The ICES aims to further build its relationship with the roundtable members to harness their networks and expand the capability of the ICES network to engage across states and territories.

Reconciliation Action Plan

An important aspect of the ABS's active commitment to building deeper engagement with Aboriginal and Torres Strait Islander peoples is reflected in its Reconciliation Action Plan, released in 2013. The plan continues to build on the ABS's commitment to showing respect for and recognition of Aboriginal and Torres Strait Islander culture, increasing the recruitment and retention of Aboriginal and Torres Strait Islander peoples in the ABS and continuing to build positive relationships between Aboriginal and Torres Strait Islander peoples and other Australians. The ABS's Senior Reconciliation Champion actively participates as a member of the Australian Public Service (APS) Indigenous Champions Network (comprising senior members of Australian Government agencies) including facilitation or support of APS Indigenous Employment Network forums. In the spirit of reconciliation, the ABS promotes external development and networking opportunities available to Aboriginal and Torres Strait Islander employees such as the APS Indigenous employee forum. It is the role of everyone in the ABS to follow through with the actions set out in the Reconciliation Action Plan, contributing to cultural change and helping achieve the organisation's objectives for reconciliation. As part of the plan, the ABS is committed to leading and coordinating statistical activity involving and relating to Aboriginal and Torres Strait Islander peoples to inform their communities and organisations, governments and the wider community.

Tackling the challenges

The ABS faces a number of challenges in continuing to collect information for and about the Aboriginal and Torres Strait Islander population. For example, during the 2011 census, diversity in geographic locations, languages spoken at home and access to information about government programs and services raised specific challenges for how best to promote the census to Aboriginal and Torres Strait Islander peoples, communities and organisations.

To attempt to address these challenges, the ABS developed the Indigenous Communication Strategy, employing an integrated communication mix focusing on high use of peer-to-peer platforms. A key component of the communication strategy was raising awareness of the importance of identifying as Aboriginal and/or Torres Strait Islander in the census. Specific messages and communication materials (tailored for urban and discrete communities) were developed, with an emphasis on the production of visual material.

In the lead-up to enumeration, the ABS actively engages with the community to identify staff to support and undertake interviewing, determine the appropriate timing of enumeration and promote a particular survey or the census. To illustrate this, in the 2011 census, the ABS worked closely with local people and their communities to plan the most appropriate approach to achieve improved outcomes. This involved discussions with communities about the best time to enumerate, whether the ABS could employ local people to assist and how to promote the census through local events and gatherings. Employing local people to work in the census meant there were people who knew the community, spoke the local language and could advise on local issues and how best to manage them. The staff were fully trained prior to undertaking census work and each received a certificate acknowledging and thanking them for contributing to its success. It has often been reported back to the ABS that people are proud to say they worked on the census and would be willing to do it again. These people's positive experiences will hopefully increase the support from the community for the work of the ABS, because without community support the ABS is unable to achieve successful outcomes.

Other challenges currently faced include balancing stakeholder needs in the Aboriginal and Torres Strait Islander community with meeting government data reporting obligations and reducing respondent burden. ABS data are used by a wide range of organisations, Aboriginal and Torres Strait Islander and non-Indigenous, for a range of purposes. The ABS works with stakeholders to anticipate these uses, but there is a tension between specificity, cost and confidentiality of data to meet these uses. An integral component of the ABS work program is the role administrative data currently play in determining population estimates and life expectancy and the increasing role they are likely to have into the future. The ABS is looking to access additional administrative data sources and pursue opportunities where this data could be effectively linked to provide relevant information that might enhance what is collected through our survey vehicles. Additional challenges encountered by the ABS in meeting these objectives—such as capturing the diversity of the population, knowledge gaps, the scale of our survey program and understanding our role—are being considered as the organisation moves forward.

Data collection

The ABS maintains an ongoing program aimed at improving relationships and ultimately making enumeration easier. The activities of the ongoing ICES program, coupled with high-level government and nongovernmental organisation (NGO) engagement, are central to the ABS's Aboriginal and Torres Strait Islander engagement strategies. While the ABS's processes and presence in the community fluctuate throughout the collection period, engagement with the community is always a primary focus.

Before enumeration

Engagement is conducted at the organisational level, before engaging with the community, in an effort to prepare and gain support for enumeration, and the ABS formed the Roundtable on Aboriginal and Torres Strait Islander Statistics to further assist these efforts. The ABS also utilises Aboriginal and Torres Strait Islander reference groups and/or technical panels along with local and national champions in planning and supporting culturally sensitive collections such as the biomedical collection of the Australian Aboriginal and Torres Strait Islander Health Survey (AATSIHS).

Culturally appropriate short videos are used on occasion to support engagement and promote participation, presenting a snapshot of what the survey is about and explaining the importance of being involved. For example, the ABS produced a short video titled 'NATSISS— It's about me, it's about us' to promote the 2014–15 NATSISS so that Aboriginal and Torres Strait Islander peoples could relate to the information collected by the survey and participate, knowing that NATSISS will tell their story. This video was used before and throughout NATSISS enumeration and was produced with the active involvement of Aboriginal and Torres Strait Islander people to tell the story.

The ABS undertakes testing of survey questions and materials to ensure these are culturally appropriate and relate to the Aboriginal and Torres Strait Islander community. An example was the development of a prompt card depicting bush tucker foods to assist people in advising what, if any, bush tucker they had consumed in the previous 24-hour period. This was field tested in a dress rehearsal of the survey prior to being used in the survey's final enumeration.

During enumeration

The aim of strategies employed before and during enumeration is to increase the participation and involvement of Aboriginal and Torres Strait Islander peoples in ABS surveys and the census. For example, in the 2012–13 AATSIHS, the ABS engaged Australian Olympic champion Cathy Freeman as survey champion to promote the importance of the data collected in the survey and improve participation. A similar approach was used for NATSISS, where a number of survey champions promoted the survey across Australia.

In the lead-up to the 2011 census, the ABS employed community coordinators in remote areas who promoted the census in the community and supported recruitment as well as planning activities such as workload management. In urban areas, the ABS employed Indigenous assistants to support or assist with completion of the mainstream census form, although, given the dispersed nature of Aboriginal and Torres Strait Islander residents in urban areas, it was often difficult to implement the strategies as planned.

During enumeration, the ICES team continues to engage with the Aboriginal and Torres Strait Islander community using existing and new collaborative partnerships with an aim to increase understanding of, and participation in, ABS collections. Where possible, the ABS employs Aboriginal and Torres Strait Islander facilitators from the local community in remote areas to assist ABS interviewers in undertaking surveys. Local facilitators are essential in providing a more positive survey experience for respondents and assist greatly with the quality of the information collected. The ABS extended the facilitator strategy to include selected nonremote and regional Aboriginal and Torres Strait Islander communities for the 2014–15 NATSISS to improve response rates. A lot was learnt from this approach, which will hopefully prove invaluable in assisting the organisation to improve its access to the Aboriginal and Torres Strait Islander urban population for future survey and census participation.

Social media is increasingly being used across all stages of enumeration. During the 2011 census, online communication and social media were employed, including YouTube video content from Aboriginal and Torres Strait Islander census ambassadors and promotion via Facebook and Twitter. Print and radio media were used heavily in line with Aboriginal and Torres Strait Islander audience communication preferences. This included media partnerships with Aboriginal and Torres Strait Islander-owned and operated media outlets, targeted editorial, media releases and interview opportunities. In addition, collaborations with technical and further education programs across northern Australia offered students working for the ABS, as part of the 2011 census program, the opportunity to receive credit towards their certificate course.

After enumeration

After enumeration, the ABS is committed to returning information collected to the Aboriginal and Torres Strait Islander community. Using its network of regional offices and the IEMs, the ABS engages with the Aboriginal and Torres Strait Islander community in local areas to discuss survey outcomes and provide statistical training in accessing and interpreting the data. The ABS returns statistical information using different means, ranging from flyers and fact sheets distributed among Aboriginal and Torres Strait Islander organisations and communities to producing audiovisual presentations. For example, the ABS is finalising an audiovisual presentation to disseminate biomedical results from the 2012–13 AATSIHS. Another example is the production of 'Census Story Books', developed as a resource to promote an understanding of the ABS and the data we collect and the story it tells for a particular region or community.

The aim of the Census Story Books is to help Aboriginal and Torres Strait Islander community members understand their community's story on a personal level and compare it with other communities within their region. This engagement tool supports the return of information in an easily understood and meaningful way, and is helping to maintain relationships with communities in the lead-up to the 2016 census and beyond. This initiative helps generate and direct discussions on how the community story in 2011 compares with now, by talking about what changes may have occurred and prompting discussions about how to ensure the 2016 census count is as accurate as possible. The Census Story Books have reached a large audience in discrete Aboriginal and Torres Strait Islander communities across Queensland, the Northern Territory and Western Australia, and helped the ICES team to engage with, and gain the support of, stakeholders and members of remote communities for data collection activities, and to promote statistical literacy.

As a national statistics organisation, the ABS has the responsibility not only to provide statistical leadership and share information with Aboriginal and Torres Strait Islander communities, but also to help educate communities in understanding and interpreting data by promoting statistical literacy. During 2013–14, the IEMs undertook a wide range of activities in remote, regional and urban areas with priority given to completing the return of information from the 2011 census and the 2012–13 AATSIHS. A popular ongoing statistical literacy program delivered by the IEMs is the ABS 'Footy Stats Program', which helps school students learn about statistical concepts such as 'data', the 'mean' or a 'census' and how to calculate a percentage using fun football-based activities.

Future intentions and options

The ABS is always looking to identify ways to improve the quality and relevance of our statistics for and about Aboriginal and Torres Strait Islander peoples. With this in mind, the ABS ICES program aims to continually improve engagement with Aboriginal and Torres Strait Islander peoples and communities by returning data to communities and undertaking activities aimed at increasing their statistical literacy, such as delivering information sessions on data about Aboriginal and Torres Strait Islander peoples. These relationships and networks play an invaluable role in communities' understanding of the importance of statistical collection activities and contribute to better outcomes.

A recent example involved the ABS working with several Aboriginal and Torres Strait Islander researchers to unlock the potential of ABS data. This included analysing the NATSISS Confidential Unit Record File using a statistical analysis platform within the confines of the ABS data laboratory.

The ABS recently undertook two reviews for the purpose of improving the quality and relevance of Aboriginal and Torres Strait Islander statistics. These reviews will help shape the future direction of the ABS's Aboriginal and Torres Strait Islander Statistics Program. A review of the ABS Indigenous Status Standard, which includes the standard Indigenous status question, involved significant consultation with government, research organisations and Aboriginal and Torres Strait Islander agencies and organisations. The review recommended further research and the ABS is currently exploring these options. The second review was of the Aboriginal and Torres Strait Islander Statistics Program to ensure its flexibility and relevance in the light of diverse stakeholder demands.

The ABS is striving to increase its relevance to the Aboriginal and Torres Strait Islander community and to make data more useful for this population. Aboriginal and Torres Strait Islander peoples have many items of particular relevance to them as a people—for example, kinship, family and community, spirituality, culture and cultural identity—and achieving optimal outcomes in Aboriginal and Torres Strait Islander data collection involves addressing the social, emotional, spiritual and cultural wellbeing of the whole community. This includes applying innovative solutions, developed in close consultation with the Aboriginal and Torres Strait Islander community, to the collection, ownership and application of Aboriginal and Torres Strait Islander statistics. Our focus needs to centre on how to better generate this information to provide a closer fit with Aboriginal and Torres Strait Islander peoples' world views, while still meeting government objectives (see Walter, and Lovett, this volume). In many cases, these objectives align, but, in some cases, there is a tension between what is measured, how it is measured, balancing cultural constructs around issues and ensuring statistical viability. Working with our international counterparts in Statistics New Zealand is providing some insight into how the ABS can better meet this changing landscape (see Bishop, this volume).

Moving forward, the ABS will attempt to address concerns in the Aboriginal and Torres Strait Islander community about the collection, use and purpose of statistics for and about their peoples. To this end, we are currently developing an Aboriginal and Torres Strait Islander Statistical Framework and Information Model and are using roundtable meetings to seek input on how to shape it from the ground up and make it useful and beneficial to the Aboriginal and Torres Strait Islander population while also meeting government requirements. The framework will be developed in close consultation with the Aboriginal and Torres Strait Islander community to ensure it is meaningful and relevant to them. It will support strength-based reporting of the Aboriginal and Torres Strait Islander population, moving away from simply measuring disadvantage and the gap with the non-Indigenous population. This is part of the ABS's role in providing statistical leadership for all Australians while seeking feedback on where the organisation can add value. More importantly, it will recognise the importance of Aboriginal and Torres Strait Islander knowledge and cultures and the need for information about their use and maintenance—again, reflecting how UNDRIP elements are interwoven in the ABS's strategies for producing Aboriginal and Torres Strait Islander statistics.

The ABS is proactively seeking collaboration across various areas with interested individuals and organisations. An integral component of this includes utilising opportunities to up-skill ABS staff and building an organisational culture that contributes to success while increasing the organisation's statistical assets through partnerships with research groups and researchers residing in or near Aboriginal and Torres Strait Islander communities. By harnessing these opportunities, the ABS will be not only investing in its own staff but also looking to work with partner organisations to build their capacity and ours and together achieve the desired outcome.

As an organisation, we are changing some of the ways we conduct our work, becoming more efficient, striving to do more with existing data sources (administrative data and surveys) and working collaboratively with the research community and Aboriginal and Torres Strait Islander communities. In addition, we aim to be more relevant, to improve Aboriginal and Torres Strait Islander peoples' experiences with ABS collections and to enhance Aboriginal and Torres Strait Islander statistics. We will continue giving something back to the community in the form of improved data access and better products, improved statistical literacy and also job opportunities. We are committed to managing this change by increasing our understanding of the environment in which we are operating and the new information options on which we can draw. We acknowledge the need to increase our awareness of the changing requirements of our key stakeholders and apply much of our energy to more effective partnerships with them and delivering benefits to both parties.

An integral part of this change is transforming people statistics to be more solution-centred, moving on from the traditional model of being focused on collections, as shown in Table 15.1.

Table 15.1 Characteristics of solution-centred and collection-centred statistics

Solution-centred models are characterised by …	Collection-centred models are characterised by …
Primary focus on information requirements	Primary focus on collection product sets
Appetite for single and multi-source statistics	Predominantly single-source statistics from ABS collections
ABS value proposition more focused on statistical leadership	ABS value proposition more focused on data supply
ABS role more defined by high value-adding activities	ABS role more defined by its collection and infrastructural capabilities
Suite of regular product sets based on (and responsive to) information requirements	Suite of regular products based on collections

Source: The author.

Through this change, the ABS aims to deliver the following:

- higher-quality statistics for policy development, delivery and evaluation
- increased responsiveness to information needs, coupled with increased flexibility
- improved measurement of outcomes for populations of interest
- assistance for Aboriginal and Torres Strait Islander people to understand data and use them more effectively through partnered education arrangements and tools.

To support this transformation process, the ABS is keen to establish key partnerships around administrative data and to seek opportunities for maximising the use of administrative and big data. We will need to partner with stakeholders to share government data and maximise a whole-of-government benefit for policy research and to develop important statistical solutions. The ABS is confident these developments, together with its existing strategies, mean it is well placed to continue to play a leading role in the future development of high-quality, relevant statistics for and about the Aboriginal and Torres Strait Islander population, and to respond effectively to the ever-increasing demand for these data.

References

Biddle N & Wilson T (2013). Indigenous Australian population projections: problems and prospects. *Journal of Population Research* 30:101–16.

Boulton A, Hudson M, Ahuriri-Driscoll A & Stewart A (2014). Enacting Kaitiakitanga: challenges and complexities in the governance and ownership of Rongoa research information. *International Indigenous Policy Journal* 5(2).

Bruhn J (2014). Identifying useful approaches to the governance of indigenous data. *International Indigenous Policy Journal* 5(2).

Jordan K, Bulloch H & Buchanan G (2010). Statistical equality and cultural difference in Indigenous wellbeing frameworks: a new expression of an enduring debate. *Australian Journal of Social Issues* 45(3):333–62.

Taylor J (2009). Indigenous demography and public policy in Australia: population or peoples? *Journal of Population Research* 26:115–30.

Taylor J, Doran B, Parriman M & Yu E (2012). Statistics for community governance: the Yawuru Indigenous population survey of Broome, Western Australia. *International Indigenous Policy Journal* 5(2).

Wereta W & Bishop D (2006). Towards a Māori statistics framework. In White JP, Wingert S & Beavon D (eds), *Aboriginal policy research: moving forward, making a difference*, Thompson Educational Press, Toronto.

Yu P (2011). *The power of data in Aboriginal hands*, CAEPR Topical Issue 2012/4, Centre for Aboriginal Economic Policy Research, The Australian National University, Canberra.

16

Indigenous peoples and the official statistics system in Aotearoa/New Zealand[1]

Darin Bishop

Introduction

The notion that data do not exist absolutely but are created through measurement highlights the importance of the measurement process in producing relevant knowledge. As Stiglitz et al. (2009: 7) have argued: 'What we measure affects what we do; and if our measurements are flawed, decisions may be distorted.'

This understanding is crucial when considering the implications and concerns raised regarding the collection, ownership and application of statistics pertaining to indigenous peoples. Many national statistics offices (NSOs) around the world have systems in place to derive statistics relating to their indigenous peoples. Arguably, New Zealand has gone further than any other nation-state in seeking to develop

---

1   The views, opinions, findings and conclusions or recommendations expressed in this chapter are strictly those of the author. They do not necessarily reflect the views of the Ministry of Māori Development (Te Puni Kōkiri) or the New Zealand Government. The Ministry of Māori Development and the New Zealand Government take no responsibility for any errors or omissions in, or for the correctness of, the information contained in this chapter. The chapter is presented not as policy, but with a view to inform and stimulate wider debate. Crown copyright © 2015.

such systems and to accommodate the data needs of its indigenous people. Notwithstanding this, significant deficiencies remain and these undermine Māori data sovereignty.

The focus of this chapter is on the measurement process, its relationship to the production of official statistics on Māori and what this may mean in terms of data sovereignty. The chapter also discusses the challenges and options for collectors and producers of official Māori statistics wanting to improve the information that is readily available.

The main body of the chapter outlines what these deficiencies are and how they undermine data sovereignty. The final section discusses what is required to overcome these deficiencies to meet the data needs of Māori, including the need for Māori to be actively involved in decision-making processes.

Measurement process

Key stages of the data collection and survey cycle are outlined in Table 16.1. For each stage, decisions are made that collectively form what I refer to as the 'measurement process'. Without an understanding of the various decision-making points, it is difficult to advocate for a more effective system for collecting data on indigenous peoples or to identify future opportunities.

In terms of the collection stage, it is important to understand not only what is collected, why and how, but also what is not collected. At the compilation stage, collectors and producers typically draw on existing statistical rules, guidelines, standards or practices to make decisions. Data users are generally not involved in this part of the process (apart from reviews of standards and classifications). As a result, users do not always understand why compilation decisions are made and what the implications are. For example, what are the data limitations for small populations when confidentiality rules are applied to the data?

At the analysis stage, questions include how indigenous peoples are considered within the analysis, if at all. And, what are the appropriate comparators when assessing indigenous peoples' progress. At the publication stage, the utility of the statistical tools and resulting statistical information for users of statistics regarding indigenous peoples is a key question.

Table 16.1 Key stages of the data collection and survey cycle

Stage	Decision-making points
Collection	Planning—formulation of objectives Conceptual measurement Consultation/engagement Selection of survey frame and sample design Questionnaire design Data collection
Compilation	Data capture and coding Standards and classifications Application of statistical rules, guidelines or practices Editing and imputation Confidentialising of data Estimation
Analysis	Comparative analysis
Publication	Production and dissemination of official statistics

Source: Adapted from Statistics Canada (2003).

In considering these issues, what is obvious is that the resulting information is not produced by chance. Rather, it involves advocacy or lobby groups who influence what is collected; it requires adequate funding and resourcing that also influence what is collected and how appropriate consultation or engagement; and subject matter technical expertise and decision-makers at each stage of the cycle who ultimately determine what data are collected and, equally, what data are not collected and reported.

The measurement process is also vital for empowering indigenous communities and assisting them to identify their own information needs. However, the ability for users of data on indigenous peoples to engage and influence decisions at each stage is both costly and time-consuming. Accordingly, the collectors and producers of official information typically shape the resulting data and information. This is despite increasing efforts by the collectors and producers to better understand the information needs of indigenous peoples, particularly in the context of Aotearoa/New Zealand.

Not surprisingly, in 2004, the United Nations Permanent Forum on Indigenous Issues (UNPFII) convened a workshop on data collection and disaggregation for indigenous peoples (UNPFII 2004). Indigenous representatives questioned the relevance of existing frameworks in reflecting their world views and drew attention to their lack of participation in data collection processes and governance (see also Kukutai & Taylor, this volume).

In addition, the UNPFII workshop identified several recommendations relating to the measurement process and data collection activities for indigenous peoples that are just as relevant today. In particular:

- including questions on indigenous identity in all relevant data collections
- following the principle of free prior and informed consent at all levels
- ensuring data collections are in accordance with human rights provisions, data protection regulations and privacy guarantees, including respect for confidentiality
- participation in all stages of data collection, including planning, implementation, analysis and dissemination, access and return, with appropriate resourcing and capacity-building to do so
- responding to the priorities and aims of the indigenous communities
- where possible, conducting data collection exercises in local indigenous languages
- developing a conceptual framework for rights-based indicators that are relevant to indigenous and tribal peoples
- collecting data specific to the situation of indigenous peoples, while also allowing comparability with other national and international populations.

Realising Māori potential

From an Aotearoa/New Zealand perspective, Māori statistics are needed for a range of reasons. Māori organisations need statistics to enable them to represent their needs to local and central governments, to perform their community-level functions and to inform their own investment decisions (see Jansen, Hudson, & Hudson et al., this volume). Here we are concerned more with the perceived needs of governments for data on Māori citizens. Within government, statistics provide the tools and evidence to assist policymakers to develop, target, monitor and report on initiatives with precision and confidence.

The New Zealand Government has tasked its agencies to deliver better public services for all New Zealanders by setting 10 challenging targets for the public sector to achieve over the next five years (SSC 2015). Furthermore, agencies and entities have developed strategies that directly impact on improving outcomes for Māori within their respective sectors (for example, Ministry of Business, Innovation and Employment 2012, 2014; Ministry of Education 2013; Ministry of Health 2014; Te Taura Whiri i te Reo Māori & Te Puni Kōkiri 2014). Each strategy has its own Māori outcomes framework and requires relevant data to assess performance and to track progress. Māori statistics are crucial to understanding and reporting the position of Māori within these priorities and strategies.

Te Puni Kōkiri (Ministry of Māori Development)

Te Puni Kōkiri (the Ministry of Māori Development) was established under the *Ministry of Māori Development Act 1991* with responsibility for promoting increased levels of attainment by Māori across a number of specified sectors. In addition to these core policy functions, Te Puni Kōkiri is charged with leading public policy in the Māori development portfolio. The ministry's advisory and program management functions have come to span a wide range of contexts, from social and economic policy as it pertains to Māori through to natural resources, the environment and cultural heritage sectors.

Te Puni Kōkiri has a wide reach despite being a small ministry. It has both a national and a local presence, providing a direct interface with *iwi* (tribes), *hapū* (subtribes) and *whānau* (families including extended families), which is important to meeting their needs as well as facilitating better Crown–Māori relationships and engagement (Te Puni Kōkiri 2015a). Within this context, the ministry needs relevant and reliable evidence to participate fully in formulating, monitoring and assessing policies and programs that contribute to improved results for Māori. The ministry is not a primary collector or producer of official statistics, meaning it relies heavily on other agencies to regularly collect, analyse and produce relevant statistical information for Māori. In this regard, it advocates for the promotion and dissemination of knowledge and encourages informed debate on emerging trends and issues for Māori.

The government's priorities, targets and strategies discussed above provide a wealth of statistical information on Māori. However, in terms of the measurement process, there is often only a small window of opportunity to influence decisions on the selected indicators and data used to measure progress for Māori within the respective strategies. This also applies when priorities, targets and strategies are reviewed or updated.

It is fair to say that the policy environment shapes the administrative records, surveys and, to some extent, the Census of Population and Dwellings in terms of what data are collected, analysed and reported in the public domain—whether they are about Māori or the population more generally. For example, the return to collecting *iwi* data in the 1991 Census of Population and Dwellings was primarily instigated by the Māori affairs portfolio, which required this information to monitor the government of the day's proposed policy to devolve delivery of social services to *iwi* (Statistics New Zealand 1988).

The 'Closing the Gap' and 'Reducing Inequalities' initiatives between the mid-1990s and mid-2000s did not lead to new data-collecting activities, but they did shape the ways in which government agencies and researchers measured and reported on Māori outcomes during that period (see, for example, Chapple & Rea 1998; Durie 2006). More recently, the government's aim to help *whānau* become more self-managing and take greater responsibility for their own development through the Whānau Ora initiative (Te Puni Kōkiri 2015b) will also influence the future reporting of Māori in the public domain by increasing the need for data that more adequately report on Māori collectives like *whānau*.

Official statistics on Māori: the Aotearoa/ New Zealand context

When considering challenges and future options for Māori statistics the starting point is to understand the adequacy of the official statistics system for users or potential users of Māori statistics. There are some fundamental principles to test the system, including whether:

- the data for Māori are readily accessible
- the data for Māori are available in a timely and ongoing manner

- it is possible to disaggregate the data for Māori by key variables such as age, sex and location (as a minimum requirement)
- the information is meaningful to stakeholders, particularly Māori
- the units of measurement include both Māori individual and Māori collective identities
- the relevant definitions, classifications and methodologies have been developed for Māori
- the system recognises the distinct Māori institutions that exist within Māori society
- the system recognises the social, economic, environmental and cultural areas of Māori development
- appropriate benchmarks and comparators have been developed for Māori within the system.

While the internet and the increased availability of reporting tools have gone some way to address issues in terms of access to information, challenges relating to measurement remain, especially in terms of measuring Māori concepts. These detailed data and information gaps are presented below.

Data and information gaps

Nearly all of the official statistical information on Māori that is available today was collected as a by-product of social and economic data collected for the total population. As such, it reflects the needs, priorities and concerns of government rather than Māori and, more than that, it reflects the fragmented and incoherent state of social statistics generally.

Despite this, official Māori statistics provide most of the data required for the measurement of socioeconomic outcomes for Māori. Coverage is at its most extensive in the demographic, social and economic areas—a reflection of the nature of the policies that successive past governments pursued in respect of Māori. Prior to the first running of the post-censual Māori social survey, Te Kupenga,[2] in 2013 (Statistics

---

2   Te Kupenga is the first national survey specifically designed to capture Māori wellbeing in New Zealand. The survey collected information on a wide range of topics to give an overall picture of the social, cultural and economic wellbeing of Māori. The survey also provides important information about the health of the Māori language and culture.

New Zealand 2013a), coverage data on Māori cultural difference or indigeneity were limited to a few variables such as Māori descent, ethnic identification, language, knowledge of *iwi* and some aspects of cultural connectedness.

In reviewing the range of official statistics relating to Māori, it is evident that in some areas national estimates on Māori simply do not exist— for example, data on *whānau*, savings or external migration (see also, Pool, this volume, on the failure of national accounts to accommodate principles of family obligation: *whanaungatanga*). In other instances, data are collected but the resulting information is reported only for the general population (for example, there is no standard reporting on Māori families or Māori households) or the data are not readily accessible in a way that has utility for Māori (for example, due to the size of the Māori sample in surveys like the Household Economic Survey). The following provide a summary of outstanding needs in specific areas.

Māori families and households

Analysis of Māori families and households could provide richer information for policy purposes. While they are a poor substitute for *whānau* (see Kukutai et al. 2016), they do offer an opportunity to look at individuals in a social context. The regional reports on Tamariki and Rangatahi prepared by Statistics New Zealand in 2001 examine the living arrangements and household circumstances of these two important subpopulations.

Currently, there is no standard output produced by Statistics New Zealand on Māori families or households. This is because, for statistical purposes, ethnicity is an individual characteristic that cannot be applied to a collective such as a family or household (see Davies & Wereta 2013). Consequently, users define for themselves what a Māori family or household is. Definitions range from ethnicity of the parent(s) and proportion of Māori in the family or household to any member of the family or household identifying as Māori. The use of different definitions means the analyses and trends are not always comparable.

Māori migration

While information exists on Māori living in Australia (Kukutai & Pawar 2013), data to track the movement of Māori leaving and returning to Aotearoa/New Zealand on a regular basis are not readily available. This information is crucial for producing improved estimates and projections of the Māori population and for understanding Māori migration patterns.

Māori business activity

The need to produce statistics on Māori businesses and Māori business activity was first discussed at the 1984 Hui Taumata (Māori Economic Summit). Despite demand and the developmental work being undertaken in Tatauranga Umanga Māori (Statistics New Zealand 2015a)—a multi-year research project that involves defining, identifying and reporting on Māori authorities and eventually Māori businesses—progress is slow.

Cultural outcomes

The existing statistics and those proposed by Statistics New Zealand are adequate for the measurement of general social and economic outcomes for Māori, but somewhat limited when it comes to the monitoring of cultural outcomes. Te Kupenga has filled some gaps in relation to cultural connectedness.

Regional data

Requirements for regional and smaller geographic units complicate the design of samples. Sampling Māori to get the same accuracy level as non-Māori requires Māori to be oversampled. In the past, Statistics New Zealand and the Ministry of Health have used booster samples to get regional data for Māori. Given the limitations, questions must be asked about the capacity of the official statistics system to meet the statistical needs of Māori communities and, indeed, the needs of other small populations.

Cost to produce new data and utilising existing data

The cost associated with conducting new surveys means it is unlikely that another national-scale Māori survey would run alongside Te Kupenga. This partly reflects the expectation that government agencies will continue to make efforts to reduce fiscal costs. It also reflects a drive to investigate alternative ways of using existing administrative records and survey data—for example, Statistics New Zealand's Integrated Data Infrastructure (IDI), a linked longitudinal dataset that covers an extended range of pathways and transitions information.

Making existing information more relevant to Māori will require further thinking, and should include an acceptance from those who lead the official statistics system that nonstandard outputs may be the way of the future within a climate of fiscal constraint.

Timeliness

Timeliness is also an issue when developing new surveys or measuring new concepts. For example, the idea of a Māori social survey was first mooted in early 2000, but, for a number reasons, the survey was not conducted until 2013.

Unit of measurement

Official Māori statistics typically use the individual as the basic unit of measurement, meaning that none of the existing data allows the observation of Māori collective entities such as *whānau* or Māori governance bodies. Accordingly, any resulting analysis is typically about Māori as consumers and producers of goods and services within the wider society, rather than as participants and contributors within *Te Ao Māori* (the Māori world). This represents a fundamental shortcoming of the official statistical system, not just in Aotearoa/New Zealand but also in other nations with indigenous populations, and the translation of indigenous concepts into existing information systems presents a significant challenge in terms of meeting state obligations under the United Nations Declaration on the Rights of Indigenous Peoples (UNDRIP).

Importance of the Census of Population and Dwellings

The census is currently the only comprehensive source of population and dwelling statistics for Māori at the tribal and subnational levels. The census provides opportunities to produce knowledge on Māori that is relevant to their information needs across a range of socioeconomic and cultural variables including ethnicity, Māori descent, *iwi* and language. Inadequacies in other surveys (for example, sample size for Māori) and administrative datasets mean that only the census can provide a comprehensive picture of Māori. Due to a combination of constraints, including costs, technical issues and small survey populations, other surveys including Te Kupenga cannot meet the specific needs of community-based Māori organisations.

For electoral purposes, the census is a key information source for determining representation in New Zealand's Parliament, including the number and size of Māori electorates. Furthermore, data are required regarding the protection of Māori culture arising from the Treaty of Waitangi. The census also provides the population frame for Te Kupenga.

Due to the rising costs of running a census, opportunities from new technologies and the increasing availability of alternative data sources, there is discussion about how New Zealand's five-yearly census will be run and how frequently it will be run in the future. These decisions are critical when considering the reliance on the census by data users of Māori statistics, the availability of alternative data sources to produce Māori statistics and the ability to produce Māori population estimates in the future (Statistics New Zealand 2015b).

Building the statistical capability of Māori organisations

Good information is a critical part of a Māori organisation's infrastructure, planning and decision-making (see Hudson, Hudson et al., & Jansen, this volume). Given the discussion about the future of the census, there is a clear opportunity to take a lead role in the design or facilitation of a statistical capability program for Māori organisations for which there are two key objectives. The first is to raise awareness and extend the use of existing official statistics by users of Māori statistics, and, second, and perhaps most beneficial, is the ability to transfer skills and capability to Māori organisations to conduct their own community surveys.

The need for an advocacy network

The number of Māori who use official statistics or have an interest in them is small (but growing) and, as a result, the Māori voice is not always heard within decision-making processes. While the Ministry of Māori Development does have an advocacy role, it is important to be able to influence outcomes both within and outside government.

An external Māori voice (such as the Te Mana Raraunga, the Māori Data Sovereignty Network) that is independent of the official statistics system can articulate Māori concerns and advocate for Māori interests in language that statisticians can understand (see Kukutai & Taylor, this volume).

Conclusion

Just over 20 years ago, Statistics New Zealand started to develop a Māori statistics framework as the basis for building a robust system of statistics for and about Māori. In 2006, that work was presented in the paper 'Towards a Māori statistics framework' (Wereta & Bishop 2006) at a meeting convened by the UNPFII to discuss indigenous peoples and indicators of wellbeing.

While the content of the framework was not necessarily a surprise to those attending the meeting, what seemed different was that an NSO was attempting to conceptually understand, measure and identify indigenous statistical needs—in this case, Māori statistical needs. Since then, Statistics New Zealand has made considerable gains in continuing to identify and meet the statistical needs of Māori. Some of the gains include:

- a review of the statistics framework and development of He Arotahi Tatauranga (the Māori Statistics Framework) (Statistics New Zealand 2014)
- statistical information (for example, *iwi* profiles) becoming more readily accessible through platforms such as the internet (Statistics New Zealand 2015c), with the challenge now being one of relevance in terms of the tools and reports that are produced on Māori, rather than access
- the first running of the Māori social survey, Te Kupenga, in 2013 with production of a series of publications on Māori culture
- a set of tier-one statistics (deemed the most important statistics for understanding how well New Zealand is performing) that includes Māori-specific statistics—namely, financial performance and position of Māori business, *whānau* connectedness, Māori cultural wellbeing and Māori language use—the significance of which is

that these statistics have priority status within the official statistics system (Statisphere 2012)

- the use of domain plans for anticipating future statistical needs and priorities for particular areas of interest including Māori environmental statistics (Statistics New Zealand 2013b)

- the (albeit slow) progress of the Tatauranga Umanga Māori project, a multi-year research project that involves defining and identifying Māori authorities, and eventually Māori businesses, and compiling statistics about them (Statistics New Zealand 2015b).

Despite these gains, Kukutai and Walter (2015) raise a number of serious issues that need to be addressed if there are to be continued improvements in the production of official statistics on Māori. These are summarised as a:

> recognition of indigenous geographic and cultural diversity; a recognition that current ways of conceptualising the data are not the only, or the most useful, set of practices; a recognition of the need for mutual capability building; and most crucially, recognition of the need for genuine indigenous decision making to shape the functionality of indigenous statistics. (Kukutai & Walter 2015: 325)

Conceptual measurement of Māori collectives and their activities continues to be a challenge. For example, it is still not clear whether it is possible to measure *whānau* through the official statistics system. The need for this information is relevant given that *whānau* outcomes are a central feature of the current government's Māori policy. In the meantime, there is scope to extend the usefulness of available data through analysis of Māori families and households disaggregated on the basis of key social, economic and cultural criteria. Discussions about the transformation and future of the census also raise issues in terms of the availability of official statistics for Māori at the tribal, regional or community level.

There remains the need for an external Māori voice in the official statistics system to articulate and promote the statistical needs of Māori at the national level and engage in the decision-making process (see also Lovett, & Walter, this volume). However, engagement comes at a price in terms of both dollars and time.

There is also scope to build the statistical capability of Māori communities and organisations. The benefits would be twofold: raising awareness and use of official statistics by Māori and the transference of skills and capability to Māori organisations to conduct their own community surveys. Also, being more informed has the additional benefit of enabling an external Māori voice and advocacy for Māori statistics. At the same time, the government and its agencies have their own Māori data needs to support their priorities for improving Māori outcomes within their respective sectors.

Finally, indigenous peoples weighing up their participation in the official statistics system and their need for data sovereignty must consider a range of issues. These include their ability to influence the measurement process; the benefit of conducting their own collections and surveys compared with using existing official statistics (including new data initiatives); their subject matter and the technical expertise required to translate indigenous information needs within the system; and their ability, ultimately, to tell indigenous stories using truly indigenous official statistics.

References

Chapple S & Rea D (1998). Time series analysis of disparity between Māori and non-Māori labour market outcomes in the Household Labour Force Survey. *Labour Market Bulletin* 1–2:127–44.

Davies L & Wereta W (2013). A demographic and statistical profile of whānau from 1975 to the present. In Families Commission (ed.), *Families and whānau status report: towards measuring the wellbeing of families and whānau*, Families Commission, Wellington.

Durie M (2006). Measuring Māori wellbeing, New Zealand Treasury Guest Lecture Series, Wellington, 1 August 2006.

Kukutai T & Pawar T (2013). *A socio-demographic profile of Māori living in Australia*, NIDEA, Hamilton, NZ.

Kukutai T, Sporle A & Roskruge M (2016). *Expressions of whānau. In Families and whānau status report 2016*, Social Policy Evaluation and Research Unit, Wellington, www.superu.govt.nz/sites/default/files/F%26W%20Status%20Report%202016_2.pdf.

Kukutai T & Walter M (2015). Recognition and indigenising official statistics: reflections from Aoteaora New Zealand and Australia. *Statistical Journal of the IAOS* 31(2):317–26.

Ministry of Business, Innovation and Employment (2012). *He kai kei aku ringa: Māori economic strategy and action plan*, Ministry of Business, Innovation and Employment/Hīkina Whakatutuki, Wellington.

Ministry of Business, Innovation and Employment (2014). *He whare āhuru he oranga tāngata: the Māori housing strategy directions 2014 to 2025*, Ministry of Business, Innovation and Employment/Hīkina Whakatutuki, Wellington.

Ministry of Education (2013). *The Māori education strategy: ka hikitia— accelerating success 2013–2017*, Ministry of Education, Wellington.

Ministry of Health (2014). *He korowai oranga: Māori health strategy, 2014*, Ministry of Health, Wellington.

State Services Commission (SSC) (2015). *Better public services*, State Services Commission, Wellington, ssc.govt.nz/better-public-services.

Statisphere (2012). *Tier 1 statistics*, Statistics New Zealand, Wellington, statisphere.govt.nz/tier1-statistics.aspx.

Statistics Canada (2003). *Survey methods and practices*, Catalogue No. 12-587-X, Statistics Canada, Ottawa.

Statistics New Zealand (1988). *Report of the review committee on ethnic statistics*, Department of Statistics, Wellington.

Statistics New Zealand (2001). *Tamariki and Rangatahi Māori regional reports*, Statistics New Zealand, Wellington.

Statistics New Zealand (2013a). *Te kupenga*, Statistics New Zealand, Wellington, stats.govt.nz/browse_for_stats/people_and_communities /maori/te-kupenga.aspx.

Statistics New Zealand (2013b). *Māori environmental statistics*, Statistics New Zealand, Wellington, stats.govt.nz/browse_for_stats/ environment/environmental-economic-accounts/environment-domain-plan/maori-environmental-stats.aspx.

Statistics New Zealand (2014). *He arotahi tatauranga*, Statistics New Zealand, Wellington, stats.govt.nz/browse_for_stats/people_and_communities/maori/how-to-think-maori-info-needs/he-arotahi-tatauranga.aspx.

Statistics New Zealand (2015a). *Tatauranga umanga Māori*, Statistics New Zealand, Wellington, stats.govt.nz/browse_for_stats/people_and_communities/maori/tatauranga-umanga-maori-2015.aspx#.

Statistics New Zealand (2015b). *Census transformation: a promising future*, Statistics New Zealand, Wellington, stats.govt.nz/about_us/what-we-do/our-publications/cabinet-papers/census-trans-promising-future.aspx.

Statistics New Zealand (2015c). *Iwi profiles*, Statistics New Zealand, Wellington, stats.govt.nz/searchresults.aspx?q=iwi%20profiles.

Stiglitz J, Sen A & Fitoussi J (2009). *Report by the Commission on the Measurement of Economic Performance and Social Progress*, Paris, www.insee.fr/fr/publications-et-services/dossiers_web/stiglitz/doc-commission/RAPPORT_anglais.pdf.

Te Puni Kōkiri (2015a). *He uru whetū, he ara haere: strategic intentions 2015–19*, Te Puni Kōkiri, Wellington.

Te Puni Kōkiri (2015b). *Whānau ora*, Te Puni Kōkiri, Wellington, tpk.govt.nz/en/whakamahia/whanau-ora/.

Te Taura Whiri i te Reo Māori & Te Puni Kōkiri (2014). *Te rautaki reo Māori: Māori language strategy 2014*, Te Puni Kōkiri, Wellington.

United Nations Permanent Forum on Indigenous Issues (UNPFII) (2004). *Report of the workshop on data collection and disaggregation for indigenous peoples*, E/c.19/2004/1, United Nations, New York, 1–21 May 2004.

Wereta W & Bishop D (2006). Towards a Māori statistics framework. In White JP, Wingert S, Beavon D & Maxim P (eds), *Aboriginal policy research: moving forward, making a difference*, Thompson Educational Publishing, Toronto.

Index

Abbott, Tony 101
aboriginal 39, 148, 166, 243
Aboriginal, *see* Australian
    Aboriginal and Torres Strait
    Islander
Aboriginal and Torres Strait
    Islander Data Archive 277
Aboriginal and Torres Strait
    Islander Social Justice
    Commissioner 238
Aboriginal and Torres Strait
    Islander Statistics Program 275,
    278, 287
ABS, *see* Australian Bureau of
    Statistics
Academy of the Social Sciences in
    Australia (ASSA) 1, 139n.1
Africa 26, 57, 67n.6
    colonisation 69
    data on 30, 277
    indigenous recognition 25, 41
    see also Central Africa, South
        Africa
African American 47, 83
Alaska Native Regional Corporation
    (ANRC) 44
Alaska Natives 44, 145, 263
    data inequity 263–4
    data on 43, 47
    identified in census 45, 263–4
    identifiers 260
    population numbers 47

American Community Survey 43,
    44n.3, 49, 260
American Indian 254, 258, 260, 268
    accurate counting of 43–5, 47,
        259, 262–3
    colonial views of 63
    culture 57–8, 255–6
    defining indigeneity 11, 41–4,
        257n.5
    federal policy 11, 257, 258
    –federal relations 256, 258, 259,
        262, 265
    identifying in census 43
    'self-governance tribes' 264
    sovereignty 11, 43, 44, 166, 254,
        263, 264–6
    subjugation 257, 258
    tribal identity 11, 42, 45, 47,
        262, 266
    undercounting 263–4
    urban 44–5
    Wars 257, 258
    see also Alaska Natives,
        American Indian and Alaska
        Native (AIAN), Bureau of
        Indian Affairs, Indian Health
        Service, National Congress
        of American Indians, United
        States
American Indian and Alaska Native
    (AIAN) 43, 47, 260, 263, 264

CAEPR Research Monograph Series

1. *Aborigines in the economy: a select annotated bibliography of policy relevant research 1985–90*, LM Allen, JC Altman and E Owen (with assistance from WS Arthur), 1991.

2. *Aboriginal employment equity by the year 2000*, JC Altman (ed.), published for the Academy of Social Sciences in Australia, 1991.

3. *A national survey of Indigenous Australians: options and implications*, JC Altman (ed.), 1992.

4. *Indigenous Australians in the economy: abstracts of research, 1991–92*, LM Roach and KA Probst, 1993.

5. *The relative economic status of Indigenous Australians, 1986–91*, J Taylor, 1993.

6. *Regional change in the economic status of Indigenous Australians, 1986–91*, J Taylor, 1993.

7. *Mabo and native title: origins and institutional implications*, W Sanders (ed.), 1994.

8. *The housing need of Indigenous Australians, 1991*, R Jones, 1994.

9. *Indigenous Australians in the economy: abstracts of research, 1993–94*, LM Roach and HJ Bek, 1995.

10. *The native title era: emerging issues for research, policy, and practice*, J Finlayson and DE Smith (eds), 1995.

11. *The 1994 National Aboriginal and Torres Strait Islander Survey: findings and future prospects*, JC Altman and J Taylor (eds), 1996.

12. *Fighting over country: anthropological perspectives*, DE Smith and J Finlayson (eds), 1997.

13. *Connections in native title: genealogies, kinship, and groups*, JD Finlayson, B Rigsby and HJ Bek (eds), 1999.

14. *Land rights at risk? Evaluations of the Reeves Report*, JC Altman, F Morphy and T Rowse (eds), 1999.

15. *Unemployment payments, the activity test, and Indigenous Australians: understanding breach rates*, W Sanders, 1999.

16. *Why only one in three? The complex reasons for low Indigenous school retention*, RG Schwab, 1999.

17. *Indigenous families and the welfare system: two community case studies*, DE Smith (ed.), 2000.

18. *Ngukurr at the millennium: a baseline profile for social impact planning in south-east Arnhem Land*, J Taylor, J Bern and KA Senior, 2000.

19. *Aboriginal nutrition and the Nyirranggulung Health Strategy in Jawoyn country*, J Taylor and N Westbury, 2000.

20. *The Indigenous welfare economy and the CDEP scheme*, F Morphy and W Sanders (eds), 2001.

21. *Health expenditure, income and health status among Indigenous and other Australians*, MC Gray, BH Hunter and J Taylor, 2002.

22. *Making sense of the census: observations of the 2001 enumeration in remote Aboriginal Australia*, DF Martin, F Morphy, WG Sanders and J Taylor, 2002.

23. *Aboriginal population profiles for development planning in the northern East Kimberley*, J Taylor, 2003.

24. *Social indicators for Aboriginal governance: insights from the Thamarrurr region, Northern Territory*, J Taylor, 2004.

25. *Indigenous people and the Pilbara mining boom: a baseline for regional participation*, J Taylor and B Scambary, 2005.

26. *Assessing the evidence on Indigenous socioeconomic outcomes: a focus on the 2002 NATSISS*, BH Hunter (ed.), 2006.

27. *The social effects of native title: recognition, translation, coexistence*, BR Smith and F Morphy (eds), 2007.

28. *Agency, contingency and census process: observations of the 2006 Indigenous Enumeration Strategy in remote Aboriginal Australia*, F Morphy (ed.), 2008.

29. *Contested governance: culture, power and institutions in Indigenous Australia*, J Hunt, D Smith, S Garling and W Sanders (eds), 2008.

30. *Power, culture, economy: Indigenous Australians and mining*, J Altman and D Martin (eds), 2009.

31. *Demographic and socioeconomic outcomes across the Indigenous Australian lifecourse*, N Biddle and M Yap, 2010.

32. *Survey analysis for Indigenous policy in Australia: social science perspectives*, B Hunter and N Biddle (eds), 2012.

33. *My Country, mine country: Indigenous people, mining and development contestation in remote Australia*, B Scambary, 2013.

34. *Indigenous Australians and the National Disability Insurance Scheme*, N Biddle, F Al-Yaman, M Gourley, M Gray, JR Bray, B Brady, LA Pham, E Williams and M Montaigne, 2014.

35. *Engaging Indigenous economy: debating diverse approaches*, W Sanders (ed.), 2016.

36. *Better than welfare? Work and livelihoods for Indigenous Australians after CDEP*, K Jordan (ed.), 2016.

37. *Reluctant representatives: blackfella bureaucrats speak in Australia's north*, E Ganter, 2016.

Centre for Aboriginal Economic Policy Research,
College of Arts and Social Sciences,
The Australian National University, Canberra, ACT, 2601

Information on CAEPR Discussion Papers, Working Papers and Research Monographs (Nos 1–19) and abstracts and summaries of all CAEPR print publications and those published electronically can be found at the following website: caepr.anu.edu.au.

www.ingramcontent.com/pod-product-compliance
Lightning Source LLC
Chambersburg PA
CBHW040141270326
41928CB00023B/3290